JOB

SEARCH

SECRETS

➤ 301 that can work for You!

MICHAEL LATAS

JOB SEARCH PUBLISHERS
St. Louis, Missouri, U.S.A.

JOB SEARCH SECRETS

➤ 301 that can work for You!

MICHAEL LATAS

Published by:
   JOB SEARCH PUBLISHERS
   1311 Lindbergh Plaza Center
   St. Louis, Missouri 63132 U.S.A.

Library of Congress Cataloging in Publication data
Latas, Michael
JOB SEARCH SECRETS - 301 that can work for You!/by Michael Latas, - 1st ed.
Includes index.
1. Job Search - Handbooks, manuals, guides, etc. I Title
2. Jobs - Handbooks, manuals, guides, etc.
3. Job Market - Handbooks, manuals, guides, etc.
4. Employment - Handbooks, manuals, guides, etc.
         1993   650.14   92-84029
ISBN 1-882904-05-2: SAN: 297-8385 $19.95 Softcover
Printed in the United States of America

Dear Job Seeker,

I dedicate this book to each of you who is seeking employment or needing to make a career change. I have written this book to you as an individual, not to you as a group. Each person is special and unique, and it is to your special and unique qualities that I appeal. I have great respect for your talents, your abilities and your work ethic; and I have confidence in you, as an individual.

I know there is room for one more "good employee" (you) to find the job you are looking for among the hundreds of thousands of businesses in the market today. Don't classify yourself as a group of the unemployed, under-employed, laid off workers, ex-military, downsized, rightsized or whatever other label might be given. Don't attach yourself to any label such as inexperienced, underqualified, overqualified, unskilled, under-educated, developmentally challenged, minority, majority, female, male, youth, old or average. You are you - a very special person with much to give to the work place.

This book gives you the do's and don'ts, ins and outs, ups and downs, the "Insider's Track" that the job search industry knows about job search success. These are not secrets to those of us in the executive search industry, but they are secrets to the majority of job seekers. This book shares them with you to help you gain job search confidence, knowledge and understanding in getting a job you want.

This book can move you ahead of your competition by giving you proven job search techniques, strategies and disciplines which will give you confidence to pursue and obtain the job that is right for you.

Much Success!

Michael Latas

Michael Latas is the president and founder of a major national executive search consulting firm: Michael Latas and Associates. He with his associates has successfully helped bring together thousands of employers and employees. After 25 years of working as a job search professional and founder of a highly respected executive search firm, he knows the "insider's track" to job search success.

A graduate of the University of Dayton with a B.S. in Business Administration, he first worked for AMF and Xerox (both new growth companies at the time) in which he rapidly moved to management positions. He subsequently became general manager for a leading search firm and Vice President for a major out-placement firm, then he founded Michael Latas & Associates, Inc. in 1975. His firm now ranks among the leading executive search firms in the nation.

Michael Latas brings more than authority and his authorship to the reader; his personal concern for those seeking employment places him in a position as a job search coach, counselor, and even a personal friend who cares to help those of you who seek a job in today's job market. He gives you a hand shake and a smile, but most importantly he gives you the know-how and confidence to get a job in today's job market.

ABOUT THIS BOOK

This book is filled with numerous first person narratives that Michael Latas and his associates have experienced as they have helped people successfully connect with jobs right for them. These stories illustrate what they have found that does and does not work in job search. The 301 All Time Most Effective Job Search Secrets that the author has discovered to make job search success come true are spelled out for you, clearly and concisely. Put them in practice, and you will be on the "Insider's Track" to a successful job search.

Michael Latas is a people person who cares. His writing reflects his personal concern for each of you who are seeking employment. His personal style makes you feel like he is sitting at your desk with you, listening to you and working to resolve your own personal job search problems. His words carry you through each phase of your job search and guide you during your job search phone conversations and in-person interviews.

Just like a coach who wants you to win the game, he often restates key points in differing ways to help you get a clear picture of what you need to do to be successful in your job search. He is powerful in action and powerful in speech. This power is a motivating force which is felt throughout this book.

Will that put you ahead of your competition? You bet it will! That is exactly what Michael Latas intends to do for you: to instantly jump-start your job search, move you ahead of the competition and help you find success in getting the job that is right for you.

That is not only what the author wants for you, it is what he expects from you. This book gives you his job search secrets. Learn from them and apply them to your job search to achieve success.

ACKNOWLEDGMENTS

Joyce Church Edelbrock served as editor, designer and publishing advisor and without whose help this book would not have been completed in a timely manner. She is a rare bundle of talent.

Carrie Roedner and Angie Prow spent untold hours typing my hand written manuscript and making corrections after corrections. Michael Latas and Associates, Inc. executive search consultants contributed to the authenticity of the text with suggestions and additions. Elaine Boughan-Lyle and Jeff Burke offered their suggestions on the cover design, Leo Kozlowski of Type Two for the cover color separations and Tom Gray and the staff at Color Art, Incorporated for printing.

I would like to give a special note of thanks to Richard Latas, Michele Latas, Mitch Latas, Sarah Aarant, Gary Jesberg, Karen Grant, Mark Zweig, Valarie Wilson, Robert Beekman, Joy Wheeler, Walter Goerss, Samuel Rusnov, Leonard Graff, Eugene Denonovich, Feyza Erenmemis, Shar Scoby, Rebecca Wagstaff, Charles Di and Nat Bodian who read the typed manuscript and offered their suggestions for improvement, additions and deletions in structure and content.

TABLE OF CONTENTS

Introduction

Section One - Understanding

Section Two - Planning

Section Three - Action

Special Section:

INTRODUCTION

Finding a job A task? A challenge? A fear? Hit or miss?
Match or mismatch? Mixed results? How can finding a job
be filled with more certainties, assurances and successes?
How can you find the job that is right for you?

This book is a collection of practical suggestions to help you
get a job. It will help you avoid the many pitfalls,
heartaches and rejections that job seekers face when they
don't have effective job search know-how. With it you can
win.

Finding A Job Versus Finding A Job Right For You

Let me qualify something from the beginning. Finding a job
is entirely different from finding a meaningful career
position that will totally meet a person's short term and long
term needs: a position that will offer continuing challenges,
provide the opportunity for complete self-actualization and
thus yield happiness. Almost anyone can find a job. Very
few people possess the knowledge and skills necessary to find
a rewarding, satisfying and meaningful career position. It is
in this career context that this book was written to help you
find a job that is right for you.

Job Search Solutions

1. <u>Luck, Know-how And Persistence Without Compromise</u>
Being in the right place at the right time with the right
people who have the right needs can play a part in anything
we do, but luck is not a reliable factor in your job search.

> The more skilled you are in finding a job:
>   the more offers you will have.

> The more offers you have:
>   the greater the possibilities are of you being
>   happy with your job search.

To bring a job search to a successful conclusion, it takes planning, preparation, study, discipline and persistence. Entirely too many people compromise somewhere in the process. What happens much too frequently is that job finding skill levels are low, so job seekers get worn down by rejection and damage to the ego. They stop short of finding the ideal job and attempt to live with a compromise. This is not necessary. A diligent and successful search can land you the job you will want to keep for the rest of your career life.

2. <u>Anything Worth Doing (Including Your Job Search) Is Worth Doing Well</u>
Some things are difficult to understand. It would seem that the hardest work of all is to be unemployed, to be under-employed, to be in a job that you don't really like, or worse yet, to have a job that you hate! Talk about hard work. To have every eight hour work day feel like an eternity; that is hard work! Whatever work it may take to remove you from any of the above situations will be short-lived and worth the effort. Agreed? So, you need to learn how to go after the job you want and get it. This is the exact intent of this book.

3. <u>Square Pegs, Round Pegs And In-Betweens</u>
Somehow, some way, hopefully, this book will help square pegs find square holes and round pegs find round holes a little easier and with less pain and trauma. And, if so, it will have made the work of writing this book all worthwhile. And as hard as it may be to believe, all of the holes are not square or round. That would make things easy. There are every conceivable shape of holes imaginable: the right shaped holes to fit everyone, including you.

There is a job right for you, now let's find it.

Section One: *Understanding*

1

SO YOU WANT TO GET A JOB?

A *Time Honored Secret To Success*

All Men Seek one goal: Success or happiness. The only way to achieve true success is to express yourself completely in service to society. First, have a definite, clear, practical ideal - a goal, an objective. Second, have the necessary means to achieve your ends - wisdom, money, materials, and methods. Third, adjust your means to that end.

Aristotle, 384-322 B.C.

THE PSYCHOLOGY OF SUCCESS

Applied To Your Job Search

How you think about yourself, your job search and your place in the work force will each affect your job search success. This chapter addresses these very personal and commonly hidden issues and will help you move forward successfully in your job search.

Need For Job Search Success

Your job often becomes your sense of identity. When people inquire who a person is, the reply is frequently, "a doctor, a teacher, a banker, an electrician, an accountant or a airline attendant." Your job is one of the most important facets of your life. It is not just your work or a means to making a living; it is a very personal expression of you, what you represent and your contribution to the world around you. It is your means to happiness and success.

Your job is then your career or at least a current or future step in that career path. Your job search is as important as your education, your training and your experience. It is fundamental to your lifestyle and your happiness. Yet, most people know little about how to get the right job. This lack of know-how makes them frightened; therefore, they suffer from anxiety when a job search is considered or becomes necessary.

Your Job Search And You

You will benefit, particularly, from help in your job search if you fit any of the following situations.

- This is the first time you (as a recent graduate) are entering the job market.

- It has been some years since you looked for a new job.

- You have been unemployed for some time.

- You are a laid off worker who has to undergo a forced career change because there are no jobs available in the area of work you have been performing or in which you are skilled.

- You have just relocated to another part of the country, world or even a nearby city.

- You are a homemaker who needs or wants to enter the job market.

- You are dissatisfied with your work that holds no future, offers insufficient money or does not inspire you.

All of you will probably suffer anxiety attacks concerning your job search. That is normal initially. There is nothing wrong with you. But you don't have to remain anxious and experience prolonged stress because you can learn how to construct a successful job search campaign. Although that would seem the natural thing to do, there is reluctance to do it among many job seekers. Panic overpowers reason, and the only thing the person can think to do is jump into the job market, prepared or not, and get it done as soon as possible.

Reasons For Job Search Anxiety

1. <u>Past Failures = Lack Of Job Search Know-How</u>
    Human nature dictates that people put off doing those things they do not enjoy doing, they do not know how to do or they do not do well. It doesn't matter what it is. Finding a job is one area in which few people excel or want to do. This is because job hunters suffer from emotional scars. They cannot forget the ups and downs, the damage to their egos, the heartbreaks, the rejections and overall disappointments they faced in the past. These feelings often stem from high school days when they looked for a part-time or summer job. This was a difficult and frustrating experience for most people. No one wants to re-live it.

    Finding a job is one of the most unpleasant experiences people face in their lives. In retrospect people do not know the real reason for the problem. They do not realize that it was not personal at all; it was due to lack of experience at job searching. After all, how often does one look for a job?

    Young people simply do not know how to get a job. They have not developed the necessary skills used in searching for a job. Parents teach job hunting to their offspring in a very limited way. All too often the only words of wisdom they preach is, "Go out and find yourself a job." Beyond that it is nag, nag, nag. Most high schools and colleges don't teach job search skills.

2. <u>Conflicting Advice</u>
    People enter the job market perhaps prepared academically but not prepared emotionally for rebuff

and rejection. The usual situation is that people look everywhere and ask everyone what they should do. Consequently, they pick up a few job search tips (usually more harmful than helpful) from other novices in job search.

Conflicting advice results...

"Send out lots of resumes."
"Don't send out resumes - no one reads them any
        more."

"Make your resume detailed."
"Don't make it over one page."

"Don't let the secretary know what you want."
"Use the secretary to get to the boss."

"Don't be too forward in your interview, just listen."
"You have to dominate... let them know who you are."
        On and on...

In actuality you are on your own - cold; so you wing it. It is scary, and you feel like your life depends on it. Fly or die. So, why should anyone like this job hunting process? It is worse than any test you had in school or any assignment you had on the job. Get it done as soon as possible is the prevalent attitude. Plunge in. Fly or die. What is a person to do? It is every person for oneself, catch as catch can. What a shame! It surely does not have to be that way.

3. Endless Unanswered Questions
    Yet the rush of doubts are ever present. Questions... An onslaught of questions... Questions which never before passed through your mind... Questions looking for answers... During the job search a strong feeling of insecurity may overcome many people due to these unanswered questions...

What about the risks involved? (There are risks.)
What should I do?
How do I handle it?
What am I going to do?
Where am I going to go?
How long is it going to take?
Should I discuss this with my family? My friends?
My co-workers?

And the list goes on and on. The major source of anxiety is the uncertainty of it all, which is coupled with a lack of practical knowledge about how to successfully launch a job hunting campaign. This book was written to answer these perplexing questions and to build confidence.

4. Need For Security
The whole world is preoccupied with the need for security; people want to feel certain about everything in life. Self-imposed high economic standards contribute towards this. Anything that disrupts harmony or has the potential to disrupt economic and personal security causes anxiety. However, these feelings will settle down as you move forward in your job hunting campaign and learn how to conduct your job search properly.

JOB SEARCH SECRETS TO SUCCESS

➤ 001 Read And Follow Instructions
The old familiar statement, "when all else fails read the instructions," applies to job hunting. Somewhere along the line everyone has encountered various do-it-yourself problems, has tried to take shortcuts or do things off the-seat-of-your-pants without success. After all, it is a quirk of human nature to follow the path with the least amount of resistance. Job hunting is no exception. It is more the rule. So, when all else fails and your own do-it-yourself efforts fail, you can now follow the

instructions in this book. These are tried and proven methods that work (providing you do) even in the toughest job markets. The bottom line is that yesterday's job hunting methods simply don't work in today's competitive job market.

➤ 002 Greener Grass

The grass may be greener on the other side of the fence; but remember, the greener and more lush the grass is the more often you have to mow it.

➤ 003 Dealing With Luck

In the course of conducting your job search you will get good breaks, bad breaks and everything in between. Learn to count on them and don't be disturbed by them. Your objective should be to keep a good level of activity going at all times; therefore, when you get a bad break or rejection it does not devastate you psychologically. You should have other leads and prospects upon which to rely. This is what is known as dealing from strength, not weakness. This knowledge will make the difference between success, or lack of it, in your job search.

➤ 004 Moving Ahead When Things Are Going Right

"When you're hot, you're hot; and when you're not, you're not." This fact of life applies to job hunting, as well as everything else. You have to learn to understand this phenomenon and capitalize upon it. When things are going good for you, put your job search activity and all follow-up efforts into overdrive. This is the time to really go for it.

➤ 005 Surviving The Job Hunting Jungle

The "law of the jungle" still applies to the "world of job hunting." You have to fight for your fair share of opportunities or perish. All the suggestions in this book will help you to the degree that you apply them and help yourself. Only you can do your job search. Only you can get yourself a job - one that you want, one at which you will be successful and will enjoy.

➤ 006 Positive Statements

If you can't say something nice, don't say anything. This is true in all walks of life.

➤ 007 Attitude Towards Rejection

There are three types of people.

- Those who simply cannot be knocked down when hit with rejection; no matter how hard they are hit.

- Those who can be knocked down but manage to pick themselves up.

- Those who get knocked out permanently!

Which one are you? With proper attitude adjustment and conditioning you can definitely get stronger in this area and grow less sensitive to things you cannot control. This will improve your endurance. Like everything else, it takes practice, experience and persistence. Prepare yourself. Learn to deal with rejection, and your job search will be easier and less threatening.

➤ 008 Optimism

You can not be too optimistic. Optimism is contagious; if you are optimistic, others around you will also become optimistic. During your job search, see yourself in the most positive situation possible. For example, when pursuing want ads or contacting companies, screen yourself "IN" versus screen yourself "OUT." Your degree of optimism will make the difference. Is the cup half full or empty? What is your outlook? Your expectations? Nothing ventured; nothing gained? Something ventured; something gained? Yes!

SOME BASIC FACTS OF LIFE

Solution Finding Versus Fault Finding

There is no denying that all jobs and all companies have some weaknesses. The easiest thing in the world is to be a full time critic or fault-finder. Really??? Does it take some higher level of intelligence to find room for improvement in this less than perfect world?

If you are a chronic fault-finder, get this through your head; the world was here long before you came along, and it does not owe you a living. You are going to have to <u>earn</u> it. It will not be given to you just because you ask or expect it. Don't make a full time profession out of fault-finding. Instead, try concentrating on solution finding. Now, there is your job.

➤ **009 NOWNESS**

TNT - Today, Not Tomorrow - is the best practice to follow in your job search. "Don't put off until tomorrow what can be done today." Live by this rule and certainly conduct your job search by it.

➤ **010 Persistence Versus Giving Up**

Persistence and determination are inherent in children. If they want something, they stick to it until they get it. How did we as adults outgrow this ability. If adults were half as persistent and determined in job search as they were when they were children and wanted something, each person would get the job each one wants. Children just don't know how to give up. It doesn't matter how many times you say, "no;" children hang in there until they get what they want. Life, for whatever reason, tends to beat many people down to where they simply stop trying.

Pick yourself up by the bootstraps, and renew your childhood enthusiasm and persistence. You will get the job you want to the degree that you pursue, persist and think positively about it.

➤ 011 The Out-Of-Work-At-Home Syndrome

If you happen to be unemployed, make it a point to arise early the same time each weekday morning. It will help keep you at your best. Otherwise, you will be inclined to develop some very bad sleep-in habits. If you are not alert, non-activity could become a habit leading to permanent unemployment. If you don't know what to do with yourself, get into the habit of exercising or taking long fast paced-walks to get your blood pumping. Some people will ride a bike, others will swim. The point is you should have purpose for getting out of bed. A cold shower will jump-start you into action. Do it, and start your day alive. Another applicable old cliche is "The early bird gets the worm."

➤ 012 The NEVER Syndrome

Never say never. The longer you look for a job, the more you will have to change your ways including how to develop a taste for eating your own words.

➤ 013 Wishing Versus Doing

Wishes don't wash dishes.

➤ 014 One Day At A Time

Take things one day at a time in whatever it is that you are doing. One day at a time is all each of us is given at best. This philosophy will reduce your anxiety to an absolute minimum.

➤ 015 Learning By Mistakes

Just remember, if you are inexperienced or new at something you are doing, it may not come easy. You are going to bruise your knuckles and skin your nose, toes, elbows and knees from the many falls you will take. This is the same with job hunting. Don't get discouraged. This is natural. Everyone goes through this very same learning process with everything in life.

➤ **016 Faith**

If you know you can, you will.
If you believe you can, you might.
If you are hesitant or have doubts, you are defeated from the start.

Surely somewhere along the way you have heard, "Faith can move mountains." Well, it can and does. History is full of examples. Faith can be the line between victory and defeat. "You gotta have faith," as the saying goes, or you are a lost soul. Learn to reach deep inside yourself in times of need when there is no place else to turn, and know you can succeed. Know and believe this every minute of every day.

➤ **017 Attitude**

You can alter men's lives best by altering their attitude. Emerson. Attitude is everything. All conduct flows from your attitude. Make it for the better. It is the only thing totally within your control.

➤ **018 Attitude/Action**

Next to attitude, action is the most important factor in your job search.

➤ **019 PMA - Positive Mental Attitude**

A Positive Mental Attitude, PMA, is a vital factor to your success in any field. It cannot be stressed strongly enough. A positive mental attitude is a habit that anyone can develop if the person will simply work at it. Everyone knows people who have strong positive, upbeat attitudes. They are refreshing to be around.

Then, there are the gloom and doom people; nothing is right nor ever will be for them; they feed off the negatives. Stay away from these people. The importance of this factor is critical in your job search.

A highly successful self made millionaire was talking to a group of sales people. He said that several years ago at age 50 he was completely down and out, actually homeless. (This was a time in the U.S. when not too many people were homeless.) One day he found himself walking down a street he had traversed often as a successful business man. He looked up at the well designed building of glass and steel in which he had once worked and walked into it. A psychologist had his old office. The man thought to himself, maybe I need a "shrink." He went into the office, made an appointment, and asked the psychologist, "How does the brain work?"

The psychologist said, "Simplistically, it is believed that the brain receives positives and negatives. It doesn't determine if the positive thought is about you or about someone else. If it is positive, the brain records it as positive. If it is negative, it is recorded as a negative. Let us say you are disturbed at the ridiculous driver in front of you. The brain only records it as a negative, whether it is justified, about you or someone else. It is just negative. If more positives are received and stored, things seem to go right in a person's life. If there are more negatives - well, you know the answer."

"You really think - *Thinking makes it so?*" He asked. He left the office saying, "If that is all I have to do is 'think success,' then I'm going to be successful again." And he was. It took work, lots of self disciplined thought, but it worked.

Just remember this: a positive mental attitude is a state of mind within your control. It evolves out of habits, knowingly or unknowingly. Habits, for better or for worse, are something you decide whether or not to develop. Your upbringing establishes your basic value system; so you may need some major or minor overhaul work done on your degree of positive mental attitude. Start now.

➤ 020 Lessons From A Turtle

The symbolic significance of the turtle came to my attention some years ago.   A turtle cannot walk sideways or backwards. The only direction it can walk is forward. This can only be accomplished when the turtle sticks its neck out. As a friendly reminder, I have kept a ceramic turtle on my desk that my daughter made when she was in the second grade.

Your job search can be rewarding in the end by leading you to a job that can offer you exciting and satisfying work, now and perhaps for the rest of your work life. But the search itself also can be an enjoyable, exciting and rewarding experience for you. Think of the people you will meet, the companies you will explore, and the opportunities you will discover. That is what your job search is: a discovery of who needs you and how you can fulfill that need.

2

BEST ALL TIME JOB SEARCH SECRETS

Knock and the door will open;
Ask and you shall receive.

Somewhere along the way you have heard this sage advice that has passed the test of time over the centuries. Apply it to your job search in every way.

AN OPEN INVITATION

Would you like a friend who has spent a quarter of a century in the job search business to sit down with you and give you the most practical, workable, success-proven tips on job search? Could you use such a friend? Of course, you could. Let me be that friend and share with you the most successful tips and untold secrets about how to find a job as quickly and easily as possible. This chapter gives a smattering of what I have said over and over to job seekers. It is an open invitation to your job search success.

➤ **021 Use Job Hunting Advice**
   The best job hunting secrets in the world will not work unless you do. Apply them, apply them, apply them. Make them work for you.

➤ **022 Control**
   More is within a person's control than most realize. Almost everything in this book is within your control. Put this knowledge into action.

YOU CAN CREATE MORE
OPPORTUNITIES
THAN YOU WILL EVER FIND

Getting a job is a creative process that only you can do for you. It is not akin to an Easter egg hunt. You just don't rush out on a bright day and find the brightly colored eggs that the bunny rabbit left for you. Don't live in fairy tales. The strongest words of advice anyone in the job search arena can give are:

> *Do not limit your search to actual job openings. To achieve maximum job hunting results, look for job opportunities.*

This sounds like a contradiction on the surface, but it is not. Many years ago I read, "You can create more opportunities than you can ever find." I knew what it said when I first read it, but I never fully <u>understood</u> what it meant. Perhaps some of you feel the same way. So let's dig into this subject.

Job seekers are obsessed with finding a job or career position on the basis of what is in it for them - what they need and want. In other words they are selfishly preoccupied, totally, with their own needs. Surely, somewhere in this great big, wide wonderful world is a company that can best meet each person's career needs.

Now, let us shift gears for a moment. Not all companies have job openings at the time job seekers call upon them or mail resumes to them. In fact, most companies would not have any actual openings for the type of background the job seeker has. Is it safe to assume that since job seekers are in pursuit of something that is of personal benefit to them that perhaps companies might also be looking from a selfish perspective? How the company can benefit by you. You can bet your bottom dollar on this.

So, what to do? Is there a better way to pursue a better job or career position? Yes, by all means. It is called pursuing job opportunities. These are not vacant positions. Almost any company will make room in the tent for a truly outstanding individual who can make an immediate contribution to the company's continued growth and profitability. The entire approach of the job seeker should be to point out the benefits that the company will enjoy by hiring that individual.

YOUR PAST ACCOMPLISHMENTS

Ask not, "what a company can do for you?"
but, "what can you do for the company?"

This key will open more doors than most people can handle. Talk about your past accomplishments and how they will enable you to help the prospective company. Do your best to make a proposition that simply cannot be refused. If you don't know what the company wants or needs, find out. If a company does not have any openings, don't let that be a deterrent. Ask what the company wants to accomplish during the next year. See if there is some niche for you, and pursue it.

➤ **023 Lint Picking**
Don't be a lint picker.

➤ **024 Game Playing**
There is no time, place or room for "game playing" when dealing with companies. Yet, this is done even in today's job market. Surely you must realize companies are not new to the business of hiring people. They know all the rules of game playing and when it is being played on them. When companies are dealing with difficult-to-find talent, they tend to bite their tongues and put up with it during expansion periods. However, companies don't forget.

Stop it if you are a game player. If there is one thing the world does not need, it is another game player who is trying to elbow one's way in ahead of the pack. It may be hard for some of you to grasp, but game playing is really not necessary if you are good. And if you are not, all the game playing in the world will not make any difference. In the end it will only work against you.

➤ **025 The Mirror Effect - Reflections**
As you give, so shall you receive. It will mirror back to you accordingly.

➤ **026 The Value Of Money**
Money is not everything.

➤ **027 Job Sources Parallel Job Hunting Success**
Lacking in total job sources? There is an important correlation of which you should be aware: the greater the number of job sources, the better the opportunities are of finding employment. Average job seekers do not use the sources that are all around them. They just stumble along hoping to get lucky and find a job. You do not need to do this. Use this book to explore your new expanded list of job sources. Do it, now, and move your job search into overdrive.

➤ **028 Persuasion**
Sincerity and a deep rooted conviction are the lubricants to persuasion. Believability is not acquired, it is earned. No person can be persuasive unless that person is believed.

➤ **029 Eliminate Pre-conceived Ideas**
Proceeding, or not proceeding, with a particular company because of pre-conceived ideas or personal prejudices is a mistake. These might be based on words spoken a long time ago. Perhaps a father of one of your friends once worked for a company from which he was

fired, and you heard him say that it was a "lousy" company for which to work. Was it, or was it the employee who was a poor worker? All you remember is the negative about the company.

Perhaps you may pre-judge a company on its appearance. You might see a corporate facility, assume it is the headquarters, and determine it is too small or unimpressive.   You might misjudge the company because the building you saw was only a branch office. Find out the facts before you draw conclusions. Erroneous assumptions about prospective employers can reduce your job market and possibly cost you the loss of a great potential job. Keep an open mind.

JOB HUNTING METHODS

There are many different methods for finding a job. Books and articles on this subject typically focus on a single method. In my opinion you owe it to yourself to become aware of all the different methods there are. Each method works. But to restrict yourself to the one "best" method is a mistake. The sooner, the quicker, the faster that you broaden your job hunting methods, the greater your prospects are for success. Each time you hear of the one "best" method, add it to your list rather than limiting yourself to it, and you will improve your opportunities.

➤ 030 Stay Flexible
The greater your flexibility, the greater your avenues are for success in job hunting and in all else. Know your options and pursue them.

➤ 031 Saying Versus Doing
Saying what you are going to do is the easy part. Doing what you said you were going to do is the hard part. Everyone resolves, "I'm going to do my best!" But what happens? Why don't people do their best? Could it be

they do not want to or they are not in the habit of doing their best. Once said, follow through deliberately and persistently.

➤ 032 Keep Your Word - Promises

Don't make statements or promises to do something unless you are prepared to do them, whatever they might be. This might require you to fill out an application, mail a resume, provide a list of references or whatever else you said you were going to do by a specific date. Do it, and do it on time. I have seen the mistake of making false promises made time after time, after time, after time, after time, after time, after time. I surely hope this point is clear to you.

I have known entirely too many people who have become their own worst enemies and hurt themselves by not keeping their word. Don't say it unless you are going to do it. This is a law in job search which is basic to good work ethics and life.

➤ 033 Mistakes And Re-making Them

"To err is human, to continue to make the same mistake is stupidity." This inscription was found in a Chinese fortune cookie. There is a lot of truth in that statement. Watch yourself. People learn from their mistakes. Right? Wrong! Because if this were indeed true the people who made the most mistakes would grow to be the wisest. And everyone knows that is not the case. For better or for worse, people tend to make the same mistakes over and over, knowingly or unknowingly because of deep rooted beliefs and convictions. Pay heed.

List your mistakes in job search. Make them a checklist of don'ts for you in the future. Be realistic.

Your Checklist Of Job Search DON'TS

_____

_____

_____

_____

_____

_____

_____

_____

_____

_____

_____

➤ **034   Capitalizing Upon Your Strengths**
Success in your job search is a matter of learning how to build upon your strengths to overcome your weaknesses. The same applies to your job.

➤ **035   Status Quo Yields Status Quo**
If you keep doing what you are doing, you will keep getting more of what you are getting. Something will have to change if you are not satisfied with the results. You will have to change the way you think, the way you act, and the way you do things. Start now.

➤ **036   The Fact About Equality**
Remember this, there is no such thing as "all things being equal." This is a myth. In a child's alphabet book the letter C was exemplified by the word caterpillar. Two cute and fuzzy caterpillars were pictured. One was stretched out beside a capital C, and one was scrunched together by a small c. The parent reading the book to her twins said, "Look, the caterpillars are twins just like you." The two caterpillars were identical, same color fuzz, same eyes, same number of legs, etc.

One child said, "But they're not equal."

"Not at the moment," the mother agreed, "no, not at the moment." Doing can make a difference in your equality at any and every moment.

➤ **037 "No Rules" Apply**
You should be aware of the rule of exceptions. This rule simply stated is that there are exceptions to every rule. Learn to capitalize on this fact. Do not allow all of the norms, hiring likelihoods, rules or your own self-imposed constraints to hold you back. There are appropriate times when rules must be broken in order to accomplish anything.

ASSUMPTIONS

Assumptions. People proceed with their lives making basic assumptions. That is human nature and it is fine, well and good when it comes to every day bread and butter type basic decisions. However, when it comes to making major decisions that affect one's life or career, do not proceed with basic assumptions but with factual information. All too often people think, act and do things on the basis of emotions which will translate into making erroneous assumptions. This is a costly mistake to make. When this occurs, people will inevitably realize their mistake later on. They then end up reflecting upon three basic questions which they ponder over, over, over, and over again:

1. What would have been?
2. What should have been?
3. What could have been?

Living a life of regrets is no way to live.

When in doubt of what to do, the best thing you can do is seek sound advice from someone whom you respect. Look to one or two good solid people whom you can trust and to whom you can turn. They may be your uncle, an old college professor or a sister-in-law. You need some objectivity at a time like this. To get it, ask for some good old-fashioned professional counsel; otherwise, you may live with regrets.

➤ 038 The Cumulative Principle
So many rain drops make an ocean. Remember, whatever you do has a cumulative effect, for better or for worse. All the many little pointers in this book will add up and make a big difference to the degree that you follow them. All the little things you think and do for good or bad make your success what it is.

➤ 039 Costs Of Job Hunting Lessons
"Every school costs money." This is a favorite quote from my mother. You will pay for every lesson you learn in life one way or the other. The school of life is expensive in time, energy, money and sacrifice - personally, emotionally and physically. Accept this and work, spend, do, learn and succeed. If you do it well, you may never have to do it again. No one beats the system. This includes job hunting lessons.

➤ 040 Company Wants Versus Hiring
Do not allow terminology such as "strongly prefer," "ideally," "a strong plus," "prefer," "it would be nice," or "it would be ideal" or other similar phases prevent you from pursuing job opportunities. These are idealistic "wish list" terms used by companies, but they are not absolute requirements. Beyond that, even certain "must have" criteria are not always cast in concrete and should not be taken literally across the board. If you do not match every specified qualification but believe you could do the job, go for it; otherwise, you might miss an excellent opportunity.

Rules are bent every day. Each specific circumstance will dictate when and how the rules can bend. Nothing is a hundred percent.

➤ **041 Sharing Information**
Share information about your job search, target companies and opportunities with others who are looking for work, and others will share with you.

➤ **042 Early Action**
Why do hunters and fishermen arise in the middle of the night to get an early start and be ready before dawn? Could it be because this is when hunting and fishing are at its best? Could this same rule apply to job hunting? What do you think?

➤ **043 Luck Versus Skills**
Luck can only go so far, then your skills will inevitably take over. Luck follows effort.

➤ **044 Action**
To convert hope into reality requires action.

➤ **045 Doing Your Best**
Do the best you can at the moment. If you make a mistake, learn from it and proceed.

➤ **046 Finding A Job During A Recession**
It takes anywhere from two to ten times or more effort to find the right job during recessionary times as would be necessary during expansion periods. You will have to conduct yourself accordingly to get the job done. You have three choices in a tight job market.

> 1. You can increase the length of time it takes to get the right job.
> 2. You can increase your activity each day.
> 3. You can do both.

➤ **047 Work/Income Relationships**
Work always precedes income.

➤ **048 Recognizing Reality**
Those of you who come to grips with the reality of the situation sooner, rather than later, will have greater success.

➤ **049 Habits**
There are habits that will help your career, and there are habits that will hinder your career. Take inventory before it is too late.

YOUR DESTINY

Those of you who know the career and specific employment you want will have much greater success getting it than those of you who don't.

Alice In Wonderland

I'm reminded of the story from *Alice in Wonderland* where Alice was walking down the road with the Queen of Hearts. They came upon a fork in the road. Alice asked, "Which fork do we take?"

The Queen of Hearts answered, "It all depends upon where you want to go. Where is it you want to go, Alice?"

Alice responded, "I really don't know."

The Queen of Hearts said, "Then, it really doesn't matter which fork you take, does it? Any road will take you there."

The sooner you crystalize your career goal, (your objective) the sooner your success will materialize. It is tough enough finding a job even when you know exactly what you want. It is surely at least ten times more difficult when you don't. Drifting is not as direct as paddling toward shore.

Direction in job search is no different from taking a trip. The first thing you must do is determine your destination, where it is you wish to go. You then plan on how you are going to get there, how long it will take, the clothes and sundries you will need, how much money you will need and other things.

If you are taking a trip, you can at least decide on your destination - California. Then once you get to California, you can better decide which city you wish to visit first. When in San Diego, you can make choices of Sea World or the Zoo.

Likewise, there is a parallel with your career. You can pursue general administrative positions that cross all industry lines which include most management trainee level positions; then, narrow it down. Please bear in mind that over eighty percent of all college graduates change jobs at least once during their first two years after college. This is the norm. So, this is not a life or death decision you have to make. Take your best shot and have at it. As you gain work experience, you will know more about the type of work you want to do and how to get a job that is right for you.

➤ 050 **Instinct**
You don't have to teach a hungry dog how to find a bone.

➤ 051 **Proceed Regardless**
Uncertainties will constantly creep into your mind throughout your job hunting campaign. When in doubt, proceed! Don't waiver and let an opportunity slip by. There is one exception; it is whether or not you should accept a position. No doubt should exist in this area.

➤ 052 **Wanting To Work**
Everybody wants a job, but nobody wants to work. If you want to separate yourself from the pack, learn to

communicate the love of your work. Your ability to do this, or not do it, will determine your outcome.

➤ 053 Finding "Good People"
The most common statement we hear in the executive search business from client companies across the land is that "good people are hard to find." This applies to all levels of employees from top to bottom. Doesn't this sound strange with so many people looking for jobs? There always has and always will be a demand for "good people." The whole world should know what this means. If you don't, you are in trouble.

Your objective during interviews is to communicate that you are indeed one of those "good people." Please understand, talk is cheap. You must then do your part to live up to your statement.

➤ 054 Open Mindedness
Don't look upon your former or present corporate competitors as the bad guys. Nearly everyone has been brain washed in this area. If there is any place that you will be placed at a premium, it is with these companies. Proceed with an open mind.

➤ 055 Too Good To Be True
Remember this in the course of your job search: if a job sounds too good to be true, be careful. It probably is.

➤ 056 How Your Work Counts
What counts most is how you work, not where you work. Joe Girard, the world's greatest salesman as proclaimed by the Guiness World Book of Records.

➤ 057 Intentions
The best intentions on your part just won't cut it. The road to failure is paved with good intentions.

➤ **058 Business Cards**

Buy some business cards to help you with your networking and job search efforts. You don't need to be a professional to have a business card. Anyone can and should have business cards. A simple white card with black print listing your name, address and phone number is all you need. These cards can be purchased very inexpensively. Using a business card is much easier than dealing with an assortment of bits and pieces of paper. Using a business card will also separate you from the masses. It represents a thoughtful touch of class. Make sure you carry your cards with you wherever you go. Hand them out generously.

➤ **059 Problem Solving**

Why is it that the easiest problems in the world to solve are other people's and the most difficult problems to solve are your own? You are not alone. Don't pick on yourself. Seek out the help you need. Don't be foolish. No one knows everything.

➤ **060 Gaining**

Remember this. No pain, no gain.

➤ **061 Finding**

Seek and ye shall find.

3

UNDERSTANDING TODAY'S JOB MARKET

The Best of Times
The Worst of Times

It was the best of times, it was the worst of times, it was the age of wisdom, it was the age of foolishness, it was the epoch of belief, it was the epoch of incredulity, it was the season of Light, it was the season of Darkness, it was the spring of hope, it was the winter of despair, we had everything before us, we had nothing before us...

A *Tale of Two Cities* - Charles Dickens

How could Charles Dickens have known back in the mid 1800's when he wrote *A Tale of Two Cities* that his words could be so aptly applied to today's job market. Recessionary times are indeed the worst of times. With this view of the job market you could close this book at this point and give up without discovering the best of times. This chapter will help you realistically look at today's tough job market and move you forward on a positive path with a better outlook about your prospects of getting a job despite the market.

TODAY'S MARKET

I will be the first person to admit that if given a choice of when to be looking for work, it would be during the best of times. Unfortunately, people are not always given a choice. However, if you happen to be caught in a job change during the worst of times, don't despair. All is not lost. In fact it is far from it. You will realize this when you put things into their proper perspective; otherwise, you could draw the erroneous conclusion that no one is hiring. That simply is not true.

Right now as this book is being readied for the printer, it is a slow economy, a slow and gloomy economy. The economy continues to sputter along in the process of slowly recovering from an extremely nasty recession that officially began over two years ago. The economic outlook is starting to move ever so slowly in the right direction at long last, but it is still a tough market.

National unemployment during the best of times runs about five and one-half to five and three-fourths percent. During a time of high unemployment, for example, at the end of July, 1992, the unemployment rate was at seven and three-fourths percent. That is a difference of two more people per hundred who are unemployed in the worst of times versus the best of times.

Please understand, I am not trying to minimize the significance of being unemployed. Being unemployed can be absolutely devastating if you happen to be one of those additional two percent of the people out of work. The biggest difference is psychological; job search attitudes are more negative during tough economic times. People don't expect to find employment as quickly as they do during better times. The point is that the statistical difference in the two extreme job market conditions is just two percent, not some astronomical difference such as ten or twenty-five percent or more. It is far from it.

A negative outlook, lack of confidence and the lack of necessary job hunting skills are much greater problems than the two percent difference in unemployment. People simply stop looking when they see and hear negatives day in and day out; therefore, they allow the negatives to overtake their lives. What a shame.

Job Openings

Just how many different job openings do you think there are in a given year? Let me shed some light on the subject that should help you see things a little more clearly:

- Over ten million people were fired from their jobs for one reason or another during 1991.

- Add to this the number of people who quit their jobs for one reason or another.

- New companies start every year and have to hire people.

- Some companies will expand even in the worst of times. Consequently, they need to hire more people.

- People retire from work each year. Companies hire replacements for training and indoctrination to take over the jobs that will be made available by people who are nearing retirement. Many people take early retirement: some of these positions are not replaced but some are.

- People die or get killed each year.

- Some people become ill and can no longer work. Short term, long term or permanent positions become available as a result.

- Confidential replacements. We deal with these needs on a daily basis in our executive search practice. Companies want to confidentially replace people who are not measuring up in their job. These services are performed quietly behind the scenes under the utmost secrecy. This is a very common practice.

Companies cannot afford to fire certain people and leave an important vacancy while they look for a replacement.

A prolonged search for a replacement contributes greatly to compromises. When this occurs, companies find themselves back in the same predicament. Finding people is not the problem. Finding "good people" is. It can take much time and effort to fill some of these positions.

Companies will use a number of different means to handle their confidential replacement openings which include blind help-wanted advertising. This is part of that "hidden" job market about which you will need to explore by networking and research.

- Casual needs are ever-present in companies. When a company finds "good people" who can improve the company's products, services, operations, productivity and profitability, the company feels compelled to hire them. Positions are simply made available for these "good people." These casual needs are being met daily throughout the nation. You must be one of the truly outstanding people to have a company make room for you, but if you are, you can fill these casual needs if you pursue them.

It is my intent to get your attention with these facts and statistics. A great deal of turnover takes place each year which creates millions of job openings. Each of these changes represents new job opportunities for the job seeker. Amazing, isn't it.

Some of you will be in regions of the country that have higher unemployment than others. But you can make up for the difference by improving your job hunting skills. That is what this book is all about. If you put into practice the suggestions and directions in this book, you will gain a major advantage over those who don't know any better.

THE CHANGING JOB MARKET

Facts And Figures
A Perspective

A good statistical overview of the job market is presented at this point to help you gain a realistic perspective. There are 127 million people in the labor force of which 117 million are gainfully employed and just under 10 million are unemployed.

If there is one thing for certain, it is change. The world is in a constant state of change. Some of this change is for the better; some of it is for the worse. Most people tend to live in a vacuum until something breaks that vacuum. Much of the time that something is change. You are not alone; everyone faces change throughout life. The only thing that anyone can change is one's perspective on how to cope with change.

New Jobs

Starting in the seventies and throughout the eighties, new jobs were created at a record breaking pace. Eighteen million new jobs were created in the U.S. during these two growth decades. The peak occurred between 1986 to 1988, during which time 66,000 new jobs were created each month; totalling 792,000 new jobs in each of the two years. In 1990, the new job machine ran down with the recession. This trend is nothing new. Economies have expanded and contracted since the dawn of civilization. Business cycles are a way of life; they have their ups and downs. The good news is that up years far out number the down years. Each down period will pass as each always has. Despite the ups and downs 117 million people remain gainfully employed in a job market that is continually changing. New job opportunities for job seekers occur as people move from one job to another.

According to a recent *Wall Street Journal* article the Conference Board stated that there were 25 million people who were unemployed at some point in time during 1991, and half of them were unemployed two different times during that same year. This figure was up from 22 million in 1990, 20 million in 1989, 18 million in 1988. It would appear that change is occurring more frequently. Each change represents an opportunity for someone.

Now, let's take a closer look at some more statistics. In 1990, the highest numbers of unemployed as a group (12.2 percent) were people who had one to three years of high school. The second highest numbers of unemployed (9.1 percent) were people with eight years or less school. (This last figure looks out of line until you realize that the total number of people with eight years or less schooling has been shrinking.) Only 5.8 percent of high school grads were unemployed. Those with one to three years of college were at 4.2 percent. And those with four years or more of college were at 2.4 percent. In 1990, the total unemployment average of all levels was 5.5 percent according to the U.S. Department of Education. The importance of getting a good education becomes self evident. The unemployment statistics for 1992 are different. For example, the figure for September of that year reached 7.8 percent, but the percentages in each group remained about the same.

New Immigrants

Job search is most difficult for immigrants who have cultural and language barriers to overcome. They come to this "Land of Opportunity" with great hopes and high expectations of finding good paying work. Legal permanent residency was granted to 704,005 immigrants in 1991. Some estimates state that there were an additional 250,000 to 300,000 illegal immigrants that year. Together, that is approximately a million new immigrants to the U.S. in 1991. The majority of these people become gainfully employed in a short period of time. They are very grateful to be in the U.S. and are very grateful for their work. Again, one must put things into proper perspective. In 1992, about thirty percent of the labor force was unemployed or underemployed in the world according to the International Labor Organization. Seven hundred million who are working only earn $2.50 or less per day. It is not hard to see why immigrants still look upon this country as the "Promised Land." You should too.

The consensus is that the recession and slow economic growth is confined to 1990-1992. An optimism about future economic improvement is gradually starting to develop. No one is anticipating any boom for the short term outlook. It is anticipated to be a steady, ever so slow progress back to a normal job market.

FREQUENCY OF CHANGE

If you follow the norm, you are going to change jobs a number of times during your career. In fact, the latest statistics available on job changes indicate that the average person will make thirteen job changes and three career changes. These statistics are staggering. Things are no longer as they once were in your father's or your grandfather's time when people went to work for a company and stayed throughout their working lives. The types of changes should come as no surprise to anyone. Changes can be seen taking place everywhere.

Job Changing Trends

The historical trend in job changing has been increasing over the years for both voluntary and involuntary reasons. Some of the statistics are startling. The Department of Labor, Bureau of Labor Statistics, October, 1992, stated that a study of people twenty-five years old and younger had been conducted over the past twelve years. It showed on average that each person changes jobs just under nine times by age twenty-five. This is not a misprint.

Eighty percent of all college graduates change jobs at least once during the first two years out of college. Some of these changes were forced; others were voluntary. People either quit or got fired for any one of a number of reasons. As mentioned earlier, over ten million people were fired in 1991. (Staggering isn't it? That is almost one in every eleven people in the labor force.)

If, on average, people start work at age eighteen and work until age sixty-fve, that would be forty-seven working years. Many job changes will take place in those years.

My reason for expanding on this subject is very simple. As people change jobs, openings are created for others to fill. This is true even in markets that are no longer expanding. Most people are not aware of these facts and nearly give up looking for work in down markets. This information should encourage you to pursue and persist with your job search until you get a job. Beyond this, if statistics are important to you, I suggest you consult with the U.S. Department of Labor; however, it is just as easy to look around at your fellow workers, friends and neighbors to see what is happening. More and more people are making more job and career changes than occurred in the previous generations.

Some job and career changes are within your control and will be brought about by your own free choice. On the other hand, some of the changes may be forced upon you and will be out of your control. The following lists some of the possibilities you may encounter.

- Mergers - being absorbed by a larger or stronger company
- Acquisitions - being acquired by someone else
- Companies being sold
- Division or plant closings
- Division or plant being moved to an undesirable location or a desirable location but you may not be given the opportunity to move

- Company headquarters being moved to an undesirable location or desirable location but you may not be asked to relocate
- Company being dissolved
- Being fired for any one of a number of reasons (Some are valid and some are not.)
- Being laid off
- Job being phased out

PAY HEED TO "THE WINDS OF CHANGE"

A special word of caution is in order before proceeding further, in what I refer to as "the winds of change." When the warm winds of stability at your present company begin to grow colder, prepare yourself for change. A message is being communicated in those cold winds. It is generally, if not always, a warning that one of the above events is going to occur. To be forewarned is to be forearmed. However, in my experience over the years, most people fail to pay heed until the last minute, if at all. It is almost as though they believe that if they disregard these cold winds of change and disregard all the tell-tale signs that the potential problem will go away. This is a mistake.

I am not suggesting that everyone abandon ship as soon as it becomes reliably certain one of these events might take place. However, I strongly do recommend that you take your head out of the sand and face reality. Start building a life boat just in case. Analyze your personal situation as objectively as possible and ask yourself the following questions:

1. What is the best that can happen?
2. What is the worst that can happen?
3. What do I realistically expect to happen?

After reflecting upon the above possibilities you will then be in a better position to determine your best course of action.

As difficult as it may be, do your best to keep wishful thinking to an absolute minimum. Wishful thinking keeps entirely too many people from taking the necessary precautions. It reminds me of people's attitude towards accident statistics. Accidents only happen to other people. A word to the wise on this subject should be sufficient.

The smartest thing one can do at a time like this is to take out what I refer to as some "job insurance." This means you should do whatever you can to protect yourself as much as possible. As an example, a prudent precaution would be to forestall any major purchases such as a new home, swimming pool, room addition, interior decorating or car. Obviously a great deal will depend upon your cash flow and cash reserves.

Sometimes the changes come about rather abruptly. Most of the time the winds of impending change will start to get colder well before the actual changes take place. It is during this time span that I say take heed and prepare.

Rumors

Rumors in companies will start slowly. Most people tend to discount this early scuttlebutt. The rumors will either die out and business goes back to normal; or the rumor mill will pick up some steam. Somewhere amidst all of these persistent rumors lies the truth; otherwise, the ship would settle down, and things would resume back to normal. Cut right down the middle of every rumor you hear from the very best to the very worst. The middle ground is the safest place to be. Regardless of how invulnerable you may feel you are, you had better make a plan of action. Your personal feelings will not have any bearing on what may inevitably happen. *Prepare thyself.*

During the third and final stage one of two things can happen. Things can either settle back down to normal or the rumor mill can run rampant. Should this occur the odds strongly favor that what you have been hearing is what you will get. This third and final stage is rather intense. You can hardly make it through the day without some discussion on the subject; it usually becomes the topic of the day. The time span from stage one to two to three will vary considerably. There is, however, some correlation as to size of the company and time span. Things move faster in small companies versus larger ones. The top Fortune 500 companies take the longest and, therefore, provide you with the longest lead time.

Each person has to assess the degree of risk one faces. Some of this risk can be very objectively measured. One is seniority. Each person then must decide on just how much risk one wishes to take. Some people will stand pat and do nothing at one extreme. Others will begin to put "feelers" out in the market place. They want to test the market. What are things really like out there in the market place? What's the job market look like? They will straddle the fence somewhat playing both ends against the middle. Others will have their job search campaign in full swing. Pay particular attention to how many fellow workers are interviewing. Next, keep a watchful eye on people who are quitting. There is a reason for this. This spells Trouble with a capital T. So, what do you do at a time like this?

1. Stand pat and do nothing?
2. Straddle the fence. Put feelers out in the market place. Explore your options. Test the waters?
3. Proceed with an all-out job hunting campaign?

Whatever you do, do so intelligently because you have assessed your personal situation and have proceeded along logically. This action is preferred to sticking your head in the sand, crossing your fingers and muttering, "I hope, I hope, I hope." That is the worst possible thing you can do.

Make up your mind what you want to accomplish and then accomplish it.

➤ 062 Job Market Perspective

You are only one person. What can you contribute to any one of the thousands of companies that are prospering even in today's economy? Is there room for one more person in all those companies? Don't think of all the people who are out of work. Think, instead, of all those who are working. There is room for one more person (you) to join the work force and make a profitable contribution to the company, yourself and the national and world economy. Go for it and get that job!

4

SPECIAL JOB SEARCH SITUATIONS TODAY

*Alone against the world -
one is one.
Together with the world -
one is all.*

How do you fit into today's job market?

The world is in an unprecedented period of transition. Today's work force is undergoing radical changes. The shift from a cold war to a peace economy has affected the world. The rise in industrialization of third world nations has created a shift in labor force from nation to nation. Competition is hard. Globalization has short circuited all avenues of trade, productivity, supply and demand, laws and equality. Another major change is the emergence from the age of industrialization into the age of communication and high technology. It simply takes fewer people with more skills to accomplish more in less time. There is a greater interdependency with less freedom to do what one wants. Big business and government regulations are yielding to growing numbers of small businesses (many at-home operations) with fewer controls.

All of these changes are not bad. Some in the long run will be very good, but the process of change has caught many people in difficult positions. Some of these situations are so difficult that it is often hard to provide for oneself and one's family in today's economy. People have a tendency to be discontent, worried and frightened while out of work.

This chapter will cover some of the most common situations today. This is not an attempt to cover all problem areas or to minimize any. Each situation is critical to those who are affected. Most of these situations are society, business, government or world imposed. Each person needs to learn how to overcome the situation and become gainfully and happily employed.

SOME HARSH REALITIES
Downsized, Rightsized Or Laid Off

Downsized, rightsized or laid off: Whatever label you wish to call it, a fancy label doesn't make losing your job any more palatable. Any way you cut it, it hurts. No matter how careful companies are in their choice of words, when people are laid off the pain is not lessened any. It still hurts. Sometimes the pain can go to the bone. Then there are those who are within throwing distance of being eligible for full or early retirement, and they get nothing but a thank you. With these people the pain cuts through the bone. Included in this group are some of the hardest working loyal company employees who gave everything possible, and still it was not enough to save their jobs. Call it what you will, the luck of the draw or being in the wrong place at the wrong time. They are the unfortunate victims of major changes in world forces including the end of the cold war that has reduced the need for defense, defense work and defense employees.

Furthermore, the globalization of the world has placed the U.S.A. in competition with all other nations whose wages, standards of living and manufacturing costs are considerably below ours. How does anyone compete with a dollar-an-hour wages? Guess what, there are a number of countries where labor is cheaper than that. Consider China, the largest country in the world with a population over 1.1 billion. There the wages are a meager fifty dollars a month. China currently produces over forty percent of U.S. textiles and many other goods. The list goes on and on, country after country. This places U.S. companies in a state of turmoil now and for some time to come. As a result, those of you who have been laid off will not be alone. Others will follow.

Just remember, "Where there is a will there is a way." Self preservation is at the top of the list of all motivational needs. Somehow, someway, the human spirit prevails through the thick and the thin. People do manage to persevere and survive through the most difficult periods in history. You will, too, even if you are currently unemployed.

If you do not fall into any of the following special employment categories, then you can proceed to the next chapter to discover new horizons and solutions.

➤ 063 Near Retirement Age

The closer you are to retirement age - the more difficult your task is and the bigger the compromise will be. Accept these factors, but don't give up. You don't have to be a statistic. There is nothing wrong with you personally. It is just that the work meter has nearly run out on you, as it will for everyone. This is the perception of most employers. Yet, experience updated to today's applications can be a powerful asset to a company. Your experience, maturity, ability to adapt and solve problems and your accomplishments are your strong points. Your health, your vigor and your enthusiasm will be concerns for employers. The big questions are simply the number of years you have to give to the company and how difficult it will be to retire you when it becomes necessary. Assess realistically what you have to give to the company, **now**. How you can be of help, **now**? Companies are always interested in the future, but **now** is more important. Short term employment, consulting or contract work are options. Your own ability to work effectively in today's work force is your best selling point.

➤ 064 Minorities

Minorities still have a difficult time advancing to top positions. Yet, your work record will push you forward to gain employment. Being a minority must be faced if you think you are being ignored or passed by because you are a minority. It is time to uproot prejudice. Persistence and facing the issues politely but firmly will carry you a long way into the work force.

➤ 065 Women In The Workplace

Women are a minority in upper level management positions and are rare in top management. Beating the system is hard; however, conditions are improving. Moving into a high level position ahead of a male counterpart will take top performance and a will to win. Always dress and act in a very professional manner. Women who have young children or wish to raise a family will have to address these issues while considering employment in relation to work schedules and travel.

➤ 066 Entering The Job Market As A Homemaker

You are special. Regardless of the reason you are entering the job market, you need to assess your skills, strengths and accomplishments. You need to transfer your homemaking accomplishments and skills into work oriented ones. You need to build confidence in yourself. You might need to go back to school and take classes in computers, for example, to up-date your skills to meet current expectations. You might also want to work part-time or accept temporary work through an agency to re-acquaint you with the world of work. If you are older than those around you, use your age to your advantage. You have experience in life that they do not. If you are confident in yourself, it shows. Frequently an employer would rather have a person who enjoys work, is dependable and thinks for herself than someone who is thinking of social life. Challenge yourself to be sharp, and you will be.

➤ 067 Recent College Graduate

No experience is your biggest problem. All want ads it seems specify "2 to 5 years" experience. How can you get a job if you do not have experience? You need to look for entry level positions. If you are a good student and a quick study, then you should be able to work your way up in the company within a short time.

A young woman graduated from college at age twenty. She received a wonderful graduation present: a trip to Australia! Instead of just taking a vacation, she used the opportunity to live in a foreign country for a while and gain some work experience. She worked as a waitress at first; then she did data entry at a newspaper office. She saw the need to help a couple of advertisers with their ad layouts. She wrote a story about her stay in Australia which was published in a local newspaper. She also helped a friend make invitations and a program for a charity ball. She supported herself fully for one year. When she returned to the States, she had a portfolio to show prospective employers.

Not everyone can go to Australia upon graduation, but many of those that have great opportunities fail to take advantage of them and put their talents to work effectively. Take every opportunity you can to build experience. Volunteer in your spare time to build credibility and a work record.

Some situations are self imposed and can be corrected when a person is willing to make adjustments in attitude, work ethic and desire.

"WANDERING" CAREER NOMADS

There are a growing number of people in the job marketplace that I refer to as the tribe of "wandering" career nomads. You may be one of them and not even know it. These include all of the people who hop, skip and jump from one job after another in search of instant fame and fortune. They graze a little here, then graze a little there and are always in pursuit of greener pastures. There simply is no holding these people down in any one place for any period of time.

- They all seek one thing: instant gratification, promotions, more money, fame and fortune, **now**.

- They all lack one quality: commitment.

- They just can't seem to stay in one job long enough to pay the price it takes to get ahead.

- They pick through and sort out all the duties they enjoy doing. They ignore those duties they dislike or pass them onto someone else.

- They never come to grips with the fact that they can only get away with this short cutting so long. When their lack of performance is about to be detected, the only solution is to get another job.

Each and every "wandering" career nomad could be a team captain of an Olympic fault-finding team if there were such a thing. They can find more things wrong with their jobs, boss, company, position, people, potential, philosophy, pay plan, benefits, working conditions, location, fellow workers or whatever, than one could think possible. They are muckrakers. Can anything really be all that bad? What do you think?

These career nomads do not fault-find with just the average run-of-the-mill companies but with some of the biggest and best companies. I can recall people who have left some of modern history's greatest growth companies including IBM,

Polaroid and Xerox. The nomads who left stated that they wanted to leave the companies because they did not offer advancement opportunities. Can you believe that? It is a fact. These are people who cannot or simply refuse to come to grips with their problems. They have totally unrealistic opinions of their capabilities that can be summed up with a favorite expression:

> *Mirror, mirror, on the wall,*
> *who is the fairest of them all?*
> And why am I?

Everybody wants to go to heaven, but nobody wants to die. There is a price to pay for whatever it is that you want from life. The more you want, the more you will have to pay. Nobody beats the system except per chance in the rarest of circumstances. A few will somehow manage to accomplish this feat though it is a long shot. These stories fly like pollen through the job market air. They encourage others and give them hope that it can happen to them.

These people know what their performance is and know that promotion is out of the question. So, what are their alternatives? Remain in the same position forever and resign themselves to the fact that this is it; this is as far as they are going to go with their careers. Or move on to yet another company where the line to the top may be shorter and they may get lucky. Whatever the odds may be against them getting lucky, it is better where the company doesn't know them. So, they move on, and on, and on until they end in the growing pool of the "Future Temporary Day Laborers of America." They complain and complain endlessly to one another about their employment war stories, and finally they end up in the book of "Who's Through In America." What a waste.

No one will argue that some people have gotten raw deals in business. That is a fact of life. But to imply that the majority of people receive raw deals is totally out of line.

Many job seekers who have been on the short end may need counseling to help them appraise the situation more accurately. If there is one thing in which career nomads truly excel, it is their creative resume writing. They certainly have much practice. Please, don't follow the path of the "wandering" career nomad.

ARE YOU A CONTRIBUTOR?

Are you a person who will do whatever is necessary to make contributions? If typical job seekers only did half of what they and their resumes state, they would literally move mountains. It is not a question of knowing what to do or how to do it; it is having the necessary self-discipline to pay the price to do whatever has to be done. Herein lies the Achilles' heel of the working population. For whatever reason, self-discipline and the "proper" work ethic are not taught much in today's world of work. The select few who are self-disciplined and have good work ethics stand out from the crowd. If you are not one, find good role models and learn from them. Do this, or suffer the consequences of settling for what life hands out to you. Nobody is going to give you anything, whether it be more money, a promotion or a job. In the end you will get exactly what you have earned. You deserve a good job if you work at it.

➤ **068 Degree Of Marketability**
Job seekers fall into one of three basic groups in regards to their marketability.

1. Above average to high demand
2. Average demand
3. Below average demand on down to special career problems

Each person has to assess which group (based upon supply/demand factors in the market place) one belongs. Also, please understand, market conditions change. In

1990, a person working in defense could have belonged to group one, but in 1992, that same person would be in group three. This grouping will dictate your expectations in finding a job along with the amount of activity necessary to do so. The lower the ranking is the greater the call for compromise. The sooner, the quicker, the faster you do, the better off you will be.

The next chapter leads you into finding solutions. Read on and move ahead in your job search.

5

WIDEN YOUR HORIZONS -

DISCOVER SOLUTIONS

Life can be beautiful;
it all depends upon the circumstances;
either you control the circumstances,
or the circumstances will control you.

➤ **069 Career Alternatives**
Do you have any career alternatives? Most people do
not. You should make a point to explore your career
alternatives from the onset of your job search or
pending job search. Most of the time people do not
consider career alternatives until they literally exhaust
themselves in their job search.   With over 22,000
different job descriptions in *The US Book of
Occupational Titles* scattered across 350 different major
industries across the millions of companies across the
land, surely, there must be more than one possibility for
you. The *Department of Commerce's U.S. Industrial
Outlook* updates and reviews the present and future
outlook of these 350 different industries. A close review
of it will help you broaden your perspective and your
career alternatives.   Do yourself a favor; conduct
extensive research in these publications. Unfortunately,
some of you will have your minds fixed on one specific
career, and your decision will be stubbornly cast in
concrete; so be it. However, you should do yourself a
favor and broaden your horizons.

DEALING WITH THESE HARSH REALITIES

Those of you who might be cut back, downsized or rightsized from long standing corporate careers need to face your situation. First of all, explore your options. Most of the people with whom I have talked over the years never considered their situations long enough to come up with career alternatives. In the meantime the company continues to remove additional chairs from the musical chair game called downsizing, cut backs and rightsizing. Each person optimistically hangs in there hoping and halfway believing that somehow "I will manage to be the person to get the last chair." Hope springs eternal. This message to you is twofold:

For those of you who are still hanging in there, get moving.

EXPLORE YOUR CAREER ALTERNATIVES,

NOW!

This is called taking out career insurance. Pay heed. Do yourself a big favor and come to grips with what has to be done,

NOW!

Don't spend any more time looking back over your working life, replaying it over and over, again and again. This is a very costly mistake financially and psychologically. Just remember; there is one thing no one can take away from you and that is your future, how you are going to spend the rest of your life. Move out of reverse gear into forward. All the talking and rationalizing on this subject will not change your circumstances one bit. You are where you are, and nothing is going to change that.

Most of you are going to have to make some major changes, now, or you will prolong the inevitable and be forced to make the changes at a later time when you will be considerably weaker financially. It is a bum deal. Despite this you must move on with your life.

Think of most major league athletes who enjoy short term fame and fortune. What happens to them? At least ninety percent inevitably have to make major adjustments at the end of their short term careers. They have to make radical changes in their careers. There is absolutely no way around this problem. Make your career adjustment work for you. The sooner you do, the better off you will be.

CAREER STEPPER
Arnold Schwarzenegger

Arnold Schwarzenegger is a classic example of a person forced to make a career change. There is a physical limitation on how long a bodybuilder can remain in world champion competition (no matter who the person is). Schwarzenegger broke all records for being the very best in the world, and still it was not enough to sustain him in that career. After peaking out in world competition as a bodybuilder, he had to step out of that career field and into another.

What to do? Arnold had always been intrigued and influenced by movies; therefore, he headed for Hollywood to become an actor. Certainly, he was well known after years of being the world's greatest heavyweight bodybuilder; and, surely, this would help him. The first thing he had to do was find an agent to represent him. He had no acting experience whatsoever; he just had a lot of drive and determination to become an actor. He was turned down (rejected) time after time... after time... after time... after time...

He was told that he had no acting experience, that he talked funny with a thick accent, that on top of all else he was built strange and that there was no way he was ever going to be an actor.   Repeatedly   he   made   the   rounds   -   all unsuccessfully.   There just did not appear to be any way he was ever going to become an actor. . . . . Really!!! According to whom???

CAREER PROFIT STEPPING

Wherever you are in your career path, you got there by applying yourself year after year, and you earned what you achieved one step at a time.   Your increases and promotions were based upon your performance.   Your progress came one step at a time.

**Laid off after 25 years
with a salary of $50,000**

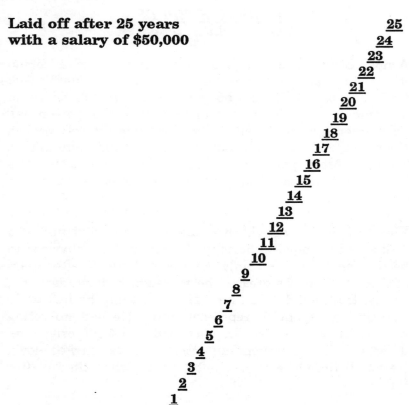

If you are a victim of company cut backs, you cannot pull the covers over your head and hope this problem will go away. It just doesn't work that way. As soon as you remove the covers to take a peek at the real world, the problem is still there. The smartest course of action is to retrace your steps, one step at a time. Test the market to see the availability of jobs for which you could qualify.

Let us assume, for example, that a person was earning $50,000 when laid off. To find a job this person may have to side-step over into other career fields. This may also call for stepping down, as well. In the new career field, a person may be offered a less advanced position with a temporary cut in pay. This person might have to pursue opportunities starting at $40,000.

One's financial standing will dictate the degree of urgency necessary. If interviews do not develop at this level within four to six weeks (this time frame will vary according to your sense of urgency), then another step down to the $35,000 - $30,000 level will be necessary. But, at the same time all job opportunities at the $40,000 and above salary level would still be explored.

You can guess what your next step should be without my prodding. After the next four to six weeks step down to the $30,000 - $25,000 level. Again at the same time keep options open for opportunities at $35,000 - $40,000 - $50,000 plus levels. If necessary for survival, this person may then have to step down to the $25,000 - $20,000 level.

Please understand, this does not mean if you side step down with a new career path that you will stay at this level permanently. It may represent a short termed step down while you learn a new career field, then step back up from there.

Career Profit Stepping

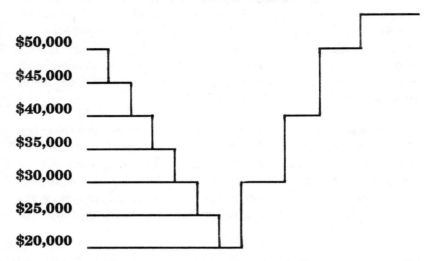

You will be amazed how quickly you can move up the stair steps to success and financial rewards. Your salary in your new career might exceed your former one.

A word of caution is in order when considering your career options. People are inclined to continue to do what they know best for better or for worse. It is fear of change that keeps people clinging to the familiar rather than reaching out for something new. This holds true regardless of how unhappy they may be and no matter how much greater the potential is for the new. This is by far the costliest career mistake that anyone can make. If you can't find employment or if you are not happy in your field, then change fields. Just remember, if you can drive a Ford, you can drive a Chevrolet. Keep this upper most in your mind.

Divorce Your House

Many people may decide or be forced to sell their homes because of finances. Face reality and be willing to make sacrifices for the bigger picture. It is not easy. Far from it, but it beats losing one's home to foreclosure as so many people do. You can always buy another home down the road after this crisis passes when you are secure in a new field.

Selling your home or other prized possessions are very difficult actions that in some cases must be taken. It is similar to amputating an arm or leg to save a life. That is a tough call to make, but what choice does one really have? You do whatever has to be done and move on with your life.

➤ 070 Career Change And Transfer Of Skills

If you change career fields, you should become acquainted with what the outplacement industry refers to as "transferable skills." These are skills that are transferable from one industry to another.

Transferrable Skills Analysis: Let us create an example such as a school teacher who wants to leave the teaching profession to enter any one of a number of different career fields. So, what are some of the skills that a school teacher may have that would be transferrable into other industries? Stop and think for a moment before proceeding. Ok, how about planning, organizing, controlling, administration, speaking skills, writing, communications and people skills for openers. Math, science or language skills may be added. A teacher might be teaching specialized courses such as advertising, sales or marketing which could lead to a job in any of these fields.

Rule of Transferrable Skills: Any person who wants to enter another field has to present oneself as a person would in that new field. For example, a teacher would need to present oneself as an advertising account executive, not as a teacher. Most skills go well beyond one career. The only industry that is interested in hiring a teacher is a school district; however, all industries need certain basic and general skills that cut across industry lines.

This same process would be followed by other career changers including ex-military or defense industry personnel. If you happen to be one, please don't use the "coded language" known only to those skilled in that field. You will improve the level of interest in your background by entering the civilian world in thought and speech. It takes real effort and determination on your part to translate your military or defense industry language back into easily understandable English. Take whatever time necessary to do it, but do it. When you have, it will do wonders to help you get a job.

SPECIAL PROBLEMS/SOLUTIONS

Broadening Your Job Search Location and Industry

I just finished talking to yet another high powered executive from the retail industry. He had an excellent record of accomplishments throughout his career and had risen through the ranks to a lofty position. The problem? His company was taken over by another firm, and it no longer had a need for him. By the time I met him, he had been unemployed for eight months and had been job hunting continuously without success. It took very little digging and probing on my part to identify his problem. His marketing plan was very simple. His objective was to find an appropriate level position offering a six figure income with a major retailer in St. Louis.

Do you have the picture yet?

Let's proceed.

How many possible major retailers do you think there are in St. Louis? A handful at best. And to compound his problem his retail background was limited to drug store chains. Is the picture starting to come into focus yet? I will be the first to agree that his retailing background should be transferrable across other retail lines. The problem in a nutshell is the extremely limited potential market for a high priced retail executive in the limited St. Louis market at any given point in time.

To illustrate this point, St. Louis has a population of about 2.4 million people in the metropolitan area. This represents less than one percent of the 250 million people in this country. St. Louis has as close to one percent of the job opportunities as it can get; therefore, he had been exploring only one percent of his job market.

What was his reason for insisting on St. Louis? He and his family were originally from New York City. They had relocated six different times. They had been living in St. Louis for three years and really liked it. They decided to make St. Louis their home. Now, there are as many different reasons for not wishing to relocate as there are people; and many of the reasons are valid. However, no matter how valid the reason for not wishing to relocate is, it will not change the fact that St. Louis or any city of similar size only represents a small portion of the potential job market.

After exhausting the very limited market in St. Louis and not finding a job there, he realized that something else had to be done. He decided to broaden his search to other industries to no avail. Now what? His lifestyle prevented him from taking any drastic cut in pay. Where do you go from here?

Let's go back to square one. He was totally unrealistic in his expectations from the start in limiting his search to St. Louis. It was one thing to start his search locally, but an entirely different matter to end it locally. He was literally up against a stacked deck within a month. His search should have been on a national level. He should start searching in those areas most desirable to him and still make St. Louis his number one choice. He would be pursuing all of the market versus a fraction of it, and he would still be covering his choice location. His prospects, thereby, would improve by a hundred fold. If there would be an opportunity in St. Louis, he would still be able to pursue it.

First, the approach taken by this executive led him nowhere. His financial picture slipped badly, and he was a pretty whipped man psychologically because of the eight months of rejection. Don't let this happen to you no matter how strong your rationalizations are. It is a perfect wager to pursue the national market, which will automatically include your local market. It is hoped that this point is clear to you.

➤ 071 Getting A Job In A Distant Area

If you have a special interest in relocating to a specific city, be sure to subscribe to local newspapers in the area. Also, you should locate any special trade publications that may be available. (St. Louis, as an example, has an excellent business paper called the *St. Louis Business Journal*. It is packed full of information covering the business scene. Job seekers would benefit greatly by reading this business publication during their job search in St. Louis. If you happen to be in construction, St. Louis also has the *Construction News and Review*, a publication covering the construction scene in the metropolitan area. The *St. Louis Post-Dispatch*, a daily newspaper, is excellent for all types of job search information.) Most large cities have similar local publications. Your chamber of commerce or library can generally provide you with the available publications within major cities.

Local newspapers are usually the only printed source of information for small towns. The editor or business editor of these small papers will usually be able to refer you to specific articles that may help you. Librarians in small communities usually keep a file of articles on business opportunities.

➤ 072 Long Distance Job Searching

Most people who wish to get a job in a distant city normally accomplish their job search in one of two ways. They can either pursue their job search via a long distance approach by mail and phone, or they can pack up their bags and move to the new city. The second move is gutsy, but it works much faster than the first approach.

There is a third approach that is one of the best guarded job search secrets. It eliminates the risk of moving first, then finding a job in the new city which may take some time. First, most people who want to move to a specific city will be moving "back home" where they have family or friends. What you do is use the address of your family or friends on your resume and letters along with their phone numbers. On the surface it appears that you currently reside in that town. Your family or friends must be willing to take your phone calls, state that you are not in at the moment, and then call you with the message. Any letters they might receive should be opened by them. If any response action is necessary, the correspondence should be forwarded or faxed to you for immediate follow-up.

If by chance you don't have family and friends in the new city, you can normally make arrangements for a small fee with an answering service to serve this purpose for you. Any phone calls you return can be handled in two different ways. First, handle yourself as though you were living in that town and do whatever necessary to arrange for an in-house interview. During the interview you can explain that you are not currently living there and that you paid your own expenses to get there because you plan to move "back home." You can be quiet at this point until the person responds. Then you can say that you are prepared to pay for your own moving expenses, if you are willing to do so. This will put you on equal footing when you are competing against local talent who will not require moving expenses. These costs to the company could work against you.

The second approach is for you to tell the company up-front on the phone that you are currently living out of town and explain your intentions to move back home. You be the judge of what approach to use. You may or may not be able to handle your own interview expense or moving expenses. When you pay for a job related move, it may be a tax deductible item on your income tax. Check out the actual cost and the effect it could have on your tax statement.

There is yet another option usually exercised by the unemployed. The person seeking employment goes to the city alone and lives with family or friends while seeking employment. Only after a job is acquired does the individual send for the family. Those without family or friends in the new city may rent an apartment by the month, (available in major markets). Others may rent a motel on a weekly or monthly basis, use the YMCA or rent a sleeping room for the duration of the job search; then they can pursue their job search. Some may find one or two part-time jobs to help meet expenses while pursuing their job search. All of these methods work. Take your pick.

➤ 073 Size Of Company

Joining the wrong sized company can be a mistake. A small, medium or large company, which one best suits your needs? The larger the company is the greater the attraction is to many people. They reason that the larger the size, the more successful the company. Size also conveys a secure company which has probably been around for a number of years; so be it. But in today's environment of downsizing, rightsizing and layoffs, security and size do not have parallels. Also, you should realize that the larger the company is the more rigid is its structure, policies and procedures. This represents a strong sense of security for many people. Everything is pretty well cast in concrete and certainty. Don't rock the boat. This is the way things are done around here, by the book.

Small companies on the other hand are loosely structured. There normally is no policy manual, and if there is it gets changed quite frequently. This can be very unsettling to many employees. Very little is unchangeable as compared to the large companies. Medium sized companies represent a blend of the large and the small. There is no such thing as the perfect sized company that is best for everyone. It is only right for you if your needs will be met and wrong if your needs will not be met. Plan your job hunting campaign and research to find the right sized company for you.

EXERCISE IN FUTILITY
Fortune 500 Companies

If you are looking for an exercise in futility in your job search, look no further. Your search has ended. Print 500 copies of your resume and mail them to the top Fortune 500 companies. Then sit back and wait... and wait... and wait... and wait... and wait... and wait some more. Talk about crushing one's ego with rejection.

Why is that? Because these 500 companies are the most highly visible household name companies in the land. On the surface it appears logical to pursue these companies. Most people like the idea of being employed by large successful firms. As a result, these firms are forever deluged with thousands of unsolicited resumes from across the land. Your resume will get mixed in with the rest. While all of this hot activity is occurring, most people fail to consider that these companies have been leading the parade in downsizing, cutbacks or rightsizing. They are getting leaner and meaner. This further compounds the potential rejection rate.

The following statistics should shed some light on this topic. In 1969, twenty-one percent of all non-farm jobs were with Fortune 500 companies. That was one job out of every five. By 1979, there were 16,193,344 people employed by Fortune 500 companies, a drop to eighteen percent of non-farm jobs. The Fortune 500 companies continued to downsize to only 11,973,236 employees in 1991, which is only ten plus percent of non-farm jobs. This is quite a drop. That is down to only one job in ten and dropping further. While at the same time small companies have expanded by over twenty million jobs.

Additionally, the Fortune 500 companies have cut over 600,000 more jobs within the past eighteen months. So there you have it.

It is one thing to selectively pursue specific Fortune 500 companies because your specific background matches their business activity. That is logical; however, just do not limit your job search exclusively to these firms. This would be a mistake.

GROWTH OPPORTUNITIES

If you are truly looking for a company with opportunities for growth, look no further; your search has ended. Do you honestly believe that there is such a thing as any company with no room for growth? No one is going to hold you back from contributing new growth to the company. Unfortunately, people seek out fast growing companies in the hopes that they will get swept up the ladder of success in the wave of growth. Joining a growth company with that rationale will not do a thing for you except get you frustrated. This is true unless you happen to be one of those rare people who will be a driving force that helps create the growth. Growth, in and of itself, just doesn't happen by itself; the right people make it happen.

I can speak from personal experience on this subject. I had the good fortune of working for two unusually fast growing Cinderella type companies at the early stages of their growth. In the early days of the booming bowling industry growth in 1960, I joined AMF. AMF had developed the first automatic pinspotters in the industry. The company enjoyed unprecedented growth. There was no such thing as a community or person who did not ultimately have access to a family fun center. This rapid growth and profitability enabled them to buy out other famous named companies that continued to fuel this growth even further; these include companies such as VOIT, Ben Hogan Golf, Hatteras Yachts, Head skies and tennis rackets, Harley-Davidson motorcycles and other top brand named companies. I was promoted to a manager within the year at AMF over other employees twice my age. If simply being in the right place at the right time was the total answer to getting promoted, all the other employees with the company prior to my joining it would have been promoted ahead of me. Such is not the case.

I left AMF after four years to join a new upstart company called Xerox. "Xerox? What was that name again?" "How in the world do you pronounce it?" "Is that an anti-freeze company?" No one could spell it correctly, and many people were even afraid to try to pronounce Xerox. I joined Xerox as a manager and shortly thereafter was promoted again. The same scenario applied here as at AMF. Being in the right place at the right time is only part of the answer to getting ahead and getting promoted.

The other key is doing what has to be done and going above and beyond the basic call of duty necessary to keep your job. Unfortunately, the majority of the people never quite see it that way. They never get the message for whatever reason. My experience and observations have taught me that people fall into one of three groups.

Group 1   These are the self-starters who go above and beyond the call of duty in every way possible. They come in early, stay late, do whatever necessary regardless of the weather or conditions and don't leave until the job is done. These are the employees commonly referred to as "good people." They are the backbone of the business, the core of the foundation that keeps companies alive, well and growing. You just can't say enough good things about them. They have strong positive attitudes towards their jobs, their fellow workers, the company and the customers. They care. They truly stand out from the crowd in every way at all levels within the company.

Group 2   Those that perform their jobs satisfactorily. They are employees who meet the basic requirements of the job. They come to work on time and put in a fair day's work. All companies need these good basic employees who make up the mass of the work force.

Group 3   Then there are those who fall short of the mark to varying degrees of doing their jobs. This group accounts for ninety percent or more of the tardiness, absenteeism, rock throwing, complaints, problems, negativism, disturbing the troops, attempts at beating the system, grievance filings, and never has a good thing to say about anything except quitting time. Just don't get caught in the vicinity of the exit door at quitting time or you might get killed by the stampede to the parking lot. Every company has its share of these people that are always being "weeded out."

So there you have it. There are many different mind sets. We don't all think alike or act alike or have the same values, that is just the way things are.

This is illustrated by a story about a guy named Herschel who worked in the maintenance shop of a major railroad. He was continually missing one day of work a week forevermore. He was continually being reprimanded for this practice. Nothing seemed to work. He simply could not make it in to work five days a week. This problem finally reached the yard superintendent, the top man, who called Herschel into his office. He proceeded to whip on Herschel with stern and final warnings and asked him why it was that he continually worked four days a week, week in and week out, to which Herschel responded, "I just can't make it on three days pay a week."

Mystery Of The Ages

Now I ask you, take a guess, give it your best shot, which group of employees do you honestly believe management regards as their promotable people? Make sure you give it some deep thought before you proceed to solve this mystery of the ages. Please keep in mind, some of the people in the second and third groups may have been hired prior to some of the people in group one. In fact some of them may have been employed from day one. Surely, many factors have to be taken into consideration. Some of the people in the second or third group may have graduated at the top of their class from the very best ivy-league schools or they may have MBA's or PhD's. They may excel in communication skills and have excellent personalities. They may dress well, look sharp and really have the proper image. What is missing? I am sure you know by now.

So, before proceeding any further with your job search you really ought to take a good look inside yourself and determine who you are, where you are, where you come from, where you want to go with your career, and then make the necessary commitment to get there. Otherwise you could end up repeating this job hunting process over and over again, like reliving a bad dream. It is up to you. For your added convenience a magic career map is included to get you where you want to go to the degree that you follow it.

Magic Career Map

The road map to mediocrity and failure is as clearly marked as the road map to success. It is as though you were actually looking at a road atlas. You first decide where you wish to go. All destinations are on the map. Just remember, hoping will not get you there. You do. Getting that job you want is one thing. Making it in that job is yet another. Just remember, getting the job you want and being a success is not a destination but a journey which you can control.

➤ 074 Starting Your Own Business

Some of you may be able to start your own business. Some may resort to this after exhausting themselves in their job search. Look deep within yourself. This may be the best thing for you. What have you always wanted to be if you were your own boss? Do you have the stamina, the persistence, the drive and the know-how to run your own business? What are all the details that you need to handle if you start your own business? If you are thinking along these lines, you should turn to the library or even take a class or two on business, business management and brush up on accounting, taxes, and the legal aspects of business. Decide if you want to buy a franchise or form a corporation, a partnership or a sole proprietorship. Will your family help you in the business or will you work alone? Will you work from your home or rent an office? These and many more questions need to be addressed. The big issue is will you have enough money to support yourself, your family and your business long enough to make it a success?

Do not stop at just one option. There are many. When your job search plan starts to develop, you will begin to see all the twists and turns it could take. This will help you focus on some avenues, but you should not discard any plausible career opportunity.

➤ **075 Change Plans**
If plan A is not working, go to plan B.

6

HOW LONG SHOULD IT TAKE?

Going With The Flow: The average person tends to drift along in life, going with the flow, without realizing what is going on. As a result these people end up becoming a mixed bag of what they wanted to become but never worked hard enough to achieve it, and what they hoped they would never become, but ended up becoming.

<u>HOW LONG WILL IT TAKE?</u>

(How Long Should It Take?)

"How long will it take to get a job?" is one of the more frequently asked questions by job seekers. The answer depends upon many factors.

1. <u>Personal Situation</u>. For many job seekers this is the first time they have ever been in the job market. For others, this is the first time they have had to compete for middle and upper management positions. Both typically suffer from anxiety attacks on this subject. After all, job hunting is a quest into uncertainties. Most people I talk to have good to excellent backgrounds. I tell them so and give them heavy assurances that if they apply themselves to the job market they will find a good job. In fact, it would be very uncommon even in today's job market not to do so.

Many employees have been cut back, downsized or rightsized from long standing careers with one company. These people are going to have a more difficult time of it. This is particularly true of middle management people. Some career fields have been terminated and will never come back. A career change is required; this will take major adjustments.

Some people have made a mess of their careers. They need to make a complete turnaround before they can land a decent job.

Still others have hopped, skipped and jumped from one job and industry to another as career nomads. They could not pull together their work history if they wanted because they have had so many different jobs. Employers will look skeptically at them. Other job seekers are close to retirement age. A high salary, long work history and prestigious position will place those near the end of their careers in the overqualified category.

Some are homemakers entering the job market after a period of time. These, too, need to prove themselves by transferability of skills.

All of the above types of job seekers are the exceptions; many of them will have to resign themselves to heavy compromises in the type of job they can get.

> *Time alone will only do one thing for you*
> *and that is it will make you grow older.*

Time alone will not get you a job. It is the amount of productive activity, coupled with time, that will make it happen.

2.   The Approach. The question really should be "How long should it take?" This is because how long it "will take" and how long it "should take" are two different things. The difference between "should take" and "will take" will be measured by the amount and type of activity

expended. This is within your control. In order to put time into perspective one must establish a basic assumption. You will be successful to the degree that you follow daily and weekly a well structured marketing plan.

A hit-or-miss (off-the-seat-of-the-pants) approach followed only when the spirit moves you will produce like results. Unfortunately, this turns out to be the most common approach. Most people suffer from a bad case of the "lazies" when it comes to doing chores. And job hunting is a chore to many people.

3.   The Level Of Position. The following rule of thumb will apply to most industry lines. The higher the position level: the fewer the number of openings, the greater the competition and the longer the company takes to make a decision. The following diagram should suffice.

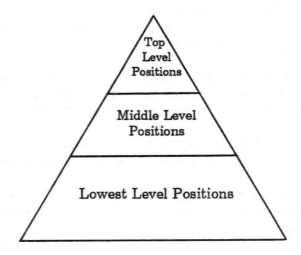

This picture makes it self evident that the higher you move up the ladder, the fewer the jobs. As a result, competition for those jobs will be greater, and the job search will take longer.

4. <u>Selectivity Of Job Seekers</u>. There is another point for you to keep in mind. Getting an offer or offers is one thing, accepting an offer is another. The degree of selectivity among job seekers is extremely diverse. It ranges from the individual who will accept the first job offer to those job seekers who persist in their job search until they get exactly what they want. Job seekers in the latter group are not people just looking for a job, but they are seeking a meaningful career position that meets their immediate needs, as well as their long range potential. These differences have to be factored in when computing how long it should take for the average person at different levels to find a job. Your degree of selectivity is a very important variable.

5. <u>Local, National, International Economic Forecast</u>. The state of the economy impacts business; therefore, it impacts hiring. The expanding, the average or the recessionary economies, each has an individual time frame. The more depressed the economy is the longer it will take a company to fill a position, and fewer expansion positions are available.

    The following ballpark figures show how long it usually takes to find a job during normal economic times.

    Executive Level Positions: 6 - 12 months or more
    Middle Management: 3 - 6 months
    Salaried Professionals: 2 - 3 months
    Hourly workers: 1/2 - 2 months

    Recessionary periods will slow the hiring process.

6. <u>Salary Requirements</u>. Another formula shows the relationship between the salary level and length of time required to find a job. The higher the salary, the longer it takes to fill the job. For example, in 1992 - a slow market year, this equates to one month required for each $10-15,000 earned.

Salary Versus Job Search Time Frames

$10-$15,000 - 1 month
$16-$20,000 - 2 months
$21-$30,000 - 3 months
$31-$40,000 - 4 months
$41-$50,000 - 5 months
$51-$60,000 - 6 months
$61-$70,000 - 7 months
$71-$80,000 - 8 months
$81-$90,000 - 9 months
$100,000 up - 10 - 12 months or more

These are only reference scales. They are nothing more, nothing less. This makes up the average length of time people take or need to get a job they want. Please understand, some people take less time, and some take more time.

7.   The Job Market - Degree Of Demand. Another big factor is the degree of demand in the market place. Certain industries (such as computers and high tech) are growing rapidly; and, therefore, they represent a higher demand for people compared to other industries (such as steel or mining). The same holds true for certain skills.

8.   Career Flexibility. Degree of flexibility on the part of the job seeker is yet another key factor. Again, the higher the level of flexibility, the greater the chances are for success. A good example of this would be a person who is a controller of a barge line company who wishes to change companies only within the barge line industry. Or a controller within a savings and loan company who wishes to remain within the savings and loan industry rather than be open to all industries. Financial skills in particular are highly transferable across most industry lines. Therefore, anyone with financial skills would be wise to expand one's

parameters as they relate to a variety of industries. Entirely too many people have self-imposed constraints in their thinking. They feel comfortable within their industry. They feel they encounter enough change by going to a new company. A new industry would represent too much change for them to handle. What if they can't cut it in the new industry? After all, each industry is different. This gnawing fear of change is prevalent among job seekers, and it works against them.

9. <u>Location Flexibility</u>. Another major variable is the degree of flexibility concerning possible locations. The greater the flexibility, the greater the job search opportunities. A good example of this would be the controller who was discussed earlier from the savings and loan industry. Let's say he now lives in Indianapolis, Indiana, and he wishes to remain in Indianapolis for any one of a number of reasons. His desire to remain in the savings and loan field and his desire to remain in Indianapolis doubly compound the problem.

From a sheer logistics standpoint there are too few savings and loan companies in any given market. It doesn't matter if we are talking about New York City, Chicago, Los Angeles or Indianapolis. The broader your geographic flexibility, the better your opportunities for success are. To restrict oneself to Indianapolis is to restrict the number of possible opportunities. It may take a long, long time! Indianapolis has a population of 700,000. That is only one-fourth of one percent of the nation's population; therefore, only one-fourth of one percent of the savings and loan market. That is placing a person in a restrictive job search market. Apply this principle to your job search, your career choice, your industry choice and your location choice. If you want a job sooner, expand your choices.

Please understand, this book is not suggesting

relocation is the ultimate answer to your job search. However, there is a definite correlation between your selected geographic area and the number of potential opportunities available there. The more flexible you are in terms of geography, the greater the number of job opportunities there are. You should at least approach this subject with an open mind.

Most people would prefer not to relocate; however, most people will relocate depending upon the opportunity. The higher up the ladder one has climbed, the greater the odds are of relocation. Lower level positions by their very nature are more plentiful; they rarely call for relocation. There are exceptions, of course, which normally occur in small towns or rural communities. The vast majority of jobs are located in or near the larger metropolitan areas of the country.

10. <u>Education And College</u>. Another important factor is the level of education and the quality/prestige of the college you attended. A highly recognized college or university that is known for its academic excellence in your specific field will carry more weight than an unknown, nondescript college. A lack of education must be compensated with other positive factors.

11. <u>Academic Success</u>. Your class standing and grade point average are additional factors that will play an important role for younger people. I am simply amazed at how youth often forgets the answer to these two questions so easily. It is called a "convenient memory" when they can't recall their standings. The truth of the matter is they chose to forget because they don't want to remember. People who graduated at the top ten and even top twenty-five or fifty percent have no problem recalling their class standing or grade point average. Other matters are often conveniently forgotten such as poor performance and the lack of the extra curricular and social activities that display leadership qualities.

12. <u>Work Experience And The Industry</u>. The next factor is your work experience. The longer you are out of school, the more pertinent your work experience becomes. The amount of experience is one factor; the type of experience is another, and the type of industry is still another. How far have you moved up or have you stood still? The industry affects this, as well as your abilities. Whether you are in a growth industry (computers/high tech/ medical) or a diminishing one (steel/shoes/ defense) is the luck of the draw. Those of you from fast growth industries will typically have an easier time of it. Those of you from the steel or shoe industry should not despair since most skills from most industries are transferable across industry lines. However, it will take more work, time, patience and persistence.

13. <u>Job Stability, Work Ethics And Your References</u>. A common thought among employment personnel is that the best measure of a person's future success is that person's past record. It is almost as certain as if it were a law of physics that states, "An object in motion tends to stay in motion." Does this apply to all people, one hundred percent? No, but what really applies one hundred percent to anything? Your past track record is going to play a valuable role in the outcome of your job search. What kind of references will you get from past employers?

14. <u>Accomplishments</u>. Another important factor is your accomplishments. This is without a doubt the area most omitted on resumes. Yet, it is probably the most important area in your favor. Most people feel very uncomfortable about making statements that could be interpreted as bragging or boastful. You must keep in mind if it is, indeed, a fact, then it is not bragging. If you choose to stretch the truth, then it is bragging and should not be stated. If you do not state your accomplishments, you are likely to lose to other job seekers who do. Furthermore, you will never get the

much deserved recognition for any significant accomplishments to which you are entitled. The more and more impressive your accomplishments are the easier it is to get a job. This is true provided you do not fall into the over qualified situation. Position your accomplishments to be applicable to specific needs of the hiring firm. This should help.

15. <u>Skills</u>. Communication skills, both written and oral, are pluses in just about every job possible. No question about it, people who have the edge here also have an edge in job hunting. All your skills are marketable. If you have only a few skills or if they are not current with the times, then you need help. For example, if you are a writer and still use a typewriter rather than a word processor, then you need to gain the skills necessary to keep pace with the times.

16. <u>Appearance/Character/Characteristics</u>. Some people appear professional; they look great, and they have an advantage over those who don't. Drawbacks in this area must be counterbalanced in other ways.

Your dress and grooming can go a long way in getting you a job. Some people have a flair for proper dress and grooming and have the right wardrobe for maximum effectiveness. Some people are down right slobs. They must clean up their act or pay the consequences. Get help if you cannot do it yourself. This is one area that is definitely within your control; yet, so many people fail miserably at it. There is really no excuse.

A great personality and charisma are selling points in your favor if you have them. Those of you who go unnoticed will have to make up for this weakness in other ways. Your character, your determination and your sincerity can all be made noticeable to your prospective employer.

17. <u>Networking</u>. The more people you know and the quicker you contact them to tell them that you are looking for work, the sooner you will get a job. Networking is the quickest way of getting a job. Even if you do not know a large number of people, you can start networking and develop a large number of contacts.

    Ask everyone you meet to help you. This will go a long way in speeding up the process of your job search.

18. <u>Resumes/Cover Letters</u>. The more resumes you send, the more contacts you will be making with prospective employers; therefore, the more job interviews you will have and the quicker you will get a job. It is not uncommon for a person who is serious about getting a job quickly to send out a thousand or more resumes with moderately customized cover letters to fit the various types of companies.

19. <u>Luck</u>. Does luck really help make a person be in the right place at the right time? I will close on this subject by sharing with you a lesson I have learned from life; the harder you work, the luckier you will get.

20. <u>Attitude</u>. The most significant variable is one that is completely within your control; it is your attitude. Your attitude will reflect your level of confidence, commitment and expectations.

    The power of positive thinking cannot be stressed strongly enough. Things pretty well happen the way you expect them to. Tell me what your expectations are and that is what will likely happen. It comes down to being a self-fulfilled prophecy. Hold your head high, keep a smile on your face and believe in yourself. The odds will weigh heavier in the favor of your expectations.

Rate Your Time Frame Factor

Consider each of the following factors that affect how long
it should take for you to get a job. Rank your time rate from
1 (short term) to 10 (long term).

	1	2	3	4	5	6	7	8	9	10
1 Personal Situation										
2 Approach										
3 Level Of Position										
4 Job Seekers Selectivity										
5 Economic Forecast										
6 Salary Requirements										
7 The Job Market/Demand										
8 Career Flexibility										
9 Location Flexibility										
10 Education/College										
11 Academic Success										
12 Experience/Industry										
13 Job Stability										
14 Accomplishments										
15 Skills										
16 Appearance/Character										
17 Networking										
18 Resumes/Cover Letters										
19 Luck										
20 Attitude										

How would you judge yourself? At this point in your career
what factors can you control to increase your job prospects?
Remember, the past is the past.

How can you present your past to be most favorable to you?

In those factors that you can control, how can you move
down a notch or two or even all the way to one?

**All twenty of these factors will play a part in
determining how long it will take for you to find the
position that will meet or exceed your short and long
range career objectives.**

What I Can Do To Improve My Time Rate

1 **Personal Situation**
_____
_____

2 **Approach**
_____
_____

3 **Level Of Position**
_____
_____

4 **Job Seekers Selectivity**
_____
_____

5 **Economic Forecast**
_____
_____

6 **Salary Requirements**
_____
_____

7 **The Job Market/Demand**
_____
_____

8 **Career Flexibility**
_____
_____

9 **Location Flexibility**
_____
_____

10 **Education/College**
_____
_____

11 Academic Success

_____

_____

12 Experience/Industry

_____

_____

13 Job Stability

_____

_____

14 Accomplishments

_____

_____

15 Skills

_____

_____

16 Appearance/Character

_____

_____

17 Networking

_____

_____

18 Resumes/Cover Letters

_____

_____

19 Luck

_____

_____

20 Attitude

_____

_____

The purpose in covering this subject so broadly is very simple. There are no quick answers. Many factors combine to play a part in how long it will take to find the right career for you. Hopefully, this will also help you plan and prepare for now, as well as in the future.

Section Two: *Planning*

7

YOUR JOB SEARCH ACTION PLAN

OVERVIEW

An Ode To A Successful Job Hunt

Oh, to know what has to be done.
Oh, to know how to do it.
Oh, to do what has to be done,
*   the way it should be done,*
*   on time - when you do it.*
Oh, to follow through, follow through,
*   follow through.*
Oh, to find the job that's right for you,
*   that's right for you,*
*   that's right for you.*
And when you do your job hunt's through -
It is all up to you.

Your job search overview is included at this point in the book to give you an insight into the total job search picture. Scan this chapter briefly and then come back to it after you have finished reading the book and are ready to construct your job search action plan.

ORGANIZING YOUR JOB SEARCH

First things first. The first step in the job hunting process is to develop a plan to achieve your objective: finding the job you want within a reasonably specified time period. This almost sounds too basic, but the truth of the matter is that most job searchers fail miserably in this area. They simply wing it off-the-seat-of-their-pants. Corresponding results occur. This is definitely no way to go. A better way involves planning.

JOB SEARCH ACTION PLAN OVERVIEW

The following is a foundation for a good basic job hunting plan. It briefly lists what can and should be done to assist you in a successful job search. Because no single job search plan can meet everyone's needs, you should make additions and deletions to suit your job search situation.

Attitude

1. Your attitude is vitally important to your job search success. Stay positive.

Survival

2. Establish and maintain an income throughout your job search.

    - If employed, you should stay employed until you find a job that is right for you. Don't quit your job prematurely.

    - Register for unemployment benefits if you are unemployed. Don't procrastinate. Benefits don't start until you sign up. Sometimes it is hard to adjust to this reality, but it helps you survive until you get a job.

    - If you are unemployed and have no unemployment benefits seek a part-time job. The added income will help sustain you. It is also good psychologically for you to be active in this work-a-day world. Temporary employment services may meet this need. If you are qualified, act as a consultant.

Preparation

3. Set aside a work space in your home which will be the center of your job search activity. Regard it as a business office. Keep all your job search materials there and stay organized.

4. Acquire the following items and use them to assist you in your job search. They will make your job search much easier and keep you on track.

    • Buy a good appointment book that provides a week at-a-glance. It should have plenty of space to book your appointments and follow-up calls.

    • Buy a large cork board to hang in front of your work space area. This is the ideal place for messages and friendly reminders.

    • Buy a telephone answering machine. Then tape a good brief businesslike message; please, nothing cute or off color when you are job hunting. Alert all family members concerning the importance of taking good clear messages and phone numbers.

    • Buy a supply of simple classic stationery and envelopes for "thank you" notes: nothing fancy or expensive, please. Either white or soft tones are preferred.

5. Your personal needs should be addressed. You should spruce up your wardrobe and grooming from your hair to your shoes and everything in between. Keep your best foot forward at all times.

Research

6. Job search literature sources are the key to successful job search. Use them thoroughly.

   - Become acquainted with your bookstore and ask the attendant for help. Ask for the job search books section. Buy the help you need. Don't skimp.

   - Become acquainted with the reference department of your main public library. Tell the librarians that you are looking for a job and ask for help concerning the special section of books on job search, resumes, careers and the like and research assistance available on companies and industries.

   - Write to publishers. Scan approximately six to eight weeks of back issue newspapers and trade publications for help wanted ads for the markets in which you have an interest. Many of these jobs will still remain unfilled; this is true particularly for the high level positions. Make sure you subscribe as soon as possible to the necessary newspapers, trade journals and publications. (It may take several weeks before you get them.) Plan ahead and you will profit by them when they arrive.

7. Job search sources and resources need to be sought out and used.

   - Depending upon your potential employment level, become listed with appropriate executive search firms or employment agencies, alumni and trade associations and all other referral services.

   - Recent graduates or seniors in college should attend campus job fairs. General and specific interest job fairs occur in cities of sufficient size and need. Attend job fairs of interest to you. Don't just browse. You must have a plan of attack to be effective.

- Trade shows and conventions are excellent avenues to pursue job opportunities. But you must work at them with a plan:

  Pre-convention/trade show activities.
  Activities while at the convention/trade show.
  Follow-up after the convention/trade show.

- Contact all chamber of commerce offices in your target areas to find out what information they have available that could help you.

- Contact and list with your trade association(s). Some are more active than others in this area.

- If you are unemployed, be sure to explore the various business-people-between-jobs organizations. Select one in which to become active. You can learn a great deal from other members and also receive support from them.

8. Be sure to conduct the necessary additional research on companies prior to your interviews. Your company research will enable you to interview much more effectively; therefore, it will help improve your opportunity for success.

Networking

9. Construct a networking list.

- To begin you should list no less than twenty-five names. Some people will start with one hundred or more names and will increase their job search success if they do. Each of these contacts could help you broaden your interviewing prospects.

- Plan on adding new people to your list daily. Cultivate extensive lists, and you will improve your interviewing possibilities greatly. This is by far the oldest, best and most tried and proven method to secure jobs. If you want to get a job quickly, increase your networking.

10. (Optional) Place ads under "positions wanted" in your specific trade publications. People do get jobs doing this. Remember, nothing is one hundred percent.

Career Options

11. Identify your career options through assistance at your public library and broaden your career outlook.

- *US Industrial Outlook* lists job prospects for over 350 industries.

- *US Dictionary of Occupational Titles* is broken down into more than 22,000 different job descriptions with new jobs being added every year.

- *Encyclopedia of Careers & Vocational Guidance* in four volumes is an excellent source.

- There are over 15 million different companies in this country. Printed material and annual reports are available on many of them if you ask.

- At the library reference department research and identify the industries, companies and positions that best meet your career needs. These will also be the same firms to which you can make the greatest contribution to their growth and profitability. These are your target companies. Then mail a resume and cover letter to each one systematically for exploratory opportunities to interview. Your sense of urgency will dictate your activity level.

- Relocation is an option. Select your location preferences. The greater your flexibility, the greater your opportunities. Pursue all options simultaneously rather than one at a time, and you will improve your opportunities proportionately.

- (Optional) Contact your city, county, state offices for available job opportunities. In 1992, these offices had 4,368,000 people working for them nationwide. They comprise the nation's largest employer by far. There are books available on how to approach these markets successfully. Ask your librarian for them.

- (Optional) Contact your federal government offices for job opportunities. Refer to federal government job source books. This is the second largest employer in the country.

- Research and identify all not-for-profit agencies and organizations. This market is the most often overlooked by job seekers.

Specific Action

12. Establish your job objective, don't state vague generalities. If you are uncertain, do some research on the subject, or turn to career and vocational counselors or college/university guidance centers for help.

13. Read a good book or two on resume writing so you will know a good resume from a poor one. Then either write your own resume which is based upon examples you found in books or use a resume writing service.

14. Never send a resume without an appropriate cover letter. Never! Books on resume writing normally include cover letter samples. A resume writing service can also write your cover letters for you. One general cover letter will not do. You will need different letters for

different occasions. Always address the cover letter to a specific person, if possible.

15. Buy/read a book or two on interviewing. Then practice what you learn. Your job search will benefit greatly from this.

16. Set appointments for interviews.

17. Follow up on all your calls and letters in a timely manner. This will produce results when nothing else will. You must be patient but persistent.

18. Review your resume and cover letters for possible areas of improvement prior to reprinting. Amend, resend, follow up; amend, resend, follow up; amend, resend, follow up.

19. Read a book on negotiating to help you during the offer stage; then practice what you have learned.

20. After you have landed a job, don't forget to inform all those in your network and all appropriate sources. Thank them for their help and consideration. They deserve it. Entirely too many people drop the ball in this area.

These activities call for action on your part. The key is:

**Make your plan workable for you; then,
work your plan to achieve success.**

The following chapters cover the points outlined in this overview. As you read on, you will see how easy it is to make your plan and put it in practice. Despite the times the goal of getting a job right for you can be obtained. Follow the directions in this book, and you will achieve success. Reread this chapter while you construct your own job search action plan to success.

8

SETTING UP YOUR JOB SEARCH

MARKETING CAMPAIGN

> *Time revolves around you*
> *if you plan your time.*
> *You revolve around time (going around in circles)*
> *if you don't.*

Nothing is easier than planning if you know what to plan for. After reading this book you will know how to plan your job search campaign successfully. Planning is one thing. Carrying out your plans is another matter. You need the determination and persistence of a bulldog to get the job done.

1. Set up your job search headquarters.
2. Understand change as it affects your plans.
3. Construct a realistic plan that you can
   achieve or you will get frustrated and give up.
4. Know what you need to make your plan come true.
   (What you currently lack and how to get it.)
5. Learn to enjoy planning your job search campaign,
   executing it and reaching success.
6. Go for it.

➤ 076 Your Job Hunting Headquarters
Set aside a specific place in your home that will be your base of operations, your nerve center, for keeping your

job search organized and on course. This is the most effective way to get yourself on track. You did this as a student. You had a place where you studied and did your homework. The sooner, the quicker, the faster, you establish your work center and get organized the more success you will have. All too many people simply hope to get lucky and get a job quickly. This rarely happens.

➤ 077 Inspiration Around You

Have inspirational messages and special incentive rewards around your base of operations that will motivate and inspire you throughout the ups and downs of your job search. You can count on getting your share of both. Continue to add new messages (books, a picture, a poem, a phrase) whenever you find them along the way. Buy a cork bulletin board. Get it large enough so it won't be too crowded or cluttered. The cost is about ten dollars, and it will serve you well throughout your job search and beyond. Keep your inspirational messages in sight.

➤ 078 Record Keeping

Failure to keep good records is a job search crime. You need to document all of your efforts like a ship's log of activity. Develop and record a workable follow-up system. Don't just drift along hoping for the best. A good follow-up program will produce results when nothing else will.

➤ 079 Selecting An Appointment Book

Buy a good appointment book/calendar with enough space to record your appointments and follow-up calls. This almost sounds too elementary, but it isn't. I have seen professionals who while working use the appointment book religiously but during job search lay it aside and don't use it again until employed. They would record interview appointments, for instance, on the refrigerator calendar, an envelope, book cover or on a scrap of paper. Does that tell you something about one's attitude about the job hunt and perhaps could be a factor in the length of time it takes to get a job? Could any appointments be missed when an appointment book is not used? The average person never gives any thought to an appointment book and does not consider it an important job search tool. Most rely on the traditional free give-away calendars from an insurance agent, garage, grocery store or other. Don't be casual about your appointments. Hit and miss approaches produce hit and miss results. This is the norm. Stop it. Start changing your ways, and this will change the results. Isn't that what you want?

➤ 080 Your Telephone And Answering Machine

A telephone answering machine (or an answering service) and a back up telephone number are necessary in today's job search. Telephone answering machines have grown in popularity to where the whole world is now accustomed to them. If you are not, you had better get in step with the rest of the world. Employed people looking to make a job change are at work all day and are not at home. The unemployed are in and out throughout the day and week. Everyone knows how frustrating it is to try to reach people who never seem to be at home. One can give up after making call after call, after call, after call, after call. Here is a classic example of opportunity knocking, knocking, and knocking at your door; and there is no one at home to open the door. This cannot be stressed strongly enough. Companies should somehow be able to get through to you during the normal business day.

You will considerably improve your odds of being contacted if you follow this advice. Yet, probably no more than five percent of all job seekers will do so. You should be able to review your phone messages at least twice during the day, so you can respond to them in a timely manner. This applies even if you have to go out of town.

➤ 081   Change Jobs When You Are Ready

The best time to change jobs is when you are ready to do so.   The time of year, state of the economy or whatever should not deter you.   While it is true that there will be fewer opportunities during slow economic times or recessions, there will be opportunities during such times that will totally meet your career needs and will slip through your fingers if you don't take action. Don't rationalize yourself out of excellent opportunities that surface even in the worst of times.   Otherwise you will live to regret it.

➤ 082   Fear Of Change

In the course of making a job change it is perfectly natural for you to feel some fear of change.   The ordeal of change is something that the world at large looks upon with great anxiety.   Even people such as a migrant farm worker experiences this feeling when switching over from picking one crop to the next such as radishes to lettuce.   We all feel this nagging fear, an uneasiness whenever we experience any change.   This is not a new experience to you.   You faced it from one school year to the next, from grade school to junior high, high school, college and so on.   Whatever you do, don't let this feeling hold you back.   It will pass very quickly in your new job as it has in the past.

➤ 083   Preparation Versus "Excusitis"

Making excuses versus preparation, is there a difference?   Entirely too many people suffer from what I refer to as a bad case of "excusitis."   This is a word I coined to describe people who are hooked on the habit of routinely making excuses and not doing what has to be done because they have an excuse not to do it.   You cannot excuse your way into getting a job.

➤ **084 Education**
If you find yourself short of the right amount of education or degree that is preventing you from getting the job you want, go back to school and get it. It is the best thing you can do to help you and your career. Go for it.

➤ **085 Cost Of Education**
A good education will cost you a lot of money. However, the lack of a good education will cost you even more.

➤ **086 Planning**
This point is going to sound trite to some of you, but it is worth the risk on my part because its importance is second to none.

> *If you fail to plan,*
> *you will plan to fail.*

People have a tendency to simply wing it off the-seat-of-their-pants in their job search. This is by far the norm. A great number of people have been highly successful in finding jobs by winging it during boom times or even during normal times. As a result they think it will always work; therefore, they continue doing it from that point forward. However, in tight job markets or recessionary times more effort has to be exerted to get a job. I honestly believe many people simply don't understand what planning means; yet, they have been planning various kinds of activities throughout their lives.

For openers, whatever you wish to achieve should be put down in writing. This is nothing more than crystallizing your thoughts - visualizing the kind of job title you wish. When it is in clear focus, write it at the top of a sheet of paper; then list the type of duties and responsibilities you would like to perform. Now, you know what you are looking for. Next, the many different things you will need to do to achieve your objective and the specific time frames to do them will come into view. Be realistic, don't short cut any step. Your basic plan is now before you. More specifics can be added at any time. Be sure to include all the advice in this book. (Refer to Chapters 9 and 10 when you research yourself to determine what kind of work you really like to do and follow Chapter 7 Action Plan Overview while you make your plan.) You are now on your way to successful job hunting.

➤ 087 Pen And Note Pad

Carry a pen and note pad with you at all times throughout your job search. Make this a habit. You will need these to write down new networking contacts. You should also be picking up new job source leads to follow throughout your job search. Furthermore, creative bursts of thought will come to you from out of nowhere that should not be allowed to slip through your memory. Jot these ideas down whenever they may occur. Be sure to use whatever time you must spend waiting in a productive manner by brainstorming within your own mind for new ideas and activities; then, write them down immediately. Keep pen and paper at your bedside so upon awakening you can record a night vision or idea. (A number of topics for this book were written following these exact same suggestions. It works.)

➤ 088 Daily To Do's

Get into the habit at the end of each day of making a list of "Things To Do Today" for the following day. Use a tablet exclusively for this purpose. You will accomplish a great deal more on a daily basis by doing this and enjoy a greater sense of accomplishment as you check off the items on your list one at a time. (Refer to Chapter 9 and check how many of the "Things I Like" and "Things I Dislike" you are actually doing.)

➤ **089 Plan Specifics With Time And Dates**
When you are planning your job search activities, always assign specific times and dates to each task to be performed. Open ended commitments rarely get done. An example of an open ended commitment would be to "contact the XYZ company" without a reference to when, where or who. A lack of specific time and date commitment will allow you to muster up all the necessary rationale to put things off indefinitely. The proper way would be to commit to contacting Bill Black, Vice President of Marketing at the XYZ company at 8:00 a.m., Tuesday, July 9; then, list what you need to accomplish from the contact. This will keep your feet to the fire to live up to that commitment.

➤ **090 Time Is Money - Your Life Is On A Meter**
Do not conduct your life as though you have a thousand years left to live. The meter is running out for everyone. Conduct yourself accordingly.

SCAVENGER HUNT

Urgency is a job hunt requirement if you happen to be unemployed or need to make a job change in a hurry. Don't become a victim of too little, too late in your job search. Today's tight and tough competitive job market calls for considerable activity to be urgently pursued.

Sometime during your youth you may have participated in a scavenger hunt at a party. Each person is usually given a list of items to find in the neighborhood. Such things as a bobby pin, a book of matches, a bottle cap, a tooth pick, or a "green" toothbrush are listed. The object is for each person or team to run (not walk) from house to house, to rapidly knock on the door and to quickly tell the occupants the items that are needed for the scavenger hunt. There is absolutely no time to waste. Every minute counts as the scavenger hunter runs through the want list and moves to the next house. The first person to return to the party with the entire list of items wins.

To be successful today your job search sense of urgency must closely resemble a scavenger hunt. You have to put your job hunting search into high gear and keep knocking on doors until you get the job that you are looking for.

Another important point comes to mind in playing this game. For some strange reason the people playing the game never feel rejected when they are turned down or could not be helped. It was nothing personal when someone did not have anything on the list. Treat your job hunting the same way, and it will help you cope with the rejection you will face.

➤ 091 Time And Consistency

Finding the right job is a full time job. You are going to have to get your priorities in order to be successful. First things first. Make the necessary time available and make the commitment to get the job done. Too many people give it the "old college try." They will test the water; if it is too cold, they will pull out for a spell; then try again later. If you work at your job search sporadically, you will get sporadic results. Only consistency will produce consistent results which will move you onward to the job that is right for you.

THE HIRING TIME FRAME

How long will it take? How anxious are you? The more anxious you are the longer it will seem to take for you to get a job that is right for you. There is no average length of time that the hiring process will take. It will vary from one company to the next, because many different factors come into play. The level of the position is a major factor. The size of the company is yet another. Larger companies take longer than smaller companies. The hiring process can take from one interview at one extreme to several months or even a year or two at the other. On average it will take from three to six weeks for most salaried positions.

There is a very strong correlation between the level of position and the length of the hiring process. The same correlation also applies to the number of people involved. Lower level positions usually require shorter hiring time frames with fewer people involved. The converse is true for higher level positions: longer hiring time frames with more people involved.

Employment agencies will fill their lower level "hot job orders" within 48 hours. One to two people will be involved with the hiring process. On the other hand, executive search firms will average weeks or months to fill their searches. Several people can be involved in the hiring process including search committees and/or members of the board of directors. Some of the more widely publicized top level positions have taken as long as a year or two; these are exceptions. Know the variations, and don't become impatient. You can always ask the company, but it cannot always pin down exact time frames.

Knowing the time frame will allow you to plan your interviews and your job hunting campaign effectively and let you know where you stand. This will also reduce anxiety that most people experience in job hunting.

Place follow-up activity at strategic points along the hiring time line. Some companies will tell you when the next step will take place during the wrap-up of your interview. If not, then ask what the next step will be and when it will take place. Whatever date is given, it should be marked on your calendar for follow-up. Do it on time.

A strong word of caution is in order. Making follow-up calls are very important. However, don't overdo them. Many people kill their chances for consideration by making a pest of themselves. Don't leave a rash of messages. If this does not kill your chances, it will surely substantially reduce your negotiating posture. It is not always easy to sit back and wait; sometimes it is nearly impossible particularly during unemployment times. The longer one is unemployed; the worse things get. All I can suggest to you is don't push too hard. It is a crazy quirk of human nature to want what is hardest to get. Now I don't make up these rules and neither do you, but we all have to live by them. The more you make yourself available, the less interested the company will be in you.

Deal from strength. Make the company seem to want you more than you want it. It takes patience. Let the company know you are interested, but not desperate. This applies whether you are employed or unemployed. The overkill position is most common when you have all of your job prospects in one basket; a single company. This is a mistake. Don't be shallow in your job hunting campaign. Don't slack off when a job offer appears. Nothing is assured until you receive an offer, accept it, then report to work. However, don't let frustration, uncertainty, rejections and fear make you accept a job offer you don't really want. Again, no matter how great the urge to do so, don't! It would be a mistake.

We, in our executive search practice, face a similar problem with our clients. What happens is that initially we will secure several prospective candidates for a particular need. The first candidate the company interviews may be exactly what is sought. The company tells us to stop our search efforts and cancel the other candidates that we have recruited for them. This is a mistake. We point out that there is no assurance that the person will accept the offer, and until this occurs the search is not completed.

The ideal situation occurs when you are dealing from strength: talking to several different companies simultaneously while continually adding new prospects.

Dealing from this position of strength allows you to nudge any company without anxiety. You can honestly let each company know you are considering another company or two. Even if you may have as many as a half dozen prospects in the works, it is bad taste and an overkill to state that you have a large number of prospects. In today's market it would seem untrue even if it is. Put yourself in their shoes. How would you feel?

> ### 092   Working At Job Hunting Until It Pays Off
Being in the right place at the right time is more than just plain luck. The more active you are in your job search, the more opportunities you make and the better you have positioned yourself to be in the right place at the right time.

> ### 093   More Work - Better Success
All things being equal (myth), the person who works twenty-five percent more at whatever that person is doing will stand out from the crowd and/or get an upper hand on the competition. This applies to your job, as well as your job search.

> ### 094   Pacing Yourself And Burn Out
Don't push your job hunting campaign seven days a week. You will burn out. Everyone needs a break from routine. The seriously unemployed can push entirely too hard in this area, because they hope that they can force something to happen. Don't do it. Take a break. It will renew you physically and mentally. It is certainly not easy for those who are financially strapped. You might ask yourself how can I go out and play golf or put my feet up and watch T.V. for a while when I need to be looking for a job? How can I afford the time? Take it. Somehow, someway, force yourself to slack off the oars and get away from your job hunting each week. Saturday is a good day for this break. Most people can get the job done working at it three, four or five days a

week. Don't keep whipping on yourself.

➤ **095 Continue Until You Are Satisfied!**

Do not stop your job hunting campaign at the first sign of a promising "potential" job offer just because things are looking positive. Wishful thinking tends to take over at a time like this. This happens particularly when the job opportunity is an unusually good one. This is a very big mistake. As the expression goes, "You can take it to the bank," there will be competition. The better the opportunity is, the more competition it will attract. Other candidates may exist despite the fact that you may not see anyone else in the reception room or because the interviewer may not make reference to other candidates. A promising "potential" job offer, the fear of rejection in further pursuit of additional opportunities and more job search frustration will provide all the necessary rationale for you to stop looking. After all, why look any further? This "potential" job opportunity has everything you are looking for. You have everything they are looking for. You got along so well with all of the people. They have conveyed to you that you all but have the job. On and on.

Just keep in mind there is no guarantee that you will get an offer until you actually receive one. Furthermore, the job is not yours until you accept. To carry this to completion, you are not an official employee until you are on the payroll and that doesn't happen until you actually start work. So, keep all of this in your mind. Keep looking with intensity. Your great "potential" offer does need special follow-up care.

➤ **096 Spending Money On Your Job Search**

It takes money to make money. It also takes money to find a job. Whatever you do, don't cut back on your job hunting because of expenses. Cut back in all other areas first, and job hunting last. Cut down on eating out, or eliminate it if necessary, and brown bag it. Some job seekers will cut down on long distance calls, mailings, driving to the library, failure to subscribe to needed publications or other necessary job hunting activities. This falls under the heading of being penny wise and pound foolish. Unemployed people in particular are guilty of this.

Unemployment can create severe financial restraints. There is no getting around it. However, being unemployed is the most costly of all, and not just from the money standpoint, but psychologically, as well. If this sounds like you, get a part-time job or two, or accept an interim position, but don't cut down on your job hunting activity. It works against you. Furthermore, the longer you are unemployed, the more difficult your task becomes.

➤ 097 Employment/Unemployment
The best time to find a job is when you already have one. This is an illustration of dealing from a position of strength versus weakness. When you are gainfully employed, you can afford to be highly selective in finding a company and position that meets your needs. Furthermore, gainfully employed people come across much more confident than the unemployed.

Unfortunately, unemployed people often carry a stigma of something must be wrong with them or they would be employed. After all, the best players in any game are on the field playing in the game. Companies don't cut back on their best people; the scuttlebutt goes on and on. Things can get very tough and demanding on the unemployed, even though everyone agrees that it is not fair. Life seems hard when the outcome cannot be seen. After all, some of the very best people have been fired for any one of a number of reasons. As an example, Lee Iacocca was fired by Henry Ford.

➤ **098 Free-lance Work**

Many of you who are unemployed have the ideal background to do free-lance work on an interim basis rather than some unrelated part-time job. Many free-lance jobs have turned into permanent career positions. Free-lancing gives both of you the opportunity to try each other on for size. It also helps pay the bills.

➤ **099 Temporary Employment**

If you still haven't found a job, be sure to register with temporary employment services (providing your background is appropriate), or find a part-time job on your own. This will accomplish several objectives. First, it will provide part-time income to help sustain you while you conduct your job search. Second, it will give you some excellent exposure to the working world. Frequently part-time employees will be assigned to a variety of firms. Many job seekers will end up with career positions with these companies after proving themselves on a part-time basis. They get exposed to the inside track and "hidden job market." Third, it will take the pressure off you to find a job and give you the necessary time to find a meaningful career position. Part-time jobs also allow you to get away for interviews, as well as the necessary time to pursue an aggressive job search. Last, but not least, working part-time will provide a psychological up lift and keep you in the mainstream of the work force.

➤ **100 Quitting Your Present Job**

Don't quit your job until you already have another.
Don't quit your job until you already have another.
Don't quit your job until you already have another.

How many more times do I have to make this statement for you to understand how important it is for you to pay heed? However, if the urge hits you in a fit of rage or emotional outburst, go outside and read this item very slowly ten times before you do anything. Bite the bullet while increasing your search activity. That is the wisest, smartest, best and most effective action you can take. But whatever you do, don't quit your job until you already have another no matter how difficult things get. It would be a mistake. If you just cannot take any time off during the day to make interviews, then schedule several interviews during one day. Use it as a personal business day or part of your vacation time. Also try to schedule evening and weekend interviews. Use your time wisely. Research the firms that you would like to pursue at night or on the weekend in the library. This will save valuable day time hours for interviews.

➤ 101 Confidentiality Of Your Job Search

In quest of something better be careful that you don't lose what you have. Very few people can maintain a confidence. In fact, it has been said that the best way to spread the word around on any subject is to say how important it is to keep the information confidential. This borders on gossip, and people in general love to gossip. So, be careful.

➤ 102 Supply/Demand Quirk

I have observed a phenomenon all of my life that people who need a job the least are the ones in most demand. Conversely, the people who need the jobs the most are in least demand. One could be led to believe that this is a crazy world we live in and rightfully so. However, this just happens to be one of those quirks of human nature. As a result people don't want what they can readily have and will fight for that which they cannot necessarily have. This is another reason for the unemployed to work part-time or accept interim work. They become more in step with the gainfully employed which somehow shows. Consulting and free-lance work are encouraged for the same reason.

➤ 103 Unemployed Advantage

There is one major advantage to being unemployed. You have the necessary time and convenience to look for another job, and you can get away for interviews. Frequently, the unemployed do not use their time to their advantage. Days without work become a downward spiral. Wondering what to do next is not very exciting; it seems hard for the unemployed to keep a fast paced agenda and use their time productively. Never become unemployed so that you will have time to look for work.

I know right about now you are probably asking yourself just how many more points are there to remember. A lot. A whole lot. But bear in mind each and every point can make the difference in your job hunting success. Would you rather not be armed with this new information? This may be why you found it necessary to buy this book. Enough said? Keep this book at your side throughout your job search and refer to it daily until you find the career opportunity for which you are looking.

➤ 104 Patience

Someone should make up a sign that says:

> *Be patient.*
> *Things will change.*
> *Nothing stays the same.*

This should help those of you on the dark side of job hunting to make it through to success. Remember this: the longest recorded rain in history lasted but forty days and nights; it too came to a halt; at long last the sun came shining through.

HOW MANY TIMES AT BAT
DO YOU GET BEFORE YOU HIT PAY DIRT?

A common mistake that job seekers make is to assume that one contact with a company is sufficient. Nothing could be further from the truth. The right hand in a company does not necessarily know what the left hand is doing. Let us look at a couple of interesting success stories. In both cases job seekers "targeted" the most desired companies that they would most like to work for. So, please keep this in mind.

The first job seeker successfully managed to secure seven different interviews (yes, I said seven) with seven different people within the same company before hitting pay dirt and landing the job of her dreams with that company. She was able to do this through an elaborate network of people she had cultivated. Talk about persistence. All of this was accomplished over a four month period of time. Talk about being in the right place at the right time. Really?

Who said you have to be at the right place at only one specific point in time? That is nothing more than a self-imposed constraint that will work against you. In baseball you get three strikes. How many foul balls or balls? The number of chances you will get will depend upon you. It is called Persistence with a capital P.

The other individual was from an advertising background. He submitted various creative approaches in which he contacted seventeen different people in that same company. The approach that generated the interview that landed him the job was his resume submitted in a bottle to a brewing company. Guess what kind of bottle he used?

There are different schools of thought on this subject. You should not get cute or too off beat with your resumes or your job hunting approach. Keep it businesslike is the soundest approach for most businesspeople. According to the book of rules on exceptions, there are exceptions to every rule and this example is one of those acceptable exceptions. Artists, musicians, entertainers and creative people in advertising, radio, and TV can successfully get away with using off beat approaches; however, most others cannot. Go to bat as often as you can to win the job.

➤ 105 Improvement
The key to improvement in anything is measurement. I don't care what it is. Can you imagine the Olympics taking place without measurements; just get out and do your best? What about baseball, golf, tennis or anything else for that matter? Ernest Hemingway is a classic example of a person who kept track of his writing. He kept a daily dairy and posted the total number of words he wrote each day. This helped him keep his feet to the fire and kept him writing even when the spirit did not move him to do so. If in the course of keeping track he ever found himself slipping behind his normal productive writing pace, he would work extra on his good days to make up for lost time until he caught up. This is called good old fashioned self-discipline. You, too, should do the same in your job search if you wish to be successful. Set a reasonable pace or daily/weekly goal you wish to achieve. Follow your plan; then keep tabs of your daily activity. You will accomplish much more activity following a plan rather than drifting along from one day through the next.

➤ 106 A Fish Swimming Upstream
A job search is in many respects like a fish swimming upstream. As long as you continue swimming you will make continuous progress. The moment you stop swimming, you will get washed backwards. Don't stop swimming until you reach your destination.

9

LEARNING ABOUT YOU

YOU

*You are the most important
person in the world to you.
Get to know yourself.
Like the good about you
and improve the rest.*

This chapter addresses some very basic issues about people.
It is placed at this point in the book because it is hard to
plan anything as important as your job search without first
addressing personal characteristics that might help or hurt
you. What about you is a go-for-it type person? What about
you isn't?

This chapter will help you in planning how to deal with
yourself and market yourself effectively. It is like looking in
a mirror and deciding if you want to see a smile or worry
lines. The truth about oneself is often painful, but the
operation to correct it is not. If you need to make some
changes, make them and make your job search campaign
work.

> **107 Be Ready - Awake, Showered, Dressed**
Wake up, shower (and shave if you are the type) and get
dressed. Casual attire is just fine, but be prepared to go
on a interview in short order. You will feel better when
you are up and ready to meet the world. Also, you will
get much more accomplished on a daily basis.

BE THE VERY BEST THAT YOU CAN BE

A favorite story of mine is about a young man who asked his mother for some advice on what he should do with his life from a career standpoint. She said that it was not her place to tell him what to do with his life now that he was grown. However, she added that should he decide to join the army, he should become a general; and should he decide to become a priest, he should become the pope. That young man was Picasso.

The moral of this story is quite simple; become the very best at what you do whether it be a butcher, a baker, a candlestick maker or whatever career you choose. The odds of finding fame, fortune and happiness favors the one who has paid the price to master one's chosen field and not the one who is the jack-of-all-trades. The generalist that knows a little bit about a whole lot of things is not likely to be able to master anything. You have to give it everything you have to master the skills of your trade or profession and never let up. There is always more to learn and master in becoming the very best at what you do. Whatever it is you decide to do, this should be your career objective in life. When you do this, your job hunting days will be over forever.

This reminds me of an interview conducted by a reporter with Pablo Cassals some years ago. Pablo was in his later years and was recognized as the world's greatest cellist. He was asked if it were, indeed, true that he still practiced playing the cello. Pablo responded immediately with a resounding "Yes! Absolutely, five to six hours a day, every day."

The reporter then asked Pablo why he felt is was necessary to practice so much when he was already considered to be the world's greatest cellist. Pablo said that if ever he missed one day of practice, he could tell the difference. He was afraid that if he missed two days in a row, the whole world would know.

You are going to have to pay the price if you want to be the very best at whatever you do. No one beats the system. This is a basic universal law. "As you give, so shall you receive." In the end, life will teach this lesson to you. "There ain't no gittin' without givin'."

The toughest school in the entire world is still the school of hard knocks. This is true despite the fact that it extracts the highest tuition. More people fight to get into it and stay there longer than all the other schools. Most people simply refuse to learn the lessons of life through other peoples' mistakes. People insist on learning themselves, the hard way. Why that is, one never knows, when it doesn't have to be that way. You figure it out.

> ### 108 Moods - Good, Bad, Ugly
Be aware of the mood you are in each day so that you can act accordingly. You will have your good, your bad, and your awful moods during your job search. Rest assured you will get a share of each. What you do is up to you. But if you are in a bad to ugly mood, take a break and turn it around.

MOOD SWINGS

Great Days, Good Days, Fair Days Or Bad Days

This falls under the quote from Plato, "Know Thyself." Or another quote that says the same thing is, "A life unexamined is not worth living." I have gotten to know myself quite well over the years, and over a period of time I have come to realize that not every day will be a great day. Through observation, reflection or self-analysis, I have formulated what I refer to as a normal month of mood swings for me. It has served me well over the years. I also believe my formula will apply to most people with slight modifications. My personal breakdown is as follows:

10	Great days
8	Good days
2	Fair to middlin', somehow-get-through-it kind of days.
2	Bad days or days that would have been spent better staying in bed for all that I was able to accomplish.
22	Total average work days in a month

Please understand, one's mood swings will not always occur the same way each month. If you pick out any twenty-two work days in succession, you will pretty well find this mix. Again, nothing is a hundred percent. The time to do any important follow-up calls or to make any new important contact calls is when you are having a great day or good day. You have more than enough great days and good days to accomplish your objectives.

A very distant third place is your fair-to-middlin' days. There are always things to be done on your fair-to-middlin' days such as your mail campaign, going through want ads or additional research at the library.

Forget your bad days, just put your job search aside and get yourself out of your lousy mood. I don't hold myself accountable for those days. Simply getting through those days is a major accomplishment in and of itself. It is more effective to postpone important follow-up calls or any new important contact calls to the next day, providing you were not told specifically to call someone that day.

The most important thing for you to remember is to maximize your efforts by fully capitalizing on your great days. These are the days that you feel like you can literally walk through walls. On these days nothing can hold you back; there are no such things as obstacles or roadblocks that can prevent you from achieving your goals. On these great days, great things happen to you. Learn to recognize and use your mood swings to maximum advantage.

YOU ARE YOU

Each person is unique. Each person's background, needs and circumstances are entirely different from all others. In light of this, people believe they have a plausible reason for taking a long time to find a job. The real reason the average job search is a lengthy process is because it is not done properly.

➤ 109   Work, Not Luck, Produces Results

When you don't know what you are doing, the tendency is to feel your way along, trust to luck, and hope for the best. Too many people rely upon luck as a major thrust. Some people seem luckier than others. The inexperienced card player relies upon luck for the very same reason. He has not developed the necessary skills to become a good card player. Learning how to conduct a successful job search campaign calls for reading, studying and practicing over a period of time. Too few people are willing to pay the price. The harder you work, the luckier you will get.

Some people believe that luck plays a part in everyone's life. But luck should not represent the cornerstone of your foundation in your job hunt. Therefore, because of ineffective job search skills, the average person sometimes dumps things into the laps of the gods. As a result, the average person will take almost any job within reason that comes along.

The degree of success one has in any field comes down to knowledge and skills coupled with action. You must develop the knowledge and skills first, then implement what you have learned. You must pay the price. Wishes don't wash dishes - at least not in my house. Somebody has to get up and do them or they will just sit there getting harder and harder to wash.

There is a story about an international concert pianist who

exemplifies this point exactly. She had been playing in Europe with great success for some years and decided it was time to visit her home town. She grew up in a very small midwestern town and was looking forward to re-visiting her family and high school friends. Her friends asked if she would conduct a recital for them which she did. After the recital one of the women commented that she would give anything, just anything, to be able to play the piano that well. There was a pause and then the concert pianist responded, "Oh, no, you would not."

The woman again said, "Oh, yes, I would, I would give just anything if I could play that well."

Another long pause... the pianist again said, "Oh, no, you would not because if you were willing to pay the price of thousands upon thousands of hours, you too could play as well; but most people will not practice that much."

Most people pay lip service rather than paying the price to accomplish whatever they wish to do. It is natural to follow the path of least resistance. And yet the path to success and happiness is not a downhill walk but an uphill climb. Could it be that too many people are trying to find the easy way? The skills necessary to find a job are not unlike skills in any other field. It takes study, practice and time to learn what to do and then doing it until success is achieved.

There is a right way and a wrong way to do anything. Judging the skills of a job seeker is like judging the skills of an Olympic athlete. Before the event begins each contestant starts with a perfect score of ten. The judge then deducts points for every error made during the performance. The athlete making the fewest mistakes is the winner. Remember, nothing is absolute. Everything is relative. No one is perfect. It is athlete against athlete and job seeker against job seeker.

The one who outperforms the other wins...

Everybody Wants a Job But Nobody Wants to Work

Hard work is not one of the more palatable subjects for a good number of people. However, as with everything in life, you get what you pay for. Most things you learn or earn will happen because of hard work.

The difference between doing what you like and what you don't like will separate you into one of two groups.

1. Those that work to live.
2. Those that live to work.

It is unfortunate, but those that work to live make up the majority of the work force. They have jobs but don't really care to work. People have asked me how can they tell when they are happy in their jobs and when they are not. I would have to answer that question the same way that I answered a question my son, Rick, at age eighteen asked me about a relationship he had with a girl.

He asked, "Dad, how do I know when I am really in love, since I have never been in love before?"

I replied, "If you have to ask the question regarding how you feel, then you are not in love. When you are in love, you will know it." The same holds true about your job. If you are really happy, you will not have to ask, you will know it.

I answered the same question another way for someone else. "If you begin to look forward to Friday more than you do to Monday, then you are no longer happy with your work." And yet, I will be the first to say that happiness is a state of mind. Further more, so is your attitude. You have much more control over your attitude than you will ever realize.

Abraham Lincoln once said, "Most people are as happy as they make up their minds to be."

Unfortunately, the most positive attitude in the world is not enough if your needs are not being met. I want to make sure this point is clear. Two of the most significant decisions a person will make during one's life will be the spouse one marries and the career one chooses. After all, people spend virtually all of their time between the two. The two go hand in hand. If you are happy in your work, this carries home with you. If you are not happy, this also carries home with you. A good balance between job and home will reflect peace of mind and happiness accordingly. Your home life can be a refuge away from work and your work can be an escape from home, but usually you take both with you wherever you go. You are the framework for each.

RESEARCH FOR HAPPINESS

People are the happiest and at their very best when they are doing what they most enjoy. Conversely, people most enjoy work that makes them happy. So, there you have it: the secret to job satisfaction and success. Find work that you do well and enjoy, then go out and enjoy yourself. This point is aptly illustrated by an old story that has been kicked around for umpteen years.

Three Stone Masons

A man was walking down the street and came upon three stone masons busy at work. He stopped and asked the first mason what he was doing, to which he replied, "I'm laying some stone, can't you see."

The man continued walking and asked the second stone mason what he was doing, to which he replied, "I'm making a living."

The man proceeded on down to the third stone mason who was whistling and chirping like a bird while working. The man asked this third mason what he was doing, to which he replied, "I'm building a beautiful cathedral."

This story sums up job satisfaction and happiness better than anything else I have ever come across. The universal problem is that the work force has too many stone masons laying stone or making a living (going through the motions of work or working for money) and not enough of them building beautiful cathedrals (seeing and enjoying the true worth of their work). I have made a profound observation over the years which is that jobs in and of themselves are neither good nor bad. They are good if you enjoy them and bad if you don't. Therefore, find the job that will make you happy, then go to work and enjoy yourself.

What Will Make You Happy

Before you begin to research the jobs and companies that can give you job satisfaction and happiness, you need to take the all-important step (missing in most job searches) of researching yourself.   Find out what makes you happy. Again quoting Plato as he said, "Know thyself." Surprisingly, people do not consider themselves thoroughly enough to get a good solid handle on themselves. They take the fast and easy approach and short-cut the process.

First, identify what it is you like to do: what will make you happy. It almost sounds too basic, doesn't it? Well, it is not. This is the magic key to finding the right job for you that will make you happy and successful. Unfortunately, too few people do this, instead they find new jobs. They hope, think and believe a new job will make them happy. "This new job is it!" This is the job which they have been looking for. They are victims of wishful thinking. They honestly believe, or delude themselves into thinking, that they can influence the outcome of their new found jobs by wishes. As quickly as the job newness becomes the sameness of past jobs, reality sets in. They find themselves in the same old rut. This practice of wishful thinking is best stated by a quote from

Emerson, "We lie the loudest when we lie to ourselves."

A Job Called Happiness

Somewhere in this great wide wonderful world are positions that will meet the needs of the most discriminating job seekers. Once you have identified your needs and abilities, these will translate into a job description or duties. (Job titles vary from one company and industry to the next and do not always convey the job description or duties.) You limit yourself when you specify specific job titles and expand your world of work possibilities when you identify with job descriptions. You need to list what you like to do and do well; then seek jobs that fit your description.

So, what job is it that will make you happy in this work-a-day world? What job will be a labor of love? Let's find out. The following approach will help you to identify your likes and dislikes which will translate later into helping you find the job that best meets your needs.

FAVORITE LIST OF THINGS TO DO TODAY

Most people are familiar with "Things To Do Today" lists. It makes good sense to write down your list of things you have to do day by day and even week by week. This is simply good basic planning. And everyone knows the importance of planning. Right? "Plan your work, and work your plan." Over the years I have observed how people cope with their planning and have concluded that most people have two different planning lists combined under the one title, "Things To Do Today."

1. The Most Favorite List Of Things To Do Today
2. The Least Favorite List Of Things To Do Today

Somehow, unconsciously the items that are from your "Most

Favorite List Of Things To Do" get done. In fact, people will go out of their way looking for more things to add to this list. In the meantime what is happening to the items on the "Least Favorite List Of Things To Do Today?" Not much, for most people. Tasks both pleasant and un-pleasant are mixed into most daily routines. People generally pick the pleasant ones at the expense of the unpleasant ones. In fact, some things are so dreadful that they get shoved aside endlessly. You are better off facing facts. Divide your list into two categories.

Things To Do Today

Most Favorite Things To Do Today	Least Favorite Things To Do Today
_____	_____
_____	_____
_____	_____
_____	_____
_____	_____
_____	_____
_____	_____
_____	_____
_____	_____
_____	_____
_____	_____
_____	_____
_____	_____
_____	_____

As the old saying goes, "divide and conquer." When you cross off each item as you accomplish it, you will find that you are doing only things you like to do. This will tend to discipline you to pick things from your "Least Favorite

Things To Do Today" list as well. In time you will start setting priorities and interspersing some of your dreaded tasks with more enjoyable ones. This technique will have a definite impact on your job search.

Unfortunately much that has to be done in a job search falls into the "Least Favorite List Of Things To Do Today." It takes a great deal of self-discipline, maturity and commitment to do what needs to be done. You will have to sell yourself with whatever words of wisdom you can to generate sufficient self-discipline and motivation to push you to do what has to be done. This is not easy, but it must be done if you are to be successful in your job search. Now that you are armed with this new found knowledge, you can proceed to the next step. Do the same thing with job related duties and responsibilities. Make dual lists:

Duties

Most Favorite Duties and Responsibilities	*Least Favorite Duties and Responsibilities*
_____	_____
_____	_____
_____	_____
_____	_____
_____	_____
_____	_____
_____	_____
_____	_____
_____	_____
_____	_____
_____	_____
_____	_____

My Favorite Activities

Make a list of the activities that you have enjoyed doing the most throughout your working career. Place these under your "Favorite" column. These are the things that come naturally and easy for you to do. They are things you welcome doing and do well. Start searching your mind and look deep within. What are the duties and responsibilities you enjoy doing?

Go back as far as you can remember and include things you enjoyed doing during your school years. Don't pooh pooh this. This is vitally important. When you feel your list is nearly complete, take the time to prioritize the items. Number your favorite activity as # 1 on the list. Work your way down the list until you have placed each item in sequence: 2, 3, 4, etc. Now, start listing your least favorite activities or tasks. Take the same approach as you did with your list of things you enjoyed the most; then, prioritize them in the same way.

Take whatever time is necessary to do this and continue to add items to both lists along the way. You may need to re-rank them in time. This will help you crystalize your likes and dislikes. This is one of the most important things you can do to help you find a job you want. Put it down on paper, don't just mull it over in your mind.

These lists will serve to stabilize your emotions and to help you proceed with your job search on a more systematic, logical basis. I refer to this as logical decisions from the head, versus emotional decisions from the heart. In our executive search practice we have found that there are people who will make their decision based upon emotions, not logic; then, they wonder why they get themselves in so much trouble in their careers.

Know what you like to do and do it.

Activities

Most Favorite Activities	**Least Favorite Activities**
_____	_____
_____	_____
_____	_____
_____	_____
_____	_____
_____	_____
_____	_____
_____	_____
_____	_____
_____	_____
_____	_____
_____	_____
_____	_____
_____	_____
_____	_____
_____	_____
_____	_____
_____	_____
_____	_____
_____	_____
_____	_____
_____	_____

➤ 110   Getting Started And Finishing

The secret to becoming successful in anything you do is learning how to do uncomfortable things until they become comfortable.

➤ 111 Divide And You Shall Conquer

Pay heed to the Napoleonic concept of "Divide and you shall conquer" principle. Rather than becoming overwhelmed by the entire process and never getting started, break down your job hunting venture into manageable parts and conquer each, one step at a time.

➤ 112 Stick-To-It-tivness

Is it the first swing of the axe or the last swing of the axe that fells the tree? It takes all of them, one swing at a time. The same holds true for job hunting. Start swinging and don't stop until you get your job.

➤ 113 Common Sense

Some people know the time of day. Others do not.

Your next step is to research industries, companies and positions that will potentially meet your needs. You need to research and list the firms to pursue in person, by phone, with resumes and through networking.

10

STATING YOUR OBJECTIVES, GOALS, SKILLS, STRENGTHS AND ACCOMPLISHMENTS

If you wish in this world to advance,
Your merits you're bound to enhance;
You must stir it and stump it,
And blow your own trumpet,
Or trust me, you haven't a chance.
Ruddigore - W.S. Gilbert

You are now about to embark upon a self analysis of what career objective(s) you wish to pursue, what your short term and long term goals are, and what your skills, strengths and accomplishments are. You will also be asked to think of the people who can support you in the way of references. Consider this chapter as a preliminary exercise in doing your research on resource publications, job search firms, prospective target companies and writing your resumes and cover letters. If you do not have a clear concept of yourself, then you will be misdirected in pursuing appropriate resources and will be handicapped in presenting yourself effectively to employers.

Use this chapter as a chart of yourself: what you have done and what you wish to accomplish. Be as specific as you can be. Use forceful words that are expressive. Take the time to enjoy yourself as you think back on all you have done.

You will be surprised how much you have accomplished and how many skills, talents and strengths you have. This is even true about people who have little or no work experience. Your school, free-lance, part-time, charity and even home experiences can be used. Think deep, not shallow, to draw out all the benefits you have as a potential employee. Even though you will probably not use all of them, many will come in handy in a variety of job search situations. This study of yourself can also open your mind to a variety of work opportunities that you might not realize you could pursue.

Pursue Your Gift

The Catholic church makes reference to priests, nuns and brothers as having a special calling to their chosen profession. The word for that special gift is charism. (It has nothing to do with the word charisma that most people know.)

Everyone has a special "gift" or special "calling." It is a natural God-given, if you will, talent or ability that everyone possesses. It is doing what comes naturally. The sooner a person identifies, pursues and develops one's own special talent, the better.

What would you really like to be doing? If you had your life to live over again, would you be doing the same thing? Please understand, some of you have, indeed, gone too far for too long. Age and physical condition may genuinely prevent you from pursuing certain careers or activities. You may have wished to become an astronaut or a professional athlete. You may have to settle for your second choice or, would you believe, your third or fourth? That beats your last choice.

When you do something that you enjoy, rather than do something just to please your family, society, your boss or anyone else, then you can reach job satisfaction. You need to change your traditional thinking about work and approach it from a positive view. It is not easy. Then again, what in life that is worthwhile is easy. Initially, start focusing on new horizons and take one or even two steps backwards. Then, think of the rewards of moving onwards into a career that will offer you job satisfaction.

DESIRES

_____
_____
_____
_____
_____
_____
_____
_____
_____
_____
_____
_____
_____
_____
_____
_____

Before you continue, make a year-by-year inventory of your life, write down all the jobs you have had, the major events in your life, the trips you have taken, relocations, business ventures and activities you have participated in. This mental picture of your life will help you remember many things that you have forgotten and will trigger the surfacing of skills, strengths and accomplishments that you didn't know you have. Put down dates and time sequences. Be as specific and detailed as you can be. Add to this list as things come to you. You will be amazed at all you have done and how much you have accomplished.

LIFE HISTORY

_____
_____
_____
_____
_____
_____
_____
_____
_____
_____
_____
_____
_____
_____
_____
_____
_____
_____
_____
_____
_____
_____
_____
_____
_____
_____
_____
_____
_____
_____

➤ 114 Skills

Make a written inventory of all the skills you have accumulated throughout your educational and work experiences. Some of these skills may go back to your high school days when, for example, you were a writer or editor for the school newspaper. Perhaps you can list skills that you acquired from a part-time job. Think about all the work you have ever done. What skills did you develop to do the work. Skills are also acquired from extracurricular activities, sports, hobbies and social events. A homemaker (wife and mother) develops an untold variety of skills. These may be acquired while running a home and nurturing a family, serving as a chairperson for a competition or being a Boy Scout leader. These skills may not seem transferable to the workplace, but they could be highly instrumental in helping you get a job.

As an example, airline companies add heavy bonus points to flight attendant applicants who have worked as food servers. Why is that? Because they have experience in dealing with and serving the public. Isn't that what flight attendants do? Yet, for whatever reason, very few people grasp the significance of this type of part-time job or work experience. This same person could pursue opportunities in restaurant management or work for a food service franchise office.

Another example might be a person who worked part-time during high school as a tire installer in a tire store. The individual may have forgotten all about the experience. Yet,the skills that were learned years ago can be directly applicable to a job today. Perhaps this person could apply for a position as a manager in a tire store or could pursue sales pertaining to tires and tire changing equipment, front-end alignment equipment or a whole variety of equipment or supplies used in a retail tire store. An engineer could pursue all the manufacturers of these products.

Now, do you see why it is important to take an inventory of the skills you have? This allows you to weave your past skills and experiences into your job prospects. It can help you identify potential career options. In the course of answering questions on the telephone or making comments during interviews you can interject your skills into the conversation whenever appropriate to show how these skills would benefit the company. Presenting applicable skills is one of the most effective communication tools you can use. Use it and use it well.

SKILLS

_____

_____

_____

_____

_____

_____

_____

_____

_____

_____

_____

_____

_____

_____

_____

_____

_____

_____

➤ 115   Strengths

First things first. Before you step into the arena called the job market, you had better prepare yourself. Get yourself organized and take a complete inventory of who you are. In the world of sales this falls under the category called product knowledge. As such, you need to know yourself (or your product) inside and out; the good, the bad, and even the ugly. The more you know about yourself, the more success you will have in selling yourself and positioning yourself to stay in contention for the job. Everyone has individual strengths, as well as weaknesses. It is vitally important to know both; so, with that thought in mind start listing yours. You may not find sufficient lines following this section to list all of yours. Don't stop just because you have reached the bottom line; take out a sheet of paper and write *STRENGTHS* across the top of it and continue listing them. Do it. Don't pooh, pooh this as merely a practice exercise. Nothing can be further from the truth.

As I sit here writing, I have reflected on the 1992, presidential debates between Bush, Clinton and Perot. Each one wanted the job as president of this country. Can you begin to imagine the planning and preparation that each candidate went through? Do you think for a moment that any one of them simply winged it? Surely no one can be that naive. Each person was researched by his staff to bring out every conceivable strength. These researchers also looked (in private) for weaknesses so they could be minimized or countered with strengths when the opposition brought the opponent's weaknesses public.

Most people don't thoroughly identify their strengths, much less their weaknesses. I cannot stress strongly enough the importance of crystallizing your strengths in writing, prioritizing them, and committing them to memory. This will enable you to insert your strengths into your interviewing at the appropriate time. You will also need this list to overshadow your weaknesses. No one is perfect. Your first attempt at listing all your strengths and weaknesses will rarely be complete, so continue to add to it throughout your job search.

Take the same approach with identifying your weaknesses. You don't want to be caught off guard and at a loss for words when being interviewed.

Now that you are ready to list your strengths and weaknesses, you might ask, what are work related strengths and weaknesses? Strengths are character traits and qualities that you exhibit. Some might be punctuality, perseverance, enthusiasm and loyalty. Weakness could be fault finding and procrastination. A strength could also be years of experience as a manager. This could be a weakness if you only managed one small toy store when you are applying for a position to manage a large electronic's store and you have no experience in electronics.

STRENGTHS

_____

_____

_____

_____

_____

_____

_____

_____

_____

_____

_____

_____

_____

_____

_____

➤ 116 Apply Your Mind

Sir Isaac Newton was once asked how it was that he came to discover the law of gravity. He stated, "By applying my mind to the problem over a period of time." The same approach should be taken to all job search problems. You have to apply your mind. This includes coming to grips with all facts about your life and your work.   You have strengths, but you also have weaknesses. These can be improved and even overcome if they are recognized. Perhaps you will need help to overcome them. If you do, then reach out and get it. Everyone needs help somewhere along the way. Don't be stubborn or foolish.   It is just too expensive, financially and psychologically. In the meantime, counter your weaknesses with strengths and proceed with confidence in your job search.

WEAKNESSES

> ## 117 Accomplishments

There are a number of people who do not really understand what accomplishments are. This is particularly true of first time job seekers and people who have been with one company since school days. All people perform various duties, responsibilities or objectives with varying degrees of excellence. Any time you achieve above average results in any area, this performance is recognized as an accomplishment. For example, a migrant farm worker may have a record of accomplishments. The worker may have been ranked in the top ten percent of all fruit and produce pickers for the past year. As a result, this worker will be in more demand than others. A secretary may be the fastest typist in the pool. A sales person may have achieved one hundred and fifty percent of last year's quota.

Whatever it is that you are particularly proud of having accomplished, you should state as an accomplishment. For every job you ever held, every extra curricular activity or other action that you have done, list your accomplishments. Then sort through them and use applicable ones in your cover letters, resumes and interviews with potential employers. This will help them view you favorably as they sort through prospective new employees. Don't hold back. Some people have a very difficult time in this area because of their genuine modesty. Just remember, if your accomplishments are facts, then it is not bragging to state them. You can state these accomplishments in your interviews with appropriate style, and you will not appear to be boastful.

A great number of jobs do not lend themselves to achieving noteworthy accomplishments. However, all people in such jobs are in the same boat; none will have any advantage over the other. Still, there can be many different things that you are particularly proud of having accomplished. These are worth stating. Just remember all people in all walks of life are graded on a curve for everything they do. This allows you to excel or stand out in a positive way from the group. These are also accomplishments. I hope this helps you get a better understanding on the subject.

ACCOMPLISHMENTS

➤ 118 Career Objective(s) - Right Or Wrong?

Your career objective(s) needs to be considered from the first moment you start thinking about your job search. Now is the time to state your career objective(s) properly. You may have a diverse background, talents and interests; therefore, you could fill several different types of positions in a variety of fields. If this is the case, then you will need to write a career objective for each field of endeavor. Do not write one all encompassing career objective. Your career objective needs to fit the job that you are applying for. Stating a career objective at the top of your resume or in your cover letter will work against you if it does not fit the job. This happens when you try to get by with only one general all purpose resume and cover letter. If you state your career objective in your cover letter, make sure it reflects the position you are pursuing. If it does not, you will have personally screened yourself out of consideration. If you are having difficulty in stating your career objectives, use resources in the library, your college placement office or other professional help.

CAREER OBJECTIVE(S)

_____
_____
_____
_____
_____
_____
_____
_____
_____
_____
_____
_____
_____
_____
_____

➤ **119 Goals**

Telling a prospective employer during your interview that your goal is to someday get into your own business is a mistake. Talk about a no brainer statement. Yet, it happens because people simply don't think. The best background and education will not compensate for such a statement. All companies are interested in hiring long term employees; even though in most cases they will have varying degrees of turnover.   Knowing that a prospective new employee is more interested in getting into one's own business in time is not in the company's best interest. Surely, you must understand this. This falls under the category of putting your foot in your mouth in a big way.

➤ **120 Be Specific In Goal Statement**

In response to the question, "What are your goals?" to say that your goal is "to go as far as your abilities will allow you to go" is not an answer, it is a built in excuse. It is the kiss of death. People who answer this question in this manner are naive to the ways of the business world. You are literally saying that you are not sure of yourself, that you are not sure what you really want or that you are not sure how far you want to go. People who know want they want specifically and are prepared make whatever commitment necessary to get there will say so specifically and are likely to succeed.

➤ **121 Communication**

The question, "Why do people have such a difficult time communicating with one another?" was asked of Plato. He answered, "Could it be because we don't all have the same definitions to the same words?" So many words and statements can be interpreted in so many different ways.   Wishful thinking tends to get mixed into our interpretations of everything we hear. Be careful, since people tend to hear only what they want to hear. This can get you into trouble.

Crystalize your short and long term goals and learn how to communicate them clearly and confidently.

During an interview you should be prepared to answer the question, "What are your short term and long term goals?" Some people simply state that their short term goal is to find a job. That certainly answers the question, but in the wrong way. Companies are much more interested in finding people whose goals are compatible with theirs and express the commitment to achieve them. The proper way to answer this question is to state your desire to learn and master the immediate job at hand while at the same time preparing yourself for advancement. Short term goals are those you expect to achieve within a year or so. Your long term goals are what you want to accomplish ultimately or the position you would like to have as the climax of your career. The following are examples of short term and long term goals.

- A degreed civil engineer may have as a short term goal of being a top field engineer for a general contractor. The long term goal could be a vice president of construction.

- A salesperson may have a short term goal to be a successful top salesperson. The long term goal could be a national sales manager.

- A person wishing to be a cook could have a short term goal as being a top cook. The long term goal could be to become a top chef.

- A management trainee's short term goal might be to join a firm as a management trainee and to learn to be a top manager. The long term goal could be in general management, managing other managers or a top executive.

- A person looking for a job in retailing could state a short term goal to become a top retail sales person. The long term goal could be a store manager.

These are just a few examples of how to crystalize your short and long term goals. Your short and long term goals may be one and the same. It may be that you want to be a teacher and become a top teacher, doing what you love best and that is to teach for a career. If that is the case, then say so. Have your thoughts clear and precise. Be brief and confident in your response.

SHORT TERM GOALS

_____
_____
_____
_____
_____
_____
_____
_____
_____
_____
_____
_____
_____
_____
_____
_____
_____

➤ **122 Human Nature**
There is a quirk of human nature that almost defies logic. Knowing you can have something seems to make it less interesting or desirable. A seed of doubt in one's mind about getting it actually makes the person want it that much more. Learn to capitalize on this knowledge.

LONG TERM GOALS

_____
_____
_____
_____
_____
_____
_____
_____
_____
_____
_____
_____
_____
_____
_____
_____
_____

➤ **123 Your References**
Select your references carefully. Ask before you use a
person as a reference. Let each reference know when to
expect calls about you. This is professional courtesy.
Also this will enable your references to gather their
thoughts about you and your background. Forewarned,
they can give a much more convincing presentation than
when they are caught off guard. Often it is not so much
what is said, but how it is said.. References which
stumble and fumble along will not seem as credible as
those that are well thought out and organized. It is also
very helpful for your references to know the kind of job
you are pursuing and any other pertinent details. You
can help or hurt yourself depending how you handle
references.

REFERENCES

Name_____
Title_____
Company_____
Address_____
_____
Phone work_____ home _____

Name_____
Title_____
Company_____
Address_____
_____
Phone work_____ home _____

Name_____
Title_____
Company_____
Address_____
_____
Phone work_____ home _____

Name_____
Title_____
Company_____
Address_____
_____
Phone work_____ home _____

Name_____
Title_____
Company_____
Address_____
_____
Phone work_____ home _____

Now you know what you want to do, what positions you want to pursue, what you have to offer an employer, what your work record looks like and what people will give you good recommendations. With this knowledge you are ready to identify target companies, discover their needs, and then let them know who you are and what you can do for them.

The information you have gained about yourself in this chapter will help you in writing your resume(s) and cover letters. Keep these facts before you while you write and use them during your phone conversations and interviews. If you do, you will realize how much you have to say about yourself that will help you land a job.

11

IDENTIFYING PUBLISHED JOB SEARCH RESOURCES

We live in the communication age.
Come of age and join the rest of the world.

A person's job search success will usually depend upon how willingly, eagerly, thoroughly and enduringly that person uses resources and resource people in bookstores, libraries and organizations. The following are primary resources everyone should use, but they are only the beginning resources you should develop in your job search.

➤ **124 On Reading Inspirational, Self-help Books**
What degree does the spirit have to move you before you do anything? This will play a major part in the success, or lack of it, in your job hunting campaign. Read motivational articles and books or turn to other inspirational resources that you have found helpful in the past. There are many excellent books available. Search them out. If you have not already done so, buy one and you will see how well your attitude, your inspiration, your spirit can be lifted out of a nonproductive mood into a productive mode.

Nearly everyone who is out of work or is living in fear of being laid off can use all the inspirational and motivational help available.

A young girl (an eleven year old newspaper delivery girl)

said, "They took away my job. I didn't do anything wrong, but they took it away. I want it back! I didn't do anything wrong!" She was downsized due to a more modernized delivery system employed by the newspaper company. Note: She did not blame herself. She knew she hadn't done anything wrong. Her youth wouldn't let her conceive that she was to blame.

As one gets older and has received numerous rebuffs, a person tends to blame oneself. This lowers one's spirit and youthful enthusiasm; so a person needs to seek something to lift one's life up. A person needs inspiration and motivation. It helps greatly, and it works. Try it. Don't hold back. When the going gets tough; don't allow yourself to slip too far down before reaching out for help. You can turn to inspirational books for help when there is no place else to go, unless you happen to be a religious person. If so, you are fortunate at a time like this. Turn to it and become inspired, then look for something good to happen.

Counselors can also help move you past the gloom and doom of depression into hope and positive action.

➤ **125 Job Hunting Books**
Be sure to read one or more self-help job hunting books before you get into the job market. People tend to lack a basic knowledge when it comes to job hunting skills. Most utilize the same job hunting approaches that they used while finding part-time jobs during high school or college days. Even many people in their mid-years lack job search skills. This is true because they have not had to face the tough job market of today's graduates; therefore, they base their job search techniques on those that worked when jobs were available for everyone regardless of talent or skills.

Books on job hunting, resume writing, interviewing, careers and opportunities are of great value to you.

These can be found in the reference department of your library and in your local bookstore. Librarians have taken the time to research and identify the most popularly requested books on these subjects. Your job search should actually begin in the library or bookstore. Each contains pure gold for you. Buy the help you need. The whole shooting match will cost you less than a single course in college.

Buying resource books will be one of the best investments you will ever make. Do yourself a favor. Don't skimp, take the time to read and follow the advice.

Make it a point to introduce yourself to the librarian or assistant in the reference department at your library and ask for help. Tell the person that you are in the process of looking for a job, and that you would like to know what information is available about various companies and industries that would be of help to you. Ask how to find company information on privately and public held companies. Librarians and reference department assistants are simply incredible. You will not believe all of the sources they have and how willingly they will help you. (I think this is one of the best examples of your tax dollars at work for you.)

Most large city libraries have dozens of books in the job search referral section. By all means, get acquainted with this section in your library. You will find much to benefit your job search. This is true for all job seekers. Don't do a once-over-lightly routine. Take sufficient time to thoroughly acquaint yourself with all the information that is applicable to you.

➤ 126 Resource "Bible" To Job Hunting

The Directory Of Executive Recruiters is considered to be the authoritative source in the industry for corporations and job seekers. Be sure to use to it. This 700 page directory lists 5,000 individuals in 4,000 offices of 2,300 search firms in US/Canada/Mexico by areas of specialization. Addresses and phone numbers are given. It includes 100 pages of text on conducting a successful job search, helpful hints, explanations of services, suggestions, and additional self-help publications.

The title *The Directory of Executive Recruiters* can be misleading; it could lead one to believe that executive search firms only deal with executives. Today, this is not the case. This industry has changed and grown considerably. Depending upon the firm, some will include salaried positions starting from approximately $40,000 and up; however, many consider only positions starting at $100,000.

Job seekers never fill out applications or sign agreements when dealing with retainer based executive search firms. All expenses are handled by client companies. Retainer based firms are only retained by corporate clients and never by individuals. Do not confuse executive search firms with executive marketing services firms that charge a service fee to the job seeker. (Executive search firms are covered in more detail in Chapter 12.)

> *The Directory of Executive Recruiters*
> Templeton Road
> Fitzwilliam, New Hampshire 03447
> (603) 585-6544

➤ **127 *U.S. Industrial Outlook***

Be sure to read the current publication of the *U.S. Industrial Outlook* printed by the Department of Commerce. This provides the current and future job outlook prospects for over 350 different industries. This should be available at your library. It will identify the up and coming growth industries, as well as those that are declining. This book offers excellent information.

Write to:
> Superintendent of Documents
> Washington, DC 20402

➤ **128** *Books Of Lists*
Most major cities have a publication called the *Book of Lists*. It identifies the twenty-five largest firms in major industries within the city. The classifications include accounting, banking, engineering, hospitals, the largest private employers and more. The list can enlighten you about the various markets in which you have an interest. It covers everything from size, number of employees, locations, type, year founded and descriptions. (Check this with the library or chamber of commerce and in the telephone directory in each major market since each Book Of Lists has its own address.)

➤ **129** *The National Ad Search*
The National Ad Search is a gem of a publication of which most job seekers are unaware. It is a weekly publication published in Milwaukee, Wisconsin, since 1970. It publishes a diversified and representative overview of help wanted ads from seventy-five leading newspapers throughout the country including Alaska and Hawaii. These ads are for salaried professional level and managerial positions, not hourly and blue collar positions.

The National Ad Search sorts the ads into job categories such as accounting, banking and finance or management, as examples. All you have to do is locate the specific section of the newspaper of interest to you to get a good overview of job openings in your category across the country. Helpful job hunting hints and suggestions to job seekers are included each week.

(To illustrate how much information is in it, the most current issue at this writing presents eighty-four pages of employment want ads.)

Subscriptions are for six weeks, three months, six
months and a year. Central libraries throughout the
country carry this publication; however, you might have
to stand in line to get it. That is why subscribing is a
good idea. Not all libraries carry this publication. Some
of you may prematurely pass on this publication,
because you may not be willing to consider relocation as
an option. However, many companies in your locale will
run help wanted advertisements in out-of-town
newspapers. They do so in the hope of attracting talent
from various competitors around the country. In this
regard, this publication will help you keep abreast of
these local needs. You will also get a good feel of the
various types of jobs in demand throughout the country.
This will prove beneficial should you decide to broaden
your search. Make it a point to look into this
publication, particularly if you are open to out-of-town
positions.

The National Ad Search
P.O. Box 2083
Milwaukee, Wisconsin 53201
(414) 351-1398

➤ **130 *National Business Employment Weekly***
This valuable publication is published weekly and is
available at major newsstands in larger cities. It
publishes want ads from all four regional editions of *The
Wall Street Journal*. Included are articles of special
interest to job seekers. It also has an "Industry
Spotlight" section featuring coverage of a different
industry each week. A "Calendar of Events" section by
region specifies people between jobs organization
meetings, various meetings, announcements, workshops
and seminars of benefit to job seekers. This publication
goes well beyond placing reprints of want ads and is
very worth while. Subscriptions are available starting
at twelve weeks or more:

National Business Employment Weekly
(800) Job-Hunt (562-4868)
(212) 808-6791

➤ **131 *The Wall Street Journal***
Most people are unaware that *The Wall Street Journal*
has four regional publications: the eastern, midwest,
southwest and western editions.   These can be
important to you if you are looking for a job in a
particular area of the country.   Asian and European
editions are also available for these foreign markets.

> *The Wall Street Journal*
> 200 Burnett Road
> Chicopee, MA 01020
> (800) 222-1940

➤ **132 Trade Publications**
Be sure to identify and use all of the trade publications
that cover the industries of interest to you.   Broaden
your scope; research related fields.   Your librarian can
help you identify these publications.   Each publication
will carry varying amounts of help wanted ads.   All
trade publications cover industry highlights and
company information that will help you in your job
search.

➤ **133 Non-Profit Job Market**
This sector all but falls between the cracks for most job
seekers.   This market is too big to be ignored.   It is
nearly out of sight for many reasons.   Review a sample
copy of *Access*, the publication that covers this market
to see if this market may serve your needs.

> *Access*
> 50 Beacon Street
> Boston, Massachusetts 02108
> (617) 720-5627

➤ 134 Government Sources Of Jobs

Failure to use all government (city, county, state and federal) sources is a mistake you should not make. You have to deal with each level of government on an individual basis. Books are available to help you tap these enormous markets. Entirely too many people overlook these sources. Every job imaginable can be found in government which is the largest employer in the country. Include all levels of government on your list of job sources.

➤ 135 *The Federal Job Digest*

This is a bi-weekly newspaper publication covering the federal job market. It covers tips for finding a federal job and gives the basic steps to apply for a federal job. Each issue contains special articles for job seekers interested in finding federal jobs. (The July 31, 1992, to August 13, 1992, issue contained 26,039 job listing vacancies nationwide.) There is a wealth of information in this publication. It covers all levels of jobs from blue collar, clerical, through top level management and executive positions. You can find this newspaper at major newsstands in larger cities, or you can subscribe direct at:

> *The Federal Jobs Digest*
> 310 North Highland Avenue
> Ossining, New York 10562
> (800) 824-5000

➤ 136 Yellow Pages Resource

Prospecting in your job search is imperative. Browse through the complete section of the yellow pages telephone directory from front to back for some thought provoking stimulation and memory jogging. It will definitely generate some job prospects for you. Libraries contain Yellow Page directories from most major cities. These are great resources for you.

➤ 137 Help Wanted Ads

Your local newspaper will list many job openings. Pursue those that are of interest to you. If you are thinking about relocating, read the classified help wanted ads from out of town newspapers. Many large cities have newsstands which carry current issues of national and international papers. Your library is also a source for these newspapers. The larger the library is the more newspapers it will carry. Respond by phone or mail immediately to each ad of interest to you.

➤ 138 Follow Up Help Wanted Ads

Follow up on all help wanted newspaper ads that are of special interest to you. Do this even if you have responded to the ad previously and have not heard from the firm. Send a second resume and cover letter. Before you do, look for ways to improve them. Give them a new slant, restate the objective, focus more on your accomplishments. Many job seekers have received interviews and job offers because of this dogged persistence.

➤ 139 Eliminating Yourself From Help Wanted Ads

Failure to respond to all classified help wanted ads worth clipping is a mistake. Why should you bother to read and clip ads, if you are not going to follow through? People do not respond because they rationalize rejection, not success. Just think about it for a moment. What happens when you don't respond? You eliminate yourself one hundred percent of the time from possible consideration. This is one of the very few things in life that is one hundred percent. Any rejection rate has to be better than that.

➤ 140 Old Ads - Go For Them

Old classified help wanted ads that were advertised 2-3-4-5-6 weeks or more ago may still be alive and well depending upon the level of position. The higher level positions take longer to fill. Don't pass up these "old" ads. An ad stays alive even longer during slow recessionary times when employers tend to be more cautious.

➤ 141 Overseas Jobs

Beware of the lure and appeal of overseas job opportunities being advertised with 1 - 800 phone numbers. These eye catching ads attract much attention. The unemployed from major corporations (including defense contractors in particular) get desperate as time passes. These ads promise large tax free salaries and free housing among other benefits. They offer adventure with the opportunity to stash away huge savings. The telemarketer at the end of the 800 number wants to sell you a list of companies in foreign markets. Hold on to your check book, no matter how promising the opportunity appears. This one point heeded will save you minimally ten times what you paid for this book.

Overseas employment opportunities are no longer what they used to be. The market has grown considerably more competitive. Wages are not what folklore would have people to believe, today. (Would you believe that painters start at $90,000 yearly tax free including housing, medical, transportation and other benefits? Give me a break.) Available positions are limited and call for very specialized skills and education.

Beware of the ancient siren calls from Greek mythology, or they will beckon you to your destruction. You must recall from your school days about these ancient sirens beckoning the sailors to their destruction and how Ulysses, being forewarned, tied himself to the mast and stuffed rags in his ears so that he, too, did not fall prey to the same siren's luring sounds. Don't be a victim.

If you are interested in foreign jobs, your research in

the library can reveal corporations that have foreign divisions. Contact them directly. There are books listing this information. Some executive search firms and employment agencies can also help in this area.

➤ **142 *The International Employment Gazette***
This publication covers job opportunities in the overseas sector. They also feature articles of special interest to job seekers interested in foreign job opportunities. Read at least half a dozen issues before you attempt to pursue overseas job opportunities. There are a number of scams that look and sound too good to be true; so be careful. This paper does a good job of pointing out this red flag to their subscribers. Pay heed to their advice. This publication is available bi-weekly at many colleges and libraries or you can subscribe direct to:

International Employment Gazette
1525 Wade Hampton Boulevard
Greenville, South Carolina 29609
(800) 882-9188

Do not limit your research in the library to these sources. Your librarian can be very helpful to you and direct you to other valuable printed sources. The next chapter extends your research to job search firms. Research these in your library as well. You will be amazed at how much you will discover and the opportunities there are for you to explore.

12

CONNECTING WITH JOB SEARCH FIRMS

Many receive advice
only the wise profit by it.
Syrus

Job search firms fall into three basic categories. There are executive search firms, outplacement firms and employment agencies. Some employment agencies refer to themselves as search firms. You need to understand the differences among these types of firms and how they can help you. You should select those that match your needs and use them to assist you in getting the job you want.

➤ 143 Executive Search Firms

Make certain you submit your resume to the proper executive search firms if you are at the appropriate level. It is a waste of everyone's time and money when specializations are ignored. This typically occurs when a well intentioned friend refers you to a firm or when you pick up a firm's name somewhere along the way. Take time to find out the area of specialization before you send your resume. Each firm has access to the hidden job market or unadvertised openings of its client companies. Submitting your resume to only one executive search firm may not be enough even though it specializes in your field. You have to expand your exposure according to your sense of urgency and need. Each search firm has its own corporate clientele, locally, regionally and nationally.

EXECUTIVE SEARCH FIRMS

Executive search firms can be an excellent source for potential employment opportunities providing you fit their area of expertise. To help you understand what you can expect, a brief overview is given here. There is a great deal of mystique to the executive search industry. Very few people really know what takes place in executive search firms, because they operate very quietly behind the scenes similar to law firms or CPA firms. How the search industry gets access to the top job openings and the "hidden job market" is one part of this mystique. Another factor contributing to this mystique is how executive search firms find the "right" candidates without placing help wanted ads in newspapers or trade publications. Just how does the system work?

The first question most often asked is, "How does one become visible to the executive search industry and receive confidential consideration for the appropriate opportunities the executive search firms are retained to fill?" The next question is, "How can a person initiate the contact with the appropriate executive search firms when one is looking for a job or wishes to make a job change?" People also want to know the procedure they should follow and what considerations, if any, can they reasonably expect from a firm.

Executive search firms are always retained by the client companies to find and appraise top talent to meet their needs. Executive search firms are never retained by individuals seeking employment or career changes. Do not confuse the executive search industry with outplacement firms or executive marketing service firms which help people find jobs for a fee.

According to the Department of Commerce there are over 2,000 executive search firms in this country. Total revenue for their services was $3.2 billion in 1991. This translates approximately 31,000 people employed within the industry of which almost half are professionals. They are retained to identify, recruit, screen and evaluate candidates for client company needs. This industry has grown considerably; yet for whatever reason, most people are oblivious to its size and scope. It fills a growing number of needs yearly.

The term executive search firm should have additional explanation before we proceed. The term can be misleading to people who may think this industry deals strictly in executive level positions. While this holds true for many executive search firms, it does not apply to the vast majority that also handle professional level salaried positions. Some firms range from $40,000 to $100,000 salary levels or more. Others start at $100,000 levels. *The Directory of Executive Recruiters* describes the salary levels and types of industries that search firms cover on a national basis. Don't tread into these waters without first checking into this directory.

Executive search firms are either generalists or specialists. Each has its own advantages. Whatever the level or industry specialization, executive search firms are selectively open to receiving resumes from individuals with the appropriate backgrounds. You can have the finest credentials in the world, but if you send your resume to a firm that specializes in banking and you are in health care, as an example, you are out of luck. We see this quite routinely in our executive search practice. There are many reasons to explain this happening, but it does not change the bottom line. Job seekers who do not match with the search firm are automatically screened out. Research the executive search firms that handle your type of background. Each firm has its own clientele so your sense of urgency will dictate how many firms in your field you should contact.

Most firms do not acknowledge receipt of resumes. Contacts are typically made with job seekers only when appropriate matches develop. Accept this fact, and don't get discouraged. There is no way possible to respond to all inquiries.

Knowing this should help reduce anxieties and that awful feeling of rejection.

We receive phone inquiries and unsolicited resumes by the numbers on a daily basis from individuals seeking to make a job change or seeking employment. People calling in are given the following message by our receptionist and secretaries:

> All we need is a single copy of your current resume, with a cover letter that can either be hand written or typed. It should give your salary and indicate, separately, if there is a bonus. We also need your location preferences and any other information you feel would be important for us to know. Upon receipt, your resume will be reviewed by our research director and his staff, and if it is appropriate, your credentials will be input into our data bank for confidential consideration against any and all search assignments that match your credentials. There are no forms or agreements to fill out now or ever and all fees are handled by our client companies. However, please understand there is no way we can predict when a suitable match will develop. Someone from our firm would be in contact with you at that time before we proceed any further. Please, mark your envelope, Attention: Research Director.

All resumes received are then sorted out by our front desk eliminating the obvious from further consideration. The remainder are passed on to our research director and his staff for further pre-screening to determine which resumes should be input into our data bank for confidential consideration against all current and future search assignments. The balance are shredded.

The first thing we do upon the acceptance of a search assignment is to review the criteria in a meeting with our research director and his staff. Procedurally, several different steps will take place simultaneously. These include researching, sourcing, recruiting, pre-screening, background checking and evaluation of prospective candidates. We utilize forty-five different methods and means to identify top talent for our clients. One of them is our computerized data bank that we search to identify all prospective candidates that potentially match the need of our clients. This is part of our standard research process.

At this point the person seeking employment or a job change can be retrieved from our data bank and be included for potential employment consideration as part of our search process. If a potential match develops, contact is then made for additional screening and discussion. The purpose of this discussion is two-fold. We need to insure that we have the appropriate match for our client before proceeding further. Secondly, we need to identify the needs and motivations of the prospective candidate. This saw cuts both ways. It does little good if the prospective candidate meets the needs of our client only to find out after the fact that the candidate's needs are not being met. This makes for a bad marriage destined to fail from the start.

Background checks are conducted. One of two things will happen next. We either move forward and present our candidate's credentials to our client, or we pass. If we pass for whatever reason, we inform the candidate and mark our files accordingly. If appropriate, we will maintain an individual's credentials in our computerized data bank for future consideration.

If all is well, we proceed to arrange for the candidate to meet personally with our client. An initial phone discussion can take place. If all remains positive, a personal meeting is arranged. Detailed feedback is shared with the client and the candidate after interviews throughout the hiring process. If something is lacking on either part or both, this is communicated. Should all continue to go well, an offer might be extended. Executive search firms often assist in final negotiations to insure that everything is fair to both parties. This is part of the process. Again, all fees are taken care of by our client companies.

Procedures will vary from one executive search firm to the next. I have pointed out our basic procedure to provide some general insights into what you can generally anticipate from an executive search firm.

CHANGING CAREER FIELDS

A strong word of caution is in order. You can forget mailing your resume to executive search firms if you are looking to change career fields. There is no such thing as a client company that will retain an executive search firm to find people, no matter how great they are, that are looking to change career fields. They don't need an executive search firm to find such people for them. Any time a client company retains an executive search firm it has some very specific talent in mind who has an outstanding track record in specific industries. I will be the first to admit there will be an occasional rare exception, and when it does occur the client will specify the person wanted. This can and does occur but not to the point that the executive search industry can afford to keep all such career changing inquiries updated in its data bank. These resumes are shredded.

OUTPLACEMENT

Outplacement firms provide job search assistance to people who need to find jobs. The outplacement business has rapidly grown in recent years, due to the advent of extensive corporate cutbacks. In spite of their growing popularity most people are still not aware of what outplacement firms do. This field has expanded so much that many people are becoming involved with one. Even the U.S. Army is providing outplacement services to assist 350,000 army personnel being downsized over the next five years to adjust and find work in the public sector. Outplacement services are becoming commonplace. In the not too distant past, employees were simply given their "pink slips" and directed to the unemployment offices at best. Now times have changed.

Broadly speaking, there are two different types of outplacement firms. First, there are outplacement firms which are hired by corporations to assist their employees being let go to find suitable employment. These services can be extended to individual employees or to entire departments, divisions, plant closings or company wide reductions. Outplacement firms may be engaged prior to announced cutbacks to assist the company in developing the best approach to take.

The outplacement firm will then meet with the individual or group and may participate with the corporation in breaking the "news" of the cutback or will completely handle this unpleasant chore for the company. The type of services provided will vary from one outplacement firm to another. They may even custom tailor a "package" if the numbers justify it. Corporate outplacement firms deal exclusively with corporate clients and will not represent individuals seeking employment assistance.

Secondly, there are outplacement firms that are also referred to as executive marketing services firms which assist individuals in their search for a job. These firms charge a fee to the individual. Now the water gets muddy, because if you look in the yellow pages for outplacement firms, you will find firms that will do both. They will work for corporate clients to assist their employees find suitable employment and/or will work for individuals. The basic difference is whether the corporate client or the individual pays the fee. In either case, the fees are paid in advance of services rendered.

Following is a sample outline of services outplacement firms provide. Services will vary from one company to the next. This outline is intended to provide a basic understanding of outplacement.

1. If a large group is involved, there will normally be an initial group meeting between the outplacement firm and the employees being cut back. The employees are then given a detailed explanation of what will take place from that point forward. Outplacement firms are professionally trained to handle this delicate task in the proper psychologically humane manner. They want to minimize the potential emotional scars and trauma of being cut back.

2. Appointments are scheduled for each individual. This initial interview or assessment meeting is intended to gain an understanding of the individual's background, capabilities and needs. A number of firms will have the individual fill out questionnaire forms to assist in this process.

3. Normally, another meeting will be scheduled to provide feedback from the initial meeting. It will outline a plan of what will take place from start to finish throughout the job search process.

4. Psychological testing and a feedback session can also be a part of the outplacement "package." In-depth interviews of the individual's entire work history, education and past accomplishments can be conducted.

5. Resume preparation is also normally part of the standard services.

6. "Transferrable skills" will be identified for those who wish or need to change career fields. This will help a person to cross industry lines and enter new careers.

7. Potential career, industry and location alternatives are explored when necessary.

8. The necessary research will be conducted to identify the potential industries, companies and jobs that will meet

the needs of the individual. These will be used for resume mailings that will be handled by the individual or the company, depending upon the "package."

9. Some firms provide access to their research libraries that can be utilized by their clientele. Included may be various publications dealing with the job market including various out-of-town newspapers.

10. Interviewing training may be provided, which could include video camera practice sessions to show improvement.

11. Progress meetings will take place throughout the job search. These will include feedback discussions from interviews. This normally continues until the person has landed a desired position.

It should be understood that outplacement firms <u>do not</u> find jobs for people nor guarantee that they will do so. Outplacement firms will assist and direct individuals with their expertise in every step of their job hunting search until they find a job. It is important for you to know the exact nature of their services and guarantees. This will help you avoid any potential misunderstanding due to wishful thinking. Make sure you understand clearly each others responsibilities in total. Remember, you can pay someone to teach you how to drive a car or how to dance, but it may not make you a good driver or dancer. It will take some practice and work on your part.

Prices will vary depending upon a number of different factors including the degree of difficulty each job seeker faces. Shop around before you decide. These services are not cheap. But what is?

➤ 144 Employment Agencies
Explore and work with employment agencies in the same way. The same principles apply. You should use

employment agencies for medium to lower level positions. It may take diligent exploration before you connect with the right ones. Your attitude in dealing with agencies will greatly affect your success.

> ## 145 Specialties Of Employment Agencies
Do not use employment agencies that do not serve your area of expertise. Most agencies specialize. They also handle different salary levels. Yellow page ads do not always state areas of specialization. Call the agency and ask. Select ones most suited to your interests for further exploration and use. Work with them, and they will work for you.

EMPLOYMENT AGENCIES

Employment agencies find jobs for people. They also fill jobs for client companies. They can be a very good job referral source if you have the appropriate background. There are an estimated 15-20,000 employment agencies in this country. The number varies according to the state of the economy. Each has its own market or specialty it services. Some are generalists while others specialize by vocation such as accounting, or by industry such as banking. Each has its advantages. As an industry employment agencies (depending upon the firm) start with entry level and secretarial positions. They handle hourly paying jobs on up to lower level management positions. They do not cater to blue collar workers, high school dropouts or upper management people. Save yourself a trip if you happen to be one of these. A select few top employment agencies do overlap with executive search firms and serve high level positions. If in doubt, call.

You should first determine which employment agencies handle people with your background. You can do this by following their advertised positions in the help wanted section of newspapers, their yellow page advertising or picking up the phone and calling.

As a comparison think of restaurants if you will. They come in every size, shape and type from carry out only, to fast food, cafeteria, home delivery, sit down casual and on up to fine dining with linens and candlelight. The same applies to employment agencies. Don't just take pot luck and call the first one listed in the yellow pages because its name begins with a series of A's. You will inevitably be walking through the wrong door to disappointment. You surely don't go to O'Reilly's Pub if you are looking for tacos or chinese cuisine; nor do you go to a fine restaurant with linens and candlelight when you want a hot dog. Just as there are appropriate eating establishments to cater to your every needs, there are employment agencies that do the same.

Companies use different employment agencies to accommodate their various needs. There is no such thing as one employment agency to handle it all. Going to the wrong agency is without a doubt the most common mistake made by job seekers. And unfortunately this ends up being reflected wrongfully against the employment agency industry because of the "bad experience." Make sure you connect with the right agency, or you will be setting yourself up for disappointment. Don't let an occasional over-zealous employment agency counselor encourage you to come in for an interview if it does not fit. Be sure to pre-screen the agency on the phone.

Upon arrival, you will be given an employment application. Fill it out neatly and completely. You might also be given a fee agreement to complete and sign. Most firms operate on an employer paid fee (EPF) basis, while a few firms also handle applicant paid fees (APF). You are not required to go out on applicant paid fee positions (APF) nor accept such a position, but it is standard practice to agree to sign the form. This is done to protect the agency from some companies which will agree to pay the employment agency fee initially in order to get a good flow of applicants to interview then change their minds in the process for whatever reasons. As a result the agency must have the complete cooperation of the job seekers up front so they will pay the fee should a decision be made to proceed and accept such a job. In most cases it is the marginally qualified applicants with little or no experience seeking basic entry level positions who will fall into the APF category.

A counselor will conduct a brief pre-screening interview. This is not the same as a job interview. The counselor simply needs to qualify certain points and fill in areas left blank on the application.

Only a small percentage of the traffic to an employment agency is considered to be highly marketable. Much effort is concentrated on these choice people. The next group of applicants are of the average every day basic type of grass roots people. The balance are marginal at best, problem applicants or upper level people whom they cannot help. Each person basically knows to which group one belongs and can anticipate corresponding results. This will dictate the number of employment agencies that should be contacted.

One of the questions you will be asked is your availability for interviews upon short notice. Another question is, "What is the minimum salary you will consider?" Don't take offense to this question since seventy-five percent of all job seekers are flexible and open to lower salaries depending upon the opportunity. The question is basically asking if you wish to be considered for a broader range of job opportunities. Interviews or "send outs" (a phrase employment agencies use when they arrange interviews) can be set up at the end of your interview with them.

Your attitude is as important as your background in regards to the amount of attention and degree of success you will have with any employment agency. As long as you are cooperative, friendly and courteous, you can expect the same treatment. Conduct yourself as such, and you will get "sent out" on interviews for employment. One strong word of caution is in order. Once a "send out" is arranged, make sure you get there on <u>time</u> and keep your appointment. If anything happens to prevent you from being punctual, make sure you call the agency and the company. If for some reason you cannot make the appointment, be sure to call as far ahead as possible and re-schedule. You don't want to be labeled as a "no show," which is the kiss of death. There are those who don't show or call ahead because they have had a change of heart or become employed. There is still no excuse for this inconsiderate behavior. Next, make sure to call the agency after each interview for feedback discussion. It needs to know how things went and the proper course of action to take.

Agencies have their own clientele with some degree of overlap. They are forever calling old and new companies on behalf of a highly placeable applicant, commonly referred to as a Most Placeable Applicant (MPA). Should you hear them mention that term in describing you, it will tell you how they look upon you and the kind of "send outs" you can expect. They will pick up other openings (job orders) while making these calls.

Quality of service will vary as much as the restaurant analogy that was used earlier. Even the finest restaurants can have a bad day at times as can agencies, so be patient and understanding.

Ninety-five or more percent of the time agencies will not charge you. They handle employer paid fees predominantly or exclusively. Remember they pay all their own bills including wages, rent, phone, advertising and all else in order to help you. They are not federally funded. So, again, watch your attitude, and you can have some good success to the degree of demand for your background. If you happen to get into the wrong agency or have a less than satisfactory experience with an inexperienced counselor, then move on down the road to the next one. Don't hold the agency responsible for the supply/demand factor for people with your background. Some of you are going to be in greater demand than others, and for some there may not be any demand. It is not the agency's nor your fault. It is being in the wrong place at the wrong time with the wrong experience.

The employment agency industry represents too many job sources to neglect it. If you live in a small town, you will have to go to the nearest large city to explore employment agencies which service your employment prospects.

➤ 146 Headhunter Relationships

Cooperate when the headhunter calls. Don't play games, be curt or rude. There is really no excuse for it. You may be completely happy at the moment and not need anything from the person. That is fine, well and good; however, don't burn your bridges. If you do, your file will be marked accordingly. What happens tomorrow when you are unexpectedly out of work? Everyone needs career insurance contacts in today's changing job climate. Use all you can get all the time. Treat people the way you want to be treated. Be sensitive to how you might help others and how they might help you.

Use the advice your job search counselor gives you. People in the job search business have helped thousands of other people get jobs. Let them also help you.

13

RESEARCH YOUR TARGET COMPANIES

Foresight is better than hindsight.
Learning before the act can prevent mistakes.
Knowing what you are getting into before you do it will keep
you out of what you don't want.

Research is the best job search tool any job seeker can use.

Job seekers often feel compelled to plunge into the job market by calling companies and asking for interviews before they know much about the companies. People even go on interviews without knowing the basics about the company. Don't fall into this trap. This chapter gives you easy and effective ways to research your target companies; this will set you way ahead of other job seekers and thrust you onto the job market prepared and confident.

To lead an untrained people to war is to throw them away.
Confucius

Don't throw away your job opportunities by being unprepared.

➤ 147 The Informed Job Searcher Wins!

There is an old Italian proverb that states,

The strong take away from the weak, but
the smart take away from the strong.

This also applies to job seekers. The stronger credentials will win over the weaker credentials. But the more informed job seekers will win over the less informed job seekers, despite their superior credentials.

> ## 148 Research Prospective Company
Always conduct research on companies prior to interviews. Being armed with this knowledge will give you an added edge. It will allow you to ask more intelligent questions and convey to the interviewer that you are not just another person looking for a job but you are truly interested in becoming part of the company. This will put you in a very select class of job seekers because few people actually research companies. Secondly, when you choose a company, you should know what you are choosing. Research can reveal positives and negatives about the company.

KNOW THY PROSPECTIVE EMPLOYER

Conduct yourself as if you were making a career-life commitment with each prospective employer. After all, isn't that your hope? Don't approach a potential job as if it is merely something to do until something better comes along.

The Better Business Bureau coined the slogan: "Investigate Before You Invest." Apply this same good advice to any prospective company you are considering. You might be investing all or part of your work life with that firm. The major reason many accept a job is because it was offered. No other reason, logic or rationale was necessary. "What have I got to lose? Right? Anything beats what I'm doing now?" (Only if you are unemployed.)

Knowing what you are getting into is worth knowing.

There are a number of sources for company information. If the company is publicly held, you can get company information from the following directories at the reference department in your main public library in major markets.

1. *Standard and Poor's Stock Guide.*
2. *Moody's* publications.
3. Corporate *Annual Reports.* **Some** are available on micro fiche. Otherwise, they are available from all publicly held companies upon request.
4. *Dun & Bradstreet Million Dollar Directory.*

In addition, most publicly held companies will provide you with available literature on the company, products or services. All you have to do is ask. Most companies look upon such a request in a highly positive manner. It reflects a serious person who is taking a long range career approach to the job, not a typical job seeker who is just looking for a job, one who is here today, gone tomorrow, another "wandering" career nomad.

There are many sources of information about privately held companies. Some possibilities are given below.

1. Dun & Bradstreet, if the company is listed.
2. *Standard & Poor's*, if the company is large enough.
3. *The INC List* of the 500 largest privately held companies in the USA.
4. Company literature on the company, products or services, when available.
5. Growth rate and track record of the company which may not be in a written form.
6. Industry standing. Where it stands within its industry or market place.
7. Overall reputation in the market.
8. Customers' attitudes towards the company.
9. Someone you know who works there.
10. Local chambers of commerce.
11. Local newspapers and other publications that could give insight about companies.
12. All else that you can find out.

Most of the above also apply to all publicly held companies as well. Please be aware that the best positions with the most outstanding career opportunities are also the ones which attract the greatest and toughest competition. You can count on it. So do your research to become an informed job seeker and gain the competitive edge over your competition.

> Just as "great battles are won in the tent" before going to the battlefield; and "great court cases are not won in the courtroom, but in the preparation," the same principle applies to the job seeker who prepares properly before interviews.

You gain a considerable edge over your competition when you display a keen knowledge and interest in the company, its products or services and other specific information. It also enables you to ask questions which show you have insight and allows you to dovetail your skills and capabilities into the company's needs.

In the course of getting to know all you can about a prospective employer, you should be talking to many different people such as friends, neighbors, relatives, customers or competitors. In your travels you will also begin to recall the many stories, both good and bad, that you have heard about various companies.

A word of caution is in order. Everything has to be put into proper prospective. I know people who work for the XYZ company who are happy because their career needs are being met. Therefore, the XYZ company is good for those people. I also know people who work for the XYZ company whose career needs are not being met. These people are not happy; therefore, the XYZ company is not the place for them. The moral to this story is quite clear. Most companies are neither good nor bad per se. They are only good in-so-far as one's career needs are being met and bad if they are not. People tend to pay too much attention to friends, neighbors, and relatives who complain and throw stones at their present companies or their previous employers. Pay particular attention to the objectivity of your sources.

Again, here is another word of caution. How many good things do people have to say about a spouse if the marriage is in trouble or has already ended in divorce? The same can be said about people who quit or were fired from a job. For one reason or the other, things did not work out. But unfortunately, most of the time they don't have much good to say about the company. Don't let their bias affect your decision about the company.

Be Alert To "Excusitis"

Most complaints and negative comments tend to come from people who are not achieving their goals. The majority of complainers have developed a lifetime habit of what I have already referred to as "excusitis." It is like a disease because it continues to get worse with time and is fatal. It is nothing more that the habit of making up excuses for all their short comings, whatever they may be. It doesn't matter what they were supposed to do, where they were supposed to be or when they were supposed to do it. They continually make up excuses. They are forever looking for some excuse like a hypochondriac is looking for a new disease to adopt. Most, if not all, will end up with an obituary in the book entitled, "Who's Through In America."

If you are not careful, you could catch this "excusitis" disease because there is so much of it around. You all know the type to which I am referring. Unless you are a very strong willed person, you could inadvertently allow yourself to be influenced negatively towards certain companies by these major league rock throwers. Be careful. There are right reasons and wrong reasons for accepting or rejecting a position with any firm. Unfortunately, people will often accept or decline a position for the wrong reasons. Could this be one of the contributing factors toward the prevailing high employee turnover?

Common Logic: Cause And Effect

I am reminded of a late night TV talk show I watched over twenty-years ago. The alarming increase in the divorce rate was the topic of discussion. A guest commented that it appeared people were getting divorced for such piddling reasons. Everyone agreed and asked why this was so?

There happened to be a popular minister on the show who answered the question with another thought provoking question. "Could it be that the reason people were getting divorced for such piddling reasons is that perhaps they were getting married for such piddling reasons?" Aha!!

Some of the reasons given for getting married were discussed:

I'm not getting any younger.
I'm tired of the single life.
I'm the last one in my circle of friends to get married.
I'm tired of the bar scene.
I don't like to sleep alone.
I don't like to eat alone.
I'm lonely.
I don't like to go out by myself.
He/she is a great cook.
I've always wanted a big wedding.
He/she's a great dancer.
He/she's a great lover.
I'd like to have someone to talk to.
I want to have a child.
My parents are on my back.
It is time to settle down.
Everybody else is getting married.
If I don't get married now, I may never do it.
I don't want to grow old by myself.
Etc., etc., etc.

Right Reasons & Wrong Reasons

There are right reasons and wrong reasons for doing almost anything. Is this the foundation upon which one builds a lasting, happy marriage? No reference was made towards loving, caring or sharing their lives forever. Could this be the problem?

The same applies with people and their jobs. There are right reasons, and there are wrong reasons for accepting any job. People who accept jobs for the wrong reasons are doomed from the start:

> *I got an offer.*
> *A friend of mine got me the job.*
> *It is close to where I live.*
> *It is an extra $500 a month.*
> *I don't like the rejection in job hunting.*
> *The commuting time is a lot shorter.*
> *I can't stand my boss.*
> *My uncle works for the company.*
> *I'll never get anywhere where I'm at.*
> *My friends are changing jobs with more money.*
> *I really like the gal/guy I'll be working for.*
> *They have an excellent benefit program.*
> *I'm tired of interviewing.*
> *Job hunting is frustrating.*
> *Anything has to be better than what I've got.*
> *The offices are beautiful.*
> *They really rolled out the carpet for me.*
> *I've always wanted to live in Florida, etc.*
> *I'm tired of looking.*
> *My neighbor is happy there.*

Again, to what degree are your career needs going to be met? What about challenge, continuity of challenge, responsibility, opportunities for advancement, duties, philosophy, growth rate, turnover, company reputation, standing within the industry, industry trend or work atmosphere?

Dig For Information

You are going to have to do some investigative digging to find out what you need to know about any prospective employer. You need to get as much information as you possibly can obtain about the company whether it is a publicly or privately held firm. Privately owned companies are more difficult to research although many privately held companies have literature available. All you have to do is ask.

In our executive search practice we have learned something somewhat startling over the years. We provide as much literature as we can get from our client companies to all candidates. When available, we give it to them prior to the interview. Half the time, client companies are late in providing the materials until after the first interview. Then again, some companies only provide company literature to candidates before their second interview. Many provide nothing at all.

Even more startling is the fact that a high percentage of candidates never take the time to read the literature. They either look upon the task as unpleasant homework, or perhaps they are fearful that they might find something unpleasant about the company or industry. Maybe they have the "ignorance is bliss" syndrome. After all, so far so good. Why mettle! Right?

We never have figured out why so many people refuse to take the time to read what we give them. Could it be that they would not believe it? Could it be that so many people are downright lazy? It may sound like unnecessary work to thoroughly research a prospective employer, but it is not. Consider the consequences of short cutting this process. The price is too high when you begin to place a value on your work satisfaction and happiness.

Life teaches that you will get out of life exactly what you put into it: no more, no less - you just cannot beat the system. *As you give, so shall you receive.* All too often job hunting campaigns are built upon a foundation called LUCK. Wow, what a way to go! You don't have to let yours be hit or miss if you research the company.

➤ 149 Searching Within A Company

Failure to pursue job opportunities in all divisions or subsidiaries of target companies is an oversight which all too many people are guilty of. The right hand does not necessarily know what the left hand is doing in a large company. One department will not know every opportunity that exists in all others. One subsidiary is not aware of the opportunities that exist in all other subsidiaries. Each tend to live in a vacuum. Be extremely thorough, and pick a company completely clean before you walk away. There is gold in those diggings. Be aware that you can spend some time trying to contact the "wrong" person in a company. Do your research; don't just rely on a secretary or switch board operator to determine the right contact for you.

THE GYPSY'S PURSE

I want to share with you a favorite saying of my mother.

> *There never has been nor ever will be enough money in the whole wide world to fill a gypsy's purse. There simply is no bottom to it. There is always room for more.*

Likewise with companies. There is no such thing as any company that has enough sales, profits, market share, enough money in their corporate treasury, successful new products, services or fame and good fortune. Show me the company that has achieved all it ever hopes to achieve. There never has been since the dawn of civilization, nor will there ever be. There is always some room for improvement. Just like the gypsy's purse, there are never "enough" improvements. There is no bottom to a company's needs. This translates into having the right people who can make ongoing contributions and improvements.

Being armed with this knowledge should enable you to literally create more opportunities for yourself than most people ever realize. So, simply looking for a new job is not the answer. It is looking for opportunities where you can make a meaningful contribution to a company's needs. Learn to convey what you can do for the company, and you will create many new job prospects for you to pursue. But remember, you need to first research the company to know what it needs.

CASUAL NEEDS

Casual needs is a term new to most job seekers. They don't know what it means. However, executive search firms, employment agencies, outplacement firms and hiring managers know it quite well. It is extremely important for you, as a job seeker, to know what this means because it can make the difference in getting or not getting a job with any specific company.

A casual need is not a specific job opening or vacancy. Companies don't actually advertise or announce positions to fill their casual needs. What they do is "keep their eyes open for exceptional talent." Interviews for casual needs are commonly referred to as exploratory interviews.

The best way to communicate this more clearly is by using the field of sports as an example. All teams will have a regulation team of players fully staffed with additional players on the bench. So, one could conclude that all the team's needs are filled. Nothing could be further from the truth. There is always room for improvement; I don't care which team might be considered. If the "right" player that truly represents a well above average track record happens to come along, room on the team is made for that person.

This same principle applies to the job search. There are from ten to twenty plus more casual needs than there are actual job openings at any one time. In order for you to be successful in this arena, you must be aware that potential casual needs exist and that whenever you are interviewed you are being considered to meet them. You must look to fill casual needs. The impression you convey must make the company conclude that it simply cannot afford not to hire you for fear that you may end up on the competitor's team. Please understand, you must have the track record to back this up. No "wandering" career nomads need apply. Pursue casual needs, and you will find a job.

Coincidentally, while editing this chapter I received a phone call from a person who was inquiring about the possibility of getting a job with our firm. He had called two days earlier while I was not available. His message stated that he was interested in talking with me about the possibility of joining our firm as an executive search consultant and would call back. Because I knew why he was calling, I decided to take his call. He had done his research well and knew who we were and was highly complimentary.

He wanted to know what my schedule looked like for the upcoming week so we could get together personally. I told him that we had no openings and were not looking to add any additional consultants at this time. He told me he understood, but he still wanted to meet me. He indicated that he was gainfully employed and under no duress to make a change. He stated, "It would be a matter of time before your company would have a need to hire someone because you are a strong progressive growth company."

He wanted to make sure that we knew who he was, his capabilities, including what he could do for us and his interest in joining our firm. He assured me that he was perfectly willing to wait in the wings for that moment to occur, and then he pressed for possible appointment times and dates. He was very professional and was not pushy; so I agreed to meet with him. He succeeded in setting an interview.

What exactly could happen from this point forward? Could we possibly make room in our company for one more good person? We certainly did not agree to get together to pass away the time of day. He did such a beautiful job over the phone that I owed it to myself to meet with him. We get job inquiries routinely which we pass on. He happened to stand out from the crowd because he had researched the firm exceptionally well.

We all know that no one gets hired without first being interviewed. He succeeded in getting that accomplished. Our first meeting was very positive. Two interviews later we made an addition to our staff.

Is the picture clear? Being persistent is one thing, but by itself it is not enough. You must also be saying and doing the right things. That is the key to opening doors for you. How many doors would you like to open? It is up to you to decide.

➤ 150 Broad Based Company Search

Do not concentrate your job search <u>exclusively</u> on the top Fortune 500 companies or the largest companies in any industry, unless you thrive on rejection. Major corporations attract entirely too many job seekers. Far more opportunities exist with small to medium sized companies. Certainly it is perfectly logical to include in your job search selected major companies that are appropriate to your background. Just don't limit your search to these companies.

➤ 151 What Is The Company Really Like?

The company, the working conditions, expectations, superiors and associates - what are they really like? In the course of pursuing job prospects with a particular company you should find out these things about the company.

- What is the company like as an employer and how respected is it in the industry?
- How stable is the company financially?
- Is it a growth company?
- Is it looking to expand into foreign markets, or could it move its local operation to Mexico or sell out to a foreign country?
- What are the people really like, and what is it really like to work with them?

This sounds almost too basic. But things are not always what they appear to be. There are some unusually successful companies that do not have a good working environment. There are some very large nationally known companies that are sweat shops. How about working for a company where no one (including salaried professionals and top management) is allowed to go out for lunch. Everyone brown bags it while being coerced into working throughout lunch. What about the firms who have extremely high turnover because of poor working conditions? What about working for a firm in which top management screams, yells and shouts while chewing out an employee to drive the point home to everyone else? How about 6:00 a.m. meetings each Saturday?

Learn these requirements during the exploration phase, not after you are on board. You can then base your decision on facts. Too many people jump from the proverbial frying pan into the fire. These things happen frequently as a result of careless research on the part of job seekers.

➤ 152 Company Culture
The company culture is probably the most overlooked

area that job seekers pursue in their job search. Is the company a ballet, live theater and arts type of company? Is it steeped in spectator sports or does it have the hunting and fishing culture? The top person in the company may be into tennis or golf. If you are in tune with this culture, you may gain points and win out on the job offer. In many companies their culture is loose or non-existent. It is a point worth exploring. It can make a difference.

➤ **153 Politics**
If your reason for leaving your present employer is because of politics, stop. Politics have been around since the beginning of time. The bigger and older the company, the more steeped it will be in politics. There is a generally accepted principle in the business world that states people will rise further in a corporation because of their political expertise than their technical expertise. You may not like this statement, but it does not change the way the world goes around. There is some middle ground called being diplomatic. It beats being a renegade by not playing by the rules of political play. It takes some practice to achieve this middle ground. But changing companies in an attempt to escape politics is not the answer. Smaller and newer firms offer better shelter to those of you who are vehemently opposed to politics. But there really is no guarantee of escape. All you can do is probe into the subject of politics before accepting any job, then hope for the best.

➤ **154 Glamour Jobs Versus Opportunity**
Don't allow glamour to overshadow opportunity. Too many people are overwhelmed by potential glamour which can take away from good solid bread and butter opportunities in basic industries. This can be extremely difficult at times, especially when the company's glamour has put some stars in your eyes.

➤ 155   Appearance Of The Company

Be careful when appraising a company that you do not misjudge it based upon the appearance of its facilities. There are some highly successful companies with excellent opportunities that you could miss out on if you judge them on outward appearances only. A classic example is the headquarters of Wal-Mart with its Spartan-like buildings and furnishings. There are many other successful companies like it. On the other hand, there are also many companies that are in serious financial trouble that are operating from very plush facilities. Things are not always what they appear to be. Would you rather work for a financially strong company or a financially shaky one? Go beyond the exterior facade to determine the real financial stability of the company. Just remember; looks can be deceiving. Look for substance, not fluff. Research the company thoroughly to learn the facts.

Use this job search tool called research, and use it well. Research combined with networking gives you the power to succeed. This combination is, in essence, knowing who you want to know and then setting out to get to know them. Apply the research information that you have learned in this chapter to the networking procedures in the next one.

14

NETWORKING -

MAKING YOUR CONTACTS WORK FOR YOU

A Case For Networking

It isn't who you are;
It's who you know.

People like people who like people.
People help people who help people.
People help people whom they like,
*   who have helped them,*
*   and who ask for help.*

Ask for help from all logical sources
*   and from many not so logical ones.*
Network, network, network.

If you could choose only one method to get a job, choose networking. People around you everyday who you know or have known throughout your life know people in positions that could be of help to you. Let them know you are looking for work. Explore possibilities. People like to help others; so, let them help you. Watch the results grow; listen to the telephone ring and find yourself going out on interviews. This chapter only briefly introduces you to networking possibilities. Your networking is up to you. Never get trapped in negative conversations while you are networking. Search out people which can help move you into a positive (rather than a hopeless) situation.

A CASE OF GROCERY STORE NETWORKING

I was in a grocery store. The lines at the check out counters were very long. The woman in front of me said, "I'm an efficiency analyst; maybe I should see the manager?"

The man in back of me replied, "I know him, he's over there stacking the racks. Come over, I'll introduce you." The two left their carts full of groceries and went over to the manager.

Within a few minutes the woman came back and removed her cart from the line. The manager was saying to her, "If you can help me schedule my employees' time to meet the flow of customers better, I'll hire you." The woman thanked the man who had made the introduction and went with the manager to his office. I don't know the outcome; I don't even know if the woman was looking for a job, but she was certainly heading for an immediate interview.

Let everyone you know (and even some that you don't) know that you are looking for a job and would appreciate help in finding one.

NETWORKING IN ANOTHER UNUSUAL PLACE

I heard of a person who literally exhausted himself in looking for work. He had an accident and was taken to the emergency room of a hospital. There he met someone in the same predicament and ended up getting a job through that chance meeting. When you are job hunting, you should be open at all times to discuss your job prospects with those you meet. You never know where an opportunity may surface. Chance favors the prepared mind.

➤ **156 Networking**
Networking is an often overlooked secret to the successful job search. A major luck factor in connecting

with the right people is who has the most friends, neighbors, relatives and connections in the right places. Who you know does make a difference. Networking through these sources will compensate for weaknesses in most areas (especially if your father owns the company). Don't hesitate to use your networking resources. You might think, "I can do it on my own." What does it prove?

Prove yourself after you have gotten the job. That is where it counts. You might have gotten into a prestigious college because your dad is an alumni, but you did not stay there or make your mark on tests because of this. Getting the right job for you is only step one. Succeeding at it is your lifetime work.

GIVERS, TRADERS AND TAKERS

In the course of your job search and networking you will discover three different types of people. Observe people and see which of the following groups they fall into.

1. **Givers**. Their giving conduct makes them stand out from the crowd. They just can't seem to do enough for anyone or the world in general. This includes favors, volunteering when no one else will, helping, giving gifts, you name it. Givers just can't seem to help their giving nature. You can always count on them. No one can give too many accolades to these Givers.

2. **Traders**. These people are willing to give or do only as much as they believe they will get back in return. They literally keep a scorecard of all conduct.

3. **Takers**. Everyone knows Takers. These are the self-centered people who are totally preoccupied with what is in it for them. That is all they think about. They are completely obsessed with themselves. They are forever

free loading at other people's expense. Takers literally will not help their mother, brothers, sisters or friends, much less strangers. They somehow manage to mingle with the rest of the world and live like parasites off others. Forget asking these people for any kind of help, contribution or consideration. Takers do not pay their own way if they can possibly avoid it. They are always looking for something for nothing. They are self consumed.

It will become self evident which of these people you encounter when networking. You won't be able to get the time of day from a Taker. It doesn't matter if it is your Aunt May. Fortunately, there are enough Givers and Traders to make up for the Takers. So, make it a point to keep doubling back for more help from the Givers and Traders. Some of you are going to be highly disappointed when being refused help from family and close friends. Their taking nature will shine through when they won't be able to think of a solitary person's name that can be of help in your networking. No one lives in a vacuum or in isolation; do they? The only people Takers will help are themselves. You will discover complete strangers (Givers) who can't do enough for you. All I can say is this just happens to be another valuable lesson in life that will serve you well.

➤ 157 Networking With Your Banker

Use your business and personal contacts for exploring job opportunities. Don't overlook your banker for help. Bankers have valuable connections. All you have to do is ask. Bankers are very active in their communities and welcome the opportunity to get to know their customers better.

➤ 158 Chamber Of Commerce

Each chamber of commerce is an invaluable source of information about the city and companies in and near it. Be sure to explore all chambers in your target areas.

Remember many companies have branch offices and facilities in many different cities in which you might consider living. The chamber can help you in all living considerations, as well as give you information concerning companies about which you might not have any knowledge.

> ## 159 Using Your Former Personnel Manager And Human Resources Personnel

Don't hesitate to ask your former personnel manager or the human resource department for help if you were let go by a company. These resource people can usually help you in a variety of ways. They normally belong to associations and have excellent networking sources beyond their close network of "buddies." They can professionally critique your resume and cover letters. They can also assist you with planning your job search. They are the professionals in dealing with employment. Pay attention to their advice. I can't stress their positive value strongly enough.

> ## 160 Past Employers Job Source

If you left former employers on favorable terms and had a good to above average work record with them, they are good potentials for job sources. People leave jobs for various reasons. Maybe it was because the immediate supervisor was a jerk and made life intolerable, yet the company was great and offered outstanding opportunities. See if the old boss is still there; if not, apply for your old job.

College graduates have a tough time adjusting to the work-a-day world and tend to change jobs prematurely. Others also leave due to impatience. Still others leave for the lure of more money or the appeal of greener grass only to discover that they made a mistake and were much happier in their old jobs.

Sometimes a fellow worker who is not happy starts

planting negative seeds into their fellow workers. The individual then quits and continues stone throwing at the company. The friend left behind begins to feel stupid because he is working for such a "lousy" company. At times the person who leaves the company can plant so many negative seeds that it actually produces a bumper crop of discontent workers. This results in a number of people leaving. Each one throws more stones at the company which stirs up even more seeds of discontent.

When reflecting back over your work life, if you conclude that you were happier with a past employer, then go talk with that person and state how you feel. Say you a made mistake by leaving the company and that you would like to come back to work for it. Reconnect with your past employers and network, network, network.

➤ **161   Direct Contact**

Knocking on doors can at times be more effective than either by phone contact or mailing a resume. Personal contact can produce results when nothing else will. Don't approach the company with a self defeating question such as, "You're not hiring anyone today are you?" or "You're not taking job applications, today, are you?" Instead, ask to speak to the person in charge of hiring in your field of endeavor. Ask for the person by name. All you have to do is call ahead and get the name and title of the person with whom you wish to speak. This works. If the person is not in, find out when the individual will be in. Then either come back at that time or ask to set an appointment. Does this work a hundred percent? No. But, what does? All I can say is there is no way you will make this work for you unless you try it. Don't lay down and die if at first you don't succeed. Be prepared for three lines of defense, and you will accomplish your objective three times more frequently. Try it. It works.

➤ **162 Prospecting Conventions And Trade Shows**
Conventions and trade shows are always good places to
find job leads. This is true only to the degree that you
work at it. First, get a list of all exhibitors or
companies that will be attending. Next, call as many of
them as you can to set an appointment to meet with
them. If no potential needs exist, ask for referrals.
Additionally, make the rounds at the conventions and
trade shows to talk to as many different companies as
time permits. Don't linger. You are not there to
socialize. Treat your available time with a sense of
urgency, or it will slip away from you before you know
it. Then, follow up on all leads or potential prospects by
phone or mail after you return home. Don't expect
immediate responses. Usually it takes some time for a
person to "catch up" after a convention.

➤ **163 Unemployed Self-Help Organizations**
If you are unemployed, make it a point to identify and
locate the various self-help support organizations.
Business-People-Between-Jobs and Executives-over-40
are just two such organizations. There are several
more. Some are local; others are national with local
groups. Some of these organizations may be based out
of church basements. You may have difficulty finding
them since there is no consistent location in the yellow
pages for them. You will have to do some digging. If
you are in a small town, you will have to drive to the
largest nearby city, if possible. These self-help
organizations serve as support groups where all the
members help one another with all aspects of job
hunting. Your networking will blossom if you take
advantage of them.

Many of these job help organizations work with
temporary agencies, consulting and telemarketing firms.
These organizations provide a stream of skilled workers
on a part-time basis. This allows the unemployed to
earn some money but remain available for interviews.

Such employment also promotes networking with a variety of companies. If you are having difficulty in locating the names of these organizations, call the employment office of firms likely to use the unemployed associated with them and ask for names and numbers of the self-help organizations they use.

➤ 164 Professional Associations

Contact all professional associations to which you belong. Ask about job leads and viable job prospects. Some associations offer more assistance in this area to their members than others. Be sure to include your alumni association. Today, alumni associations have become increasingly active in job networking and assistance than at anytime in the past. College and universities don't hesitate to ask you for help; now let them help you.

➤ 165 Not-For-Profit Organizations

Do not overlook not-for-profit organizations in your job search. These include schools, universities, the Red Cross, associations, museums, the zoo, and many, many others. Entirely too many people wear blinders for one reason or another and completely overlook these organizations as potential employers. Every conceivable type of job is available in this gigantic arena. You may be driving by such organizations every day of your life but never give them a thought. Learn to open up your eyes and ears. This field is fertile. Visit your library and research local and national not-for-profit organizations. Network and get involved with fund raisers. You never know where you might meet your future boss.

➤ 166 Position Wanted Ads

Placing an ad under positions wanted in various trade publications can pay dividends. People do get hired doing this. It is another iron you can put in the fire.

Research the publications.   The more targeted the reader is, the more effective the results of the ad should be. But there are no guarantees.

> **167 Help From All Sources**
Learn what personnel and human resource people can and cannot do for you. Likewise know how executive search firms, employment agencies, outplacement firms and others can help you. The sooner, the quicker, the faster you learn who can help you and use the help available, the better off you will be in your job search.

Network.

Network.

Network.

It isn't how much you know; it is who you know. So get to know as many people as you can. Always be alert to making a good first impression. Networking is akin to running for a political office or pledging a fraternity or sorority. You never know who will influence a decision for or against you. Always be personable. *Smile and the whole world smiles with you.*

Your networking should begin the day you decide to look for work and should not conclude until you have secured the position. Do not forget those who have befriended you. Write thank you notes, take them out to lunch or at least offer to do a favor for them. You never know when these same people can help you again. And even if they cannot, remember their help, and help others as you were helped.

15

ALL ABOUT YOUR RESUME(S)

> **My Resume**
>
> *It matters what I say.*
> *It matters the way I say it.*
> *It matters the way it looks.*
> *It matters the way it reads.*
> *It matters how well it represents me*
> *   in person and while I'm not around.*
> *My resume is important.*
> *It tells "This is my life."*

Forty years, thirty years, twenty years, ten years or zero years work experience. How can it be effectively presented on a page or two? "Help, what do I do now, coach?"

You are right; help is needed and probably from a writing and a job search coach. I have not known a single person who could not improve on resume writing with the help from a professional in this field. How you present yourself in your resume can directly affect the number of responses you receive from it. Little things can screen you out. Take the time to gather all the data about you that is necessary to write your resume, read books on resume writing, and ask for help and have a professional critique it after it is written.

This chapter is not meant to tell you how to write your resume. Entire books are written on this subject. Read one or two of them to help you in this endeavor. Each book will shed a little different light on this all-important subject.

This chapter is meant to give you the advice I give those who come to my office. It is a collection of highly valuable little things that can make your resume represent you in the most favorable way possible and still represent you honestly.

ANSWERS ABOUT RESUME(S)

The work you did in assessing yourself in the previous chapter about your career objective(s), goals, strengths, skills and accomplishments should be before you as you contemplate the actual writing of your resume. Before you begin, you will also need to seriously consider the following most frequently asked factors about resumes, what your resume should look like and how many, how often, and to whom they should be sent.

➤ **168 Effective Resume**
Your resume should be current and do the best job possible in representing your background, education, capabilities and accomplishments. During an interview this will serve as a foundation to allow you to discuss your past job history with ease. It allows you to put your best foot (work) forward. You should never have to apologize for your resume. After all, if you can't handle something as important as it, how will you handle some of the routine, mundane aspects of your job? Resumes will either precede you and/or be left behind after interviews. They should represent you in your most realistic favorable light. You will not be present to defend yourself in either case, nor should you have to. Your resume should stand on its own merit without the need for apologies or explanations.

➤ **169 Old Resumes And Apologies**
Using an outdated resume, then falling all over yourself apologizing for it, is no way to go. Get your act together. Please.

> ## 170   How Many Resumes
Previously, fifty resumes were more than enough to find a job. Now, 500 to 1,000 may not cut it. The numbers game has increased considerably. Would you believe, it may take 1,500 to 2,000 or more resumes before some people find a job? You do not need to print large quantities all at once. Reprint when needed. Critique your resume each time before you go to press and make improvements in it.

> ## 171   One Or More Versions Of Your Resume?
One general all-purpose resume for all occasions will not work. You need to slant your resume to fit certain jobs to get maximum results. Anytime you have enough specific background and experience to custom-tailor your resume for a specific job, do so. This allows you to target your prospective employers. Having only one resume would be like having one suit of clothes for all occasions. You would not always be dressed appropriately, would you?

> ## 172   Length Of Resume
A resume should not exceed two pages. One page will do for beginners. An exception might be three pages for seasoned executives. Longer resumes will work against you.

> ## 173   Photos
Do not send your photo with your resume. PERIOD!

> ## 174   Don't Explain Leaving Employment
Do not list reasons for leaving your present or past employers on your resume. This subject is handled during interviews and only when you are asked. Keep your answers brief, positive and professional.

> ## 175   Salary In Resume
Do not list your present or past salary history on your

resume. This is discussed during interviews. Occasionally, you will see a help wanted ad which requests salary expectations. Write salary "open" as your response.

➤ 176 Age In Resume
Do not state your age on resumes.

➤ 177 Writing An Effective Resume
Don't make the mistake of writing your resume based on the advice from a well meaning friend who lacks professional resume writing experience. Use samples in books about writing resumes to pattern yours, or use a resume writing service. I have seen entirely too many bad resume examples come across my desk. A poor resume will produce poor results and will beat you down with rejection. Don't let this happen to you.

➤ 178 Lies And Stretching The Truth
Don't lie on your resume or company applications. It can cost you a job, even long after you have been employed by a company. Studies have shown that as many as forty percent of all resumes present gross exaggerations, misrepresentations or a combination of both. This trend has been building steadily over the years as the competition for the better jobs has increased. As a safeguard to our executive search firm and our clients, we do a very thorough job of background checking on candidates we present to our corporate clients. Our personal experience does not reflect as high a percentage of fabrication as the studies above. However, the mainstay of the executive search pool of candidates are gainfully employed versus unemployed or on the job market. We do see a trend in what Mark Twain referred to as "stretchers" or Huckleberry Finn's "stretching the truth."

Outright lies are also on the rise, as well. It is a serious mistake to allow yourself to get caught in the rationalization process which might let you (in self defense) justify doing what you hear others are doing. If you do, you will pay a price; it will hang over your head.

In our executive search practice we do not submit candidate written resumes to client companies. We submit what is referred to as a biographical sketch of the candidate's background, experience, education and any special certifications. This is presented in a factual manner without the fluff, bragging, salesmanship or creative resume writing techniques of "stretchers."

The information we present is secured from extensive interviews and background checks. Once we find misleading claims or lies, we withdraw the culprit from contention and mark the person's files permanently closed.

Examples of these lies include people who claim they have degrees when they don't, jobs or titles they never had, incomes they never earned, years spent with companies that don't exist, dates that don't jive, accomplishments that never happened, number of people managed that never existed. The list goes on and on and on. It is limited only by the perpetrator's imagination. Enough said on this subject. Be straight forward and honest.

THE APPEARANCE OF YOUR RESUME

After you have decided what to write in your resume, you need to consider the appearance of your resume. This, too, is a reflection of you. The paper, the quality of the type reproduction, the layout - all will make an impression.

GREAT CREDENTIALS
POOR QUALITY RESUME

I just got off the phone talking to a former executive vice president from a general contracting firm. We have known each other over the past few years. He called me for help. He had mailed a copy of his resume to me earlier in the week and asked if I would critique it for him. I did. The format was excellent. He was a degreed civil engineer. He had a stable working history. He really had an excellent, well balanced background along with a strong record of accomplishments. That was the good news. The bad news was that it was done on a home computer print out on a dot matrix printer on the typical low quality computer paper. Computer print outs of this type would lead anyone to believe that he was a rank amateur who was making mass mailings. No one wants to hire someone in that scenario. An executive vice president using this approach??? Common sense would dictate that a top executive should present one's credentials with class.

Master copies of your resume(s) should be typed on a high quality electric typewriter or on a computer/word processor and printed out on a laser printer. Copies should be professionally printed on a high quality offset press. This level of person should also use a high quality rag-content paper and matching envelopes.

After my stern lecture he openly admitted he had also been doing his cover letters on this same computer printer. What a way to go... Need I say more?

➤ **179 Paper Selection**

Use white, off-white, light beige or grey paper. Select quality paper for resumes and cover letters. Become sensitive to the difference between copy paper and fine paper suitable for resumes and letters. This can be driven home by comparing fine china to paper or styrofoam dinner plates. Don't fall into the trap of buying the bargain basement printing jobs that you will see advertised. What kind of impression do you want to make to get a good job? Yes, a good impression, make one!

➤ 180 Personal Note And Stationery

Buy a good supply of business quality personal stationery and matching envelopes for your follow-up notes. This does not have to be expensive; to the contrary, expensive stationary is an overkill. A variety of attractive selections are available at a reasonable price. Select white or soft tone colors. Having this stationery on hand in advance of a specific need will prompt you to use it in a timely manner rather than as an after thought. Also, buy a roll of stamps. You will need them.

➤ 181 Typewriter, Word Processor, Desk Top Publishing

Use a quality typewriter, word processor or desk top publishing program on your computer. Print out with a quality laser jet printer. Never use a manual typewriter with white out corrections. It doesn't matter how good a typist you are; a poor quality machine will produce poor quality results. If you do not have access to a quality electric typewriter or computer, you can rent computer time at many quick printing shops or use a professional typing service. Many are listed in the yellow pages under the heading of Typing Services. Refer also to Resume Writing Services in your yellow pages directory. Make sure you distinguish between a company that just wants your print order and one that can be of professional help to you in writing, designing and printing your resumes and cover letters.

➤ 182 Resume Writing Services

Shop around for a resume writing service before selecting one. Some services will do better than others for your field of specialization because of their familiarity and understanding of it. Ask to see samples of their work. The right service can present your background and capabilities very effectively. (Even if you intend to use a resume writing service, read a book on writing resumes so you can intelligently judge the quality of the service.) Also, have your resume critiqued by another professional. You will pick up pointers that will improve it.

➤ 183 Selecting A Resume Writing Service
Don't just shop price. The most expensive resume writing service doesn't necessarily make it the best. Neither does the cheapest make it the poorest.

➤ 184 Resume Software
Excellent resume writing software packages are available to assist you with your resumes if you have a personal computer. Investigate them at normal software outlets.

➤ 185 Resume - Presentation/Accuracy
Never mail a resume or cover letter with typo's or overstrikes, even if you specify that you are not a skilled typist. This kind of rationalization will kill your chances of obtaining the job. If you do not type well use a typing service or a resume service. It is the best investment you can make.

➤ 186 Proof Reading
Never male a resume or a cover letter without proofreading it for misspelled words and grammatical errors. Do yourself a very big favor and have someone proofread it for you. No one can proofread one's own writing. Select someone who is skilled with the English language. Everyone makes misstakes. No one misspells words knowingly. Misspelled words and errors in grammer will weigh very heavily against you. The

record number of misspelled words that I have seen was twenty-seven on a two page resume. It is hard to believe isn't it? (Three misspelled words were intentionally used in this paragraph. Did you catch them? What was your reaction? Do you, now, get the message?)

➤ 187 Copier

Poorly copied resumes create bad impressions. The second or third generation tattletale grey copies that are fuzzy to read should never be considered. Should more be said? Who was so important that the other person got the original copy? Resumes should be professionally printed.

➤ 188 Printing

Obtain quality printing for your resume. Always have your resumes printed on a high quality offset press or laser jet printer. Talk to a printing firm which takes pride in its work; don't use a low quality bargain basement printer. You may have to buy your own stationary with matching envelopes from a stationary store for some of the smaller printers. But be selective, and don't press the printer to do it overnight. Take the time and spend the money to get a good professional quality resume.

SUBMITTING YOUR RESUME(S)

➤ 189 Submit To Prospects & Networking Channels

It is hard to determine how many resumes you should have printed because you will never know in advance how many companies you will need to submit resumes. The one rule is to submit to every possible prospect. Send your resumes to friends, acquaintances and business associates who might be able to help you. Send your resumes to target job search firms that might be interested in you. Send your resumes long distances from home if you need to broaden your job search base. Send your resumes to former employers, your college placement offices and associations. All the research you have done concerning networking and job prospects will be the basis of your mailing list for your resumes. Of course, you send selective or customized resumes to target companies in response to ads or other leads you receive. The point is that a company cannot become interested in you if it does not know about you.

➤ 190 Re-submitting To Target Companies

Never assume that a single submission of a resume to any one select target company is sufficient to get the job done. You may need to repeat the process time and time again on a periodical methodical basis through different sources within the company. Review your approach including your resume and cover letter with each submission. Try to improve with each submission. Less than one in a hundred job seekers will do this. If you are that one, then you have a one hundred percent better prospect in getting a job as a result. People generally conclude that one resume per company is enough. Furthermore, people hesitate to re-send a resume to a company that has rejected it. Why continue to pursue the same source which will surely reject it again? One rejection from any company is more than enough. Why punish yourself? Right? Wrong. This is not a suggestion that you follow this procedure for all companies; to the contrary, do this to pursue your select target companies that are of the highest level of interest to you. Include additional companies along the line for further pursuit. It works! No matter what you may think or feel or believe, it works to the degree that you pursue it.

➤ 191 Re-send Your Resume

If you have not received a reply from a resume which you submitted in response to a help wanted ad, should you re-submit your resume when you see the same ad run again? The answer is yes, certainly. Review your cover letter and resume closely and improve them if possible before re-sending them. Companies are often unrealistic in their initial demands and expectations. In time they have to come down to earth. Many people have been hired on their second go-around.

➤ **192 Follow Up On Your Resume**
When a key target company does not respond to your resume, follow up and follow through. Be persistent.

RESUME MAILING RETURN RATE

Your rate of success from sending resumes to target companies that you have researched will vary from one industry to the next. Your rate of return will also vary according to economic times as follows:

1.   An expanding market may result in three to five interviews per hundred resumes mailed.

2.   A normal market may result in one to three interviews per hundred.

3.   A tight or recessionary market may only produce a single interview per hundred.

As mentioned throughout this book there are many other variables, too numerous to repeat here again. Everybody needs some point of reference for planning purposes. Many of you will go way beyond these averages; however, this will be offset by those of you that won't. Entirely too many job seekers have unrealistic expectations and as a result get beat up and beat down with rejection in spite of the fact that their rate of return may be considerably better that average. It is important for you to have this perspective so that you can generate sufficient activity to secure interviews. Most job seekers fall considerably short in this area because they just don't know any better.

WHAT HAPPENS NEXT?

Resume Screening Process

Resumes will be initially scanned and sorted. Surely you must realize that people who review and pre-screen resumes do not read every resume word for word. What most people do initially is scan the resume lightly to determine if it is indeed worth the further investment in time. It either is or it isn't.   The person reviewing the resume will be approaching this task on the basis of what is in it for them and not you. They will be asking themselves if this person is worthy of further consideration.   They do not take a humanitarian approach to give all resumes fair and equal consideration. They want to utilize whatever time they have available on those resumes that survive the initial cut.

The approach most commonly used to pre-screen resumes is referred to as a "negative biased" approach.   It is also referred to as screening for "knock out" factors. These are the resumes that will be weeded out because they are lacking certain "must have" skills, education, years of experience, salary, industry, location, special registrations such as a CPA, or must be an MBA, or must be a licensed professional engineer referred to as a P.E., or any one or more criteria any job seeker responding to the ad must have for further consideration. Often times, secretaries or a personnel clerk in major corporations pre-screen. This screening process sorts resumes into either two or three categories.

1. Basically qualified
2. A "maybe" possibility
3. Not qualified

Another word of caution is in order. "Must have" criteria might not hold true. Furthermore, you will routinely see terminology such as "prefer" or "strongly prefer" or "ideally" which is separate and not the same as "must have" criteria. Do not eliminate yourself from consideration any time you see this terminology. The company is letting you know it is willing to bend the rules for consideration providing you meet the other basic criteria.

The initial pre-screen scanning process takes from a few seconds to perhaps a minute. The number of responses determines how much time can actually be spent on each resume. Ask yourself, "What is it that I can do to create the best first impression in order to survive this preliminary cut?" Following the pointers in this chapter will help.

Now, let's discuss the outcome of this initial pre-screening process.

1. Good quality paper and printing/typing is something the employer feels and sees from an aesthetic standpoint. This is much better than a second, third, fourth generation copy from a poor copy quality copier. Many companies won't even bother to read unacceptable quality resumes, regardless of one's background. This is an area that is one hundred percent within your control. Please, don't flunk here.

2. Next is a crisp, clear and to the point cover letter that will capture the reader's attention and stimulate interest in your resume. Custom-tailor your cover letter to each situation. The cover letter is like an appetizer, inviting the reader to carefully review the resume.

3. Then comes your resume. What does it convey about you? How does it set you aside from others? How do you fit the job description? This is the big one. Is it easy to read? Is it designed effectively? Have you given your name, address, and phone number(s) so you can be reached? What about the content and order of presentation? Follow the standard chronological resume

format in which you outline your employment history and education. First, list your most current position with accomplishments and work backwards. This is by far the most widely accepted resume format.

There are other resume formats that center on your accomplishments, area of expertise and education. Use which ever type best fits the situation. Many samples are provided in books on resumes.

If you have a great deal of diversity, group your work experiences in categories and start with the experience that is most closely related to the job offering.

If you have a short work history or if it is not related to the job, then first state your educational experiences, and briefly point out how they have prepared you for the work.

Your career objective, if stated, must match the needs as given in the ad or job description as much as possible, otherwise don't state it.

What happens next?

Those of you who make the preliminary pre-screening cut will then be reviewed more closely for consideration for an interview. This can take place preliminarily over the telephone, or you could be invited in for a personal interview. Should a preliminary phone discussion take place, don't work against yourself and contribute to your own demise. Do whatever you can within your power to keep your conversation short, to the point, and positive. Suggest that you get together for a personal meeting. Once the preliminaries (confirming a mutual interest and match exists) are out of the way, your objective should be to arrange a personal interview. Keep this uppermost in your mind. People don't get hired over the phone for any meaningful job, but they do get screened out of consideration quite routinely. Pay heed to this all important advice.

Your resume is important. Take the time to make it be responsive to the needs of the company. If you can customize it to the specific company, do so. Most of the time you will not need to do this; your cover letter will do that for you. The next chapter will show you the importance of writing effective cover letters and how they work together with your resume to spark an interest in you by the company.

16

YOUR COVER LETTERS, APPLICATIONS

AND THANK YOU NOTES

Words, words, words.
Why do they fail me now?
Why do I have to spell them a certain way?
Why do I have to use periods and commas, too?
Word, words, words.
I have no alternative but to use them
and use them well!

COVER LETTERS

A companion to the resume is the cover letter. Your cover letter introduces your prospective employer to your resume. Without the cover letter your resume appears like a stranger knocking at the door. The cover letter helps you shake hands and greet one another like someone introducing you to a stranger. Your cover letter makes a first impression; make sure it is a good one.

➤ **193 The Cover Letter**
Do not send a resume to a prospective employer without a cover letter. This happens frequently. You will see the importance of writing a good cover letter for each resume sent out when you read a book on writing cover letters. You will also see how to construct good cover letters. Be sure to do your homework in this area. It can really pay good dividends.

TYPES OF COVER LETTERS

You will need cover letters for the following situations:

- Specific job openings within companies.

- Exploratory job opportunities for companies you have researched that you would like to work for. This is for your resume mailing campaign.

- Newspaper help wanted ads, as well as trade publications.

- Executive search firms/employment agencies and other referral sources such as college placement offices, alumni associations, trade associations, etc.

- Letters with resumes to all people on your networking list.

- Other situations require you to write letters during your search. Get help when needed.

➤ **194 Customize Cover Letter**
Using only one general all-purpose cover letter for all occasions is a mistake. It is like "To Whom It May Concern" or "Dear Occupant" letters. The generic resume and cover letter denote a message of a mass mailing, which normally conveys a problem candidate. Don't give that impression. Make the company feel you are particularly interested in it. There is a need for a general cover letter, but this should only be part of your repertoire. Use your general letter as a guide. Custom-tailor it to each prospective employer whenever possible. This will give you maximum results.

➤ **195 Cover Letter Overkill**
Do not overkill in your cover letters. They should

always be short and specific to get attention. They should elicit a reaction from the reader to read more about you in your resume. Two and three page cover letters are overkill. Someone once said, "If you can't write your idea on the back of a business card, it won't be read." Be brief and interesting, but most of all match the employer's needs.

➤ **196   Accomplishments - Cover Letter/Resume**
Highlight your most applicable accomplishments in present or past positions in your cover letter even though they are stated in your resume. Your specific accomplishments are definitely attention getters. Everyone routinely uses them quite generously in today's tough competitive job market. Sometimes this practice borders on bragging or tooting one's own horn, but when they are stated correctly your accomplishments are a matter of record. If you have difficulty with this, then I strongly suggest that you go to a top professional resume writer who will routinely dig and pry to uncover accomplishments in your present and past activities of which you are particularly proud. They will incorporate these facts into your resume. This will put you on equal footing with the rest of the job seekers. Omitting accomplishments may convey you don't have any.

JOB APPLICATIONS

➤ **197 Job Applications**
Fill out job applications with care when an application is mailed to you. Your best bet is to make a copy of the application and practice filling it in properly. This way you will have a spare form just in case you make a mistake.

- Type in the information if you can do so without making mistakes. White out is tacky on applications.

- Print or hand write the information as legibly as you can. Use black ink.

- Do not write off the top of your head. Think your answers through or even use a note pad to jot the answers down before you write them on the application.

- Avoid cross-outs and misspellings.

- Stay within boundaries whenever possible.

- Be brief and to the point.

- Be complete in supplying all the applicable data.

- Draw lines through non applicable spaces.

- Do not say, "see my resume" even if the requested information is given on the resume and it is submitted with the application.

- Be prompt in returning the application.

- Come to any interview prepared to fill out an application. You will need your references, phone numbers and addresses, dates of employment and salaries.

- Be prepared to explain gaps in your employment history. Give a very brief explanation with dates: sabbatical, maternity leave, career change. Be prepared to state the type of position you are seeking and your philosophy or why you would benefit the company should you obtain the position.

- Attach a resume to your job application. (If applicable)

- In a few days follow up with a letter which re-states your interest in the company and mentions that your application and resume are on file. Include at least one of your accomplishments and tell how it would be applicable to the company.

➤ **198 Salary Expected**
State "open." Your salary expectations should only be discussed during the interview. If your expectations appear too high on the application, this will screen you out of contention.

FILLING OUT JOB APPLICATIONS

Most people fill out job applications very poorly. People tend to be impatient while answering routine questions and go over them hurriedly. After all, applications are such a pain-in-the-neck to fill out. No one will argue this point. When you have launched an aggressive job hunting campaign, you will literally get writer's cramp filling out repetitive questions. It is so much easier to write, "See Resume" across the application. All I can say is this is a mistake. Don't do it. My best advise is to fill out all job applications neatly and completely. Applicants who have poor writing skills should take the extra time to write legibly. Most companies will let you take the application home. Do so if it will help you do a neat and careful job.

You may be asked to fill out an application before you interview, after you interview or just prior to being hired. I have even heard of companies that will have the candidate fill out an application after the person has been hired to comply with company requirements. Others do not use applications at all. Regardless of the situation, it does not change the importance of writing neatly and being thorough.

You will not get a second chance to make a first impression. When the person reviewing your application scans it initially, you are making that first impression. A sloppy job, poor handwriting, sketchy answers and blank spaces not filled in all go against you. A number of people reviewing applications will go no further than the initial scan if it is not neat and complete. Can you blame them? They feel your application is a preview of coming attractions. A lack of attention to detail is reflected here. Sloppy, incomplete work is something no employer wants.

Furthermore, your company job application will remain in your personnel file throughout your career with that company. It will be reviewed at salary review times for potential salary increases. It may also be reviewed when your name comes up for a possible promotion. So, stop and think for a moment. How do you want your superiors to look upon you? Your paperwork will either reflect positively or negatively on you. It is up to you.

Duties and general descriptions of past jobs should be well thought out and stated as clearly and briefly as possible due to limited space on the form.

Dates, including month and year are always requested. Don't guess. You should know them, and be specific.

The "salary desired" question is best answered with the word, "open." A figure that is too high can knock you out of contention. It is not ever worth the risk. Putting too low a figure can possibly sell yourself short. You may be requested to state your current or previous earnings. Most companies will use your current salary as a starting point for negotiations.

Reasons for leaving positions may be asked on job application forms. Due to space constraints, your answers need to be short and well thought out in advance. I have seen poorly written and/or highly negative reasons for leaving past employers. If you do this, you are giving your prospective employer a negative impression before anyone from the company gets to meet you.

Now is a good time to acquire a few standard job applications and practice filling them out. Learn how to express yourself effectively within the allocated space. This may sound too basic for most, but it is well worth the practice. It is extremely important to express yourself clearly and in a positive manner. You might be asked what you could contribute to the company and be given two lines or a full page to answer it. Be prepared.

Names, addresses and phone numbers may be asked for references. Have these handy. When you give these references you can indicate if you will allow them to be checked at this time. If you are still employed and do not wish to jeopardize your current position unnecessarily, state so beside the reference. If, indeed, there is continued mutual interest and if the references are tantamount to a possible job offer, then allow them to be checked. References should not be carelessly tossed about and given indiscriminately. If your present employer finds out you are interviewing, it could cost you your job. Normal precautions are in order.

Most applications will have a disclaimer above your signature line. It typically states that the above information is true, to the best of your knowledge, and if you should be hired and it is found that you provided false information, it can be grounds for dismissal. Many companies wish the applications to be filled in completely so they have protection against misrepresentation.

THANK YOU NOTES

➤ **199 Thank You's**

Send thank you notes and letters to people who have helped you network, to some secretaries who were very personable and always to those who interviewed you from companies in which you have a keen interest.

Thank you notes will help separate you from the pack. Your note should express your appreciation for the time and courtesy extended to you and include an expression of interest in the company on your part. Also, be sure to point out what it is about your background and/or abilities that will allow you to make a contribution to the company's continued growth and profitability. This letter should be brief, friendly, well composed and to the point. Three brief paragraphs will do just fine. Lengthy letters are overkill. Your thank you messages can be typed or legibly hand written on quality paper or business type note cards. Either are acceptable. Again, don't overkill. And most importantly, be sincere. Don't just go through the motions because an expert in the job search business told you it was a good thing to do. Your sincerity (or lack of it) will show through.

17

EFFECTIVE TELEPHONE TECHNIQUES

The tone of your voice tells more about you than you would ever imagine. It can stimulate interest or disinterest, reflect a mood of hope or despair and evoke a response of welcome or rejection. The tone of your voice is up to you and the impression you want to make.

Ring!

Now what do you do?

This chapter gives you a few basic points about making a good impression (and often the first impression) over the telephone or answering machine. Don't take this chapter lightly. After all everyone uses the phone everyday. Right? How hard can it be to say the right thing to a prospective employer so the person on the other end of the line will want to invite you for an interview? All your work up to now is dependent upon your effective telephone presentation. Learn to make telephoning work for you. You need to have everything that you might possibly need to use or reference at your fingertips so you can function effectively.

➤ 200 Phone Conversation's Purpose
Remember this, people don't get interviewed and hired over the phone. At best they get pre-screened in or out. Your objective on any preliminary phone discussion is to be as courteous, personable, businesslike and as brief as you can be; and yet, do whatever is necessary to arrange a personal interview.

➤ **201 Appointment Book**

To schedule dates and times always have your calendar or appointment book in front of you during telephone conversations. This type of positive expectation will increase the odds of this occurring in your favor. This also prevents you from fumbling around or having to call back to set a mutually convenient date and time. Bring your appointment book with you to your interview, so you can schedule a second interview or follow-up activity.

➤ **202 What's In It For Me?**

When most job seekers respond by phone to help wanted ads, they will state the reason for calling by saying one of the following:

> *The ad caught my attention.*

> *The job sounds interesting to me.*

> *The job is the type of position for which I am looking.*

A word of caution is in order. The above statements convey a message of "What's in it for me?" That is not what companies are interested in. They are interested in "What's in it for them?" So you want to make sure you cover this very important point. Be sure to tell them how your background and proven track record fits their objectives (providing it is indeed true); then, press on for a personal interview.

PLAN YOUR CALLS

Plan your calls before you make them. This includes your phone calls and personal contacts. Don't wing it. Like anything else there is a right way and a wrong way including how to make a proper call. Most people are poorly prepared to accomplish the right objective during the call. The standard method of practice is to mull around in one's mind the need to make the call, then justify why it should be done, procrastinate a while, then finally make the call.

There is a much better way, and it is the only way to proceed. First, have a clear cut objective of what it is you wish to achieve. The average person will simply state the objective: to call XYZ company. Wrong! You need to state your desired objective: what you wish to achieve when you call XYZ company. As an example, if you are responding to a help wanted ad, your objective should be: to call XYZ company and if the position appears to be interesting to arrange for an interview. You should have your appointment book/calendar in front of you in anticipation of arranging an interview. This is the proper approach instead of simply picking up the phone and responding to the ad.

Next, in order to accomplish this objective you must prepare yourself for the possible outcome once you get someone on the phone. The better the match is between the requirements listed in the ad and your background; the better your chances are of achieving your objective. One of four situations will occur that you should anticipate.

1. What is the best that can happen?
2. What is the worst that can happen?
3. What do you realistically expect to happen?
4. What curve balls, if any, can you possibly anticipate?

The company's objective is to screen out - to interview only those that appear qualified. Companies will be screening you and your background initially on the basis of what you may be lacking. This is also referred to as screening for "knock out factors" or using a "negative biased" approach. Therefore, the employer will tend to confront your weaknesses up front more times than not. This is the norm. You should minimize your weaknesses with your strengths. This works.

Keep your thrust positive and press for the interview.

The company may counter a second time. Respond with your secondary strengths and accomplishments and press for the interview. A few companies will counter a third time. If you can manage to hang on to the ropes, you can still press forward for an interview and get it. This is your objective. With practice you can become quite proficient. Work your accomplishments, skills and strengths into the conversation whenever possible. Your success, or lack of it, will relate to your preparation and persistence. Burn this lesson permanently into your mind, and practice it each time you plan to call anyone on the phone or make a personal contact; then watch what happens.

This lesson is worth its weight in gold to a job seeker. After all, no one ever gets hired until interviewed in person. This procedure and strategy will work equally well throughout your interviews, that is unless you are totally unqualified or very marginally qualified. Just remember to plan for a minimum of three lines of defense, and you will do well in setting interviews.

➤ 203 Your Skills, Strengths & Accomplishments

While you are talking on the phone, always have a list of your strengths, skills and accomplishments before you. You might consider this unnecessary. After all you know yourself. But in time of pressure it is good to have a memory jogger. You do not want to hang up the phone and then say, "Oh why didn't I remember to say this or that?" These lists will help you immeasurably.

➤ 204 Getting And Using Name And Title

Be sure to properly identify each person with whom you will need to communicate or interview. Get the correct spelling of each name, mark the pronunciation so you can remember it and write down each title. Doing these simple things will gain points and provide additional confidence for you. By doing this, you put yourself ahead of your competition because most people are very bad at remembering names.

➤ 205 Write Down Names, Dates, Addresses

Do not rely upon your memory to remember important names, dates, follow-ups or results of your activity. Record them so you can keep track of them in an organized manner. Don't just write things down on scraps of paper. Otherwise, your job search becomes a muddle, and you will let too many things "fall between the cracks" of non-accomplishment. Use your appointment book. Have it with you at all times. Always make notes in it at the conclusion of every phone call and interview!

➤ 206 Ask About The Length Of Interview

Be sure to ask the approximate length of the interview beforehand; so you can plan your time and presentations accordingly. The average interview will run from one to two hours. A few can run a little less. Out of town interviews can run from one to two hours to a half day, a full day or more. This will vary from company to company. Your interviewing objective must be accomplished within the specified time frame. Plan accordingly. Interviewers can run behind and make you wait and run overtime and make you late for another interview. Plan for these variables in your schedules.

➤ 207 Phone Messages Taken By Friends & Family

Coach all household members, roommates guests or baby sitters, how to answer the phone and take messages correctly. Many a job prospect has lost out because of "cute" or "off color" answering machine messages or rudeness and because messages were lost or never given to the job seeker. All members of the household must be on notice throughout the entire job search. Each needs to be reminded how to be polite and to take messages properly. Correct spelling of names and the correct phone numbers are essential. This is serious business. This sounds basic and elementary doesn't it? Well, it is not. Don't let this message slide by the other members of your household. This can get trying when people are unemployed over a period of time. However, don't slack off here, or it will come back to keep you unemployed. "Hey dude, what's up?" is no reception that a prospective employer wants to hear. People judge you by your family and friends. Attach a pen and message pad to each phone in the house, so a message can be taken at any time without delay.

> **208 Collect Phone Calls**
Do not make collect telephone calls to job prospect companies unless you are instructed specifically to do so. This holds particularly true for follow-up calls after interviews - it is tacky.

> **209 Electronic Phone Tagging**
The telephone is one of your most important job search tools. It is your most direct and immediate link to each prospective employer. As stated earlier make sure your prospective employer can get in touch with you. In today's world of answering machines, playing phone tag has taken on new dimensions: two way recorded messages. Always be prepared to meet with an electronic mail message. Know what you want to say so you do not falter. Your message is the first impression; make it a good one. When the party returns your call, be prepared. Keep a list of the people with whom you have left messages so you will know what company the person is representing.

If the person returns your call while you are not at home, make your recorded message on your answer phone productive for the caller. Let the person know when you will be able to return the call; then return it on time. Recorders or answer phones are never very clear. Speak distinctly and politely, and spell your name if it is difficult. State your phone number slowly enough so it can be received immediately. Be pleasant businesslike and courteous. Sound upbeat and positive.

➤ 210 Smile Over The Phone

Always smile while you are talking on the telephone. The smile goes through the lines and is picked up on the other end of the line just as clearly as if you were on a television screen. Your words come out differently when you are smiling. The tone, the purpose, the interest, the excitement, they are each controlled by a smile. If you wear a dead pan expression on your face, your voice will be a monotone reflection of it. To check on yourself, place a mirror where you can catch a glimpse of your smile while you are talking on the phone. See yourself smiling? See that twinkle in your eyes?

**What you have to say is important,
but how you say it is crucial!**

18

SUCCESS PROVEN ELEMENTS
OF INTERVIEWING

Face to face we stand -
alone or together?

Interviewing is such an important part of getting a job that three chapters have been devoted to it. This chapter will give you the basic components of interviewing, Chapter 19 will give you many personal do's and don'ts to effective interviewing, and Chapter 20 will provide you with astute interviewing questions. Being nervous during an interview is usually based on not knowing what to expect, not feeling confident in yourself, and not knowing what to ask. These chapters give you interviewing ammunition that will make your interviewing a winning experience for you.

INTERVIEWING OVERVIEW

How to interview? Are you good, fair or weak at interviewing? Can you judge this for yourself? There are many books on interviewing. They can help set some standards for you. The objective of this section is to pinpoint major interviewing weaknesses and highlight success proven interviewing techniques. What can you learn about interviewing? A great deal that will make a positive impact on your success! Many people fail badly at interviewing. They do not know what they are doing wrong. Amazing? No, not at all. It is hard to see yourself as others see you. When you become aware of effective interviewing skills, then you are more likely to see your weaknesses and overcome them.

There is a vast difference between thinking something may work and knowing something will work. The difference lies between the degree of <u>un</u>certainty at one extreme to the degree of certainty at the other extreme. Thinking, hoping or wishing something badly enough will not change it into reality. The answer lies in being forearmed with the knowledge of knowing what works and what does not. How much is two + two? It is four. Do you think it is four, or do you know it is four? You know it is four. You should not have to drift around in a field of uncertainty and do what you think, believe or hope will work. You need to take the necessary time to learn what has worked for others and what will work for you. Once you <u>know</u> what things work in an interview, then you can do them. Your job hunting campaign will be a success accordingly.

The average resume leaves a lot to be desired, but the average interviewing conduct is even worse. Usually it takes a lot of work to generate an interview, so don't treat it lightly. Poor interviewing skills cause rejections. People get beat down by continuous rejections, lower their sights and accept a succession of compromises. If this downhill slide continues long enough, the person might eventually find a job, but at what level and for what reason? The job seeker will point a finger at all the wrong things. The very last thing that will be blamed is interviewing skills. People blame all of the following factors.

- Education
- Years of experience
- Type of experience
- Number of jobs held
- Age
- Income requirements

However, the company had this information about the

applicant before the person was invited to the interview. There are valid reasons for companies to reject candidates. All that is suggested is that entirely too many people literally reject themselves from consideration because of the way they handle themselves during interviews, not because of their lack of job requirements. Sharpening your interviewing skills will do wonders for your ability to get a job.

Many misconceptions exist about interviewing. It is an information gathering session for <u>both</u> parties. The interviewer is pre-screening the applicant, and the applicant is pre-screening the company. The gathering of information is supposed to be a two way street. The majority of people do not realize this. Too many people feel intimidated by the interviewing process. They feel morally obligated to answer all questions, even those of a personal nature. Yet, people being interviewed feel apprehensive about asking questions for fear of asking the wrong questions and looking foolish. As a result, their information gathering ability is extremely curtailed. Strive to achieve a balance. Ask as many questions as you are asked.

HIRING PROCESS STAGES

Hiring is a process that is broken down into four different stages. All of these stages can take place in a single interview, but in most cases two, three, four or possibly more interviews will occur. This will vary from company to company. It is important for you to know how many interviews are anticipated with each company so that you can plan accordingly.

1. <u>Pre-screening</u>: The first stage is the initial pre-screening which determines who will make the initial cut and be invited back for a personal interview. This could be determined from a resume, phone conversation, a referral or in person as a drop in requesting a job and filling out an application. This initial stage is normally

very brief and consists of confirming that you warrant further discussion and consideration. Your objective is to arrange a personal interview. Think of playing baseball. You have to get on first base in order to get into a scoring position; then, comes second base, third base and finally home plate - likewise with the four hiring stages. Your object is to keep from getting "thrown out" as you round the bases. Keep this mental picture in your mind. This vivid parallel will help you understand the hiring process.

2. <u>Making A First Impression</u>: The second stage takes place during the initial personal interview. This conversation will put your "first impression" to the test. The first few moments will be vital. This discussion will be general in nature. Each person will qualify each other to confirm a potential match and to determine if there is a need for further discussion. If there is no fit, the process will end here. The chemistry/personality factor will carry a lot of weight at this juncture even to the point of unfairness. It will work for you or against you.

3. <u>Covering Specifics</u>: The third stage involves getting down to specifics. It will cover in greater detail all general areas mentioned in stage two. This will include the candidate's background and capabilities, and the specifics of the job in its entirety. This process will identify the final candidate(s).

4. <u>Detailing The Offer/Negotiations</u>: The last stage is the offer/negotiation stage. The job offer is given with a detailed review of the position including where it fits within the company and the job potential. It will state the salary. Ideally, it will also give the bonus structure if applicable, salary reviews, fringe benefits (including vacations, retirement plans and perks, if any), working hours and parking assignment. A tour of the facilities and/or work area/office will usually take place at this

time. However, some firms simply give a dollar offer. They may ask if you have any questions and address only those asked. Larger firms will give you a fringe benefit booklet covering company policy in total. Both parties can resolve any remaining unanswered questions. A few firms will simply mail the job offer and wait to hear from you by a designated date.

This is a brief description of what generally takes place in the four hiring process stages so you can prepare for them. Notice that fringe benefits including vacations and retirement are not discussed until stage four. There is a proper time and place to discuss everything, the proper protocol to be in step with the rest of the world. Otherwise, it will go against you.

As covered in Chapter 6 the hiring time frame covering the above stages will vary according to the level of the position. Higher level positions usually have longer hiring time frames.

THREE TYPES OF INTERVIEWS

Not all interviews are the same. There are different types of interviews for different purposes. Each type calls for specific interviewing strategies; so be prepared to meet each type appropriately.

1. Interviews For Specific Job Openings. These are the most prized and sought after by job seekers because interviewing is taking place to meet a specific need within the company. These are actual position openings the company is looking to fill.

2. Exploratory (Casual Need) Type Interviews. There is no specific job opening at the company, but it just might make room for one more "good person."

3. <u>Courtesy Interview.</u> There are no needs, actual or otherwise. This occurs when someone is doing a favor by talking with you about the industry, careers in the industry and may also provide advice and counsel you about your job search. The courtesy interview can also be an excellent source for referrals. This type of meeting, brought about by family, friends and networking, can provide a motivational uplift to a job seeker.

It takes interviews to get a job. Do whatever necessary to get interviews. Pursuing all three types of interviews will improve your odds and will be a key to your success.

➤ 211 Preconceived Ideas

Entirely too many people will not proceed to a first interview because they are not convinced they would accept a job offer should one be made. How does anyone make such decisions before the first interview. This is like a child who refuses to try a new food just because it is new. The child has made up its mind before, rather than after, trying. Could this childhood resistance to trying something new linger into adulthood? There is a little bit of kid in everyone, but some have considerably more than others. Don't put yourself into an offer/decision stage until you actually have an offer. I am not referring to wild goose chasing, but legitimate job opportunities within your respective field.

➤ 212 Make The Most Of Your Interviewing Time!

The average person has only two to three interviews with a prospective employer and spends less than four hours interviewing. Can the company and the job prospect learn if they are compatible in this short period of time? Is it any wonder that the match fails to be perfect? Really!!! Give me a break. Research is necessary.

➤ 213 Improving Your Interviewing Skills

Interviewing skills play a much larger role in securing job offers then most job seekers are aware. Read at least one book on developing your interviewing skills. Then practice, practice and practice until you are confident that you can do it right. Don't just wing it, or you will lose out to people more skilled at interviewing regardless of your credentials. Strong interviewing skills will help to overcome other weaknesses. It is within your control to be strong at interviewing. If you are not a natural conversationalist, you will have to work harder to perfect your interviewing skills. Regardless of your natural talent, you can become effective at interviewing.

➤ 214 The Effect Of A Positive First Impression

First impressions are lasting ones. They are formed instantly within the first few moments when people meet. This applies to both the candidate and the interviewer who greets and meets with the prospect. The balance of the interview will be spent reconfirming those first impressions. I cannot stress strongly enough how important it is for you to be prepared to make a great first impression. <u>Do</u> <u>not</u> talk about "no-brainers" such as how bad the traffic was or how much difficulty you had in finding the office. Whatever you say, make it positive. Period!

CHEMISTRY MATCH

A primary factor in the job search is human relations. That is how well you react to another and vice versa. The chemistry/personality/philosophy match between the job seeker and employer (or interviewer) is critical. People don't hire people they don't like. After all, employer and employee have to be able to see eye to eye, get along, and be able to communicate, inspire, motivate, build a productive relationship and be a team together day in and day out. It is equally important for the employee to feel a bond with the management team and associates.

A personality clash with the initial pre-screener can take you out of contention pre-maturely. A personality match can keep you in it. However, unless you develop the necessary skills to get past the pre-screeners and become one of the final candidates, you will never get to the point where chemistry/personality/philosophy with the employer will separate the winner from the losers.

I Don't Like You

Awareness of the logistics in the selection process go above and beyond base credentials of candidates. Knowing this will help you cope with rejection which is part of the job hunting process. Here are the variables:

- You like them, but they don't like you.
- They like you, but you don't like them.
- Neither of you like each other.
- You both like each other.

That breaks down to one chance in four for a compatible match.

This applies in the social world, as well as the business arena. An incident occurred back in the middle of the nineteenth century at Oxford University in England that provides a good illustration of this "I don't like you" fact of life. It has been called *The Wells Syndrome*.

The Wells Syndrome

A student was sitting in a class that a Doctor Wells was conducting. The student was inattentive and totally preoccupied with what appeared from a distance to be doodling. The professor asked him what he was doing. The student replied, "Nothing," and attempted to cover his handiwork.

Doctor Wells walked over to the student's desk and pulled the paper from beneath the student's arms to see what he had written. What he saw was a statement written that read as follows:

> *Doctor Wells, I do not like thee.*
> *I do not know why I do not like thee.*
> *All I know is that I do not like thee.*

Everyone is equally guilty of feeling this way about certain people and nothing can be done to eliminate it. Again, this too falls under the basic laws of human nature.

➤ **215 First Impressions And The Receptionist**
Always treat receptionists and secretaries with professional respect and courtesy. They can make you or break you. Don't be sexist or condescending by saying such comments as, "Hey honey, get me a cup of coffee ... double cream and sugar and make sure it is hot." Please.

EXPECTATIONS

I was early for an appointment with the president of a client company which was a furniture manufacturer. While I was waiting in the reception room, I observed three different approaches to employment. A blue collar worker walked in off the street and asked the receptionist, "They're not hiring anybody, today, are they?"

She said, "No." He turned around and left.

A few minutes later a second person entered. He said a cheerful good morning with a smile on his face, and asked the receptionist for an application to fill out. She gave him one. He filled it out, gave it back to the receptionist, thanked her, told her to have a good day and left.

A third person came in and asked for the name of the cutting room foreman. She then asked to see him. The receptionist said, "I don't think we're hiring, today."

The job seeker responded by stating, "I understand, but I'm highly skilled in upholstery. When he meets with me for only a minute, he'll want to keep me at the top of his list to call when an opening becomes available. I can make him and this company some money; it'll only take a minute."

The receptionist sat there for a moment and almost looked blank as she sized up the situation; she then asked the woman to have a seat. The receptionist made a phone call. A man came in and was introduced to her. They talked for about two minutes at which point he led her into the office. What happened next, I don't know. But, she did get an audience with the person she wanted to see.

Many basic job search truths are in this little story. Unfortunately, you would have to be sitting in my chair to get the whole picture. I saw it this way. The first person that came in was a sorry sight. He literally looked like a homeless person. He needed a haircut and shampoo badly. His white T shirt needed a good washing and bleach job. His trousers were originally plaid dress slacks but were now permanently stained with spots and were rumpled. His shoes were grungy. This is a sad scene to experience because this person may have been homeless and was really desperate for work.

Setting this type of person aside surely you must appreciate the need for good grooming with clean clothes and shoes.

Unfortunately, some people just overlook their appearance. They are accustomed to living slovenly and simply don't know or don't care that they make a poor or rebellious impression. They just don't seem to understand. They normally end up in the day labor pool working only when needed for minimum wages. This person was screened out by the receptionist based on sight alone.

The second person that asked for an application was also a blue collar laborer dressed appropriately with clean jeans, shirt and shoes. He looked the part. His cheerful "good morning" with a bright smile on his face helped him get the application. He passed the initial screening. The third applicant was also presentable and appropriately dressed.

It would seem people make things happen the way they expect them to. The first applicant was already defeated when he walked in the door. The second person was positive and upbeat and was successful in securing an application. But, that is all he asked for, expected and got. Period. It was apparent that the woman was determined and prepared to get through to talk with the foreman or possible employer which she did. If she had taken the same approach that the first two did, what do you think would have happened?

Expectations and determination can set you apart from the crowd. It can also be said that first you have to be hungry. The story about the cheetah comes to mind. The cheetah is the fastest animal in the world and can hit bursts of speed up to sixty miles an hour. Its speed and its killing ability, one would think, would enable a cheetah to catch any animal it wants. But this is not the case. Studies show on the average a cheetah catches its quarry on the tenth attempt. It is apparently not hungry enough early on. As the hunger grows, so does its determination. Another factor is motivation. The cheetah is running for its dinner. The quarry is running for its life. The same factors apply to job seekers.

> ## 216 Follow up After Interviews

Be sure to follow up on all interviews of interest. Call or write. Don't just pacify your conscience with attempts to follow up and then drop it, continue until you do. Once you get the person on the phone be sure to express your appreciation for the opportunity you had to interview. Let the person know about your keen interest and desire to proceed to the next step. Then highlight a point or two showing how you and your background would enable you to meet the company's needs. Ask what the next steps are. Be specific about your availability for a subsequent interview or offer to submit work samples, references or other assistance.

You don't want to be a nuisance by making excessive calls or leaving too many messages. It doesn't matter how important it is for you to get feedback from the company, you must restrain yourself from overdoing it. Use some discretion. One or two messages in a week are fine, but three or four in a given day are out. You can ease your way around some of this problem by not leaving a message each time you call. Most frequently you will not be able to talk to the right person, so ask when you should call back. The person to whom you wish to speak may be in a meeting ending in a half hour. Don't leave a message but call back at that time. The person may be out to lunch and not be expected back until 1:30 PM. Again, you can call back then rather than leave a message. With practice you can learn how to finesse your way around and get through to the right person. Always be courteous to the secretary. Each relationship you build can help you reach the desired person. Don't be rude or demanding, and don't sound weary.

> ## 217 Preparation For Second Interview

Do additional in-depth research prior to the second interview. Don't just rely upon conventional library resources or published company literature. Though you should read everything you can about the company, there are more direct ways to gain information about it. I will give you an example.

My daughter, Michele, is in the highly competitive fashion industry. She is very thorough and pays acute attention to detail. Her research into the company she joined included shopping the market where she lives in New York City. This consisted of many phone calls and leg work to personally visit the stores where the clothing was being sold. She wanted to see the lines, the types and sizes of stores, the position of the goods physically within the store, how they were displayed and priced. She talked to the sales clerks, met some of the managers and owners and asked volumes of questions while trying on some of the clothes to get the feel of them.

She took notes and was prepared to ask specific questions of the interviewer while commenting about her observations. What kind of impression do you think she made?

Add this personal observational research to the typical information available on most companies in the form of literature, financial information, and you now begin to get a comprehensive picture of the company. Often people lose out to those who may be less qualified but do a much more thorough job on their company homework and interview preparation. Is there a need to say more?

➤ 218 Ask About Advancement Opportunities

While being interviewed you should ask if opportunities for advancement are open or limited to this division or other divisions, locations, subsidiaries or other. If you have done your research thoroughly enough, you should know the answer. If it is a dead end job, then you would not ask it. If there is room for advancement, this conveys to the company that you are interested in a long-term career commitment. It also gives you a much better picture of where you might be able to grow within the company.

➤ 219 Attention To Details
Attention to detail is the religion of success.
                    Napoleon

When Napoleon didn't follow his own advice, he failed. Pay heed. Detail every possible situation you might encounter in each of your interviews and you will move your job search to a successful conclusion.

19

THE DO'S & DON'TS OF INTERVIEWING

The company wants me;
  The company wants me not.
The company wants me;
  The company wants me not.
The company wants me;
  The company wants me not.

Pluckin' a daisy's petals to determine if a company wants to hire you is just about as unreliable as trusting the daisy to your fate with love. Don't trust your job search to chance. This chapter covers a wide variety of common and not so common, human behaviors during interviews. Some of these are just common courtesy; some are common sense; some are nearly ridiculous, but they all happen. Make sure you eliminate the don'ts, and do the do's to presenting yourself as a desirable candidate for a job.

➤ 220 Health And Your Interview

Do not go on an interview if you are not feeling well, no matter how tempted you may be. There is no way that you can be your best under these circumstances. Call and reschedule.

➤ 221 Being On Time

Know the true value of time; snatch, seize, and enjoy every moment of it. No idleness, no laziness, no procrastination; never put off till tomorrow what you can do today. Chesterfield

Don't be late for interviews. Always leave extra early for all interviews to allow an extra cushion of time for potential traffic problems, getting lost or finding a place to park your car. I have seen many people gain extra points by being early for interviews. Then there are those who work against themselves by being late and coming in huffing and puffing, falling all over themselves with apologies and wasting valuable interviewing time. They end up parting with yet another apology. What a poor impression to make on a prospective employer! Being late is no way to go.

Being early is an expression of interest on your part. It allows you to get acclimated to your surroundings, observe the company in operation, catch your breath, go to the rest room, take a breath mint, straighten your clothes, gather your thoughts, and review the questions and points you want to cover in your interview.

PUNCTUALITY

There are three types of people when it comes to punctuality.

1. Those who make it a point to be early wherever they go, with a good margin for safety.

2. Those who somehow manage to get there on time, within a minute or two one way or the other by the skin of their teeth.

3. Those who are forever running late. Being on time is the exception for this group. And when they are on time, they somehow manage to get in just under the wire by five seconds at best.

Which are you and what kind of impression are you conveying? This can help or hurt your career progress.

➤ 222 Your Appearance

Dress and look your best for all interviews. Conduct yourself as though your future and your career depend upon it; they do. This is an all-important area that is well within your control. There is no excuse for poor dress and grooming. Looking sharp can make up for a multitude of weaknesses. This is definitely an area in which you can excel and gain an important edge over the average job seeker. Good grooming can be accomplished despite your size, your natural beauty, your age, your overall appeal and even your clothing budget. Make sure you are groomed to match the business. If you do not have the knack of good grooming, ask for help.

➤ 223 Make-up And Clothes

Some women need to guard against excessive use of make-up. False eyelashes and the like will work against you in interviews. The whole world knows this - except perhaps the person who does it. Make-up should enhance your appearance, not totally disguise you. Likewise this applies to clothing. Look at yourself factually in the mirror in good light; is there anything that would suggest that you are ready for a date, or do you look like you are ready for the office? There is a big difference.

➤ 224 Your Smile

On a number of occasions I have seen a bright shining smile be the deciding factor among the final candidates for a position. Smile!

➤ 225 Hand Shake

A good firm, friendly hand shake will gain positive attention. A loose, limp handshake will do the opposite. This is such a simple little habit that is done so routinely that few people think of it. Think about your hand shake. Make it firm and friendly, but no bone crushers, please. Look the person in the eye and smile while you are shaking hands. Believe me, "Little things do make a big difference."

➤ 226 Eye Contact

Poor eye contact during interviews is very unsettling and uncomfortable to interviewers. Look at the person eye to eye. Be attentive. Some job seekers have a difficult time doing this. They will nervously glance at various things around the office, look out the window, stare down at the floor or become captivated with their hands as they fidget with some object in them. If this resembles you in any way, stop it. This conveys a lack of interest on your part. Practice in front of a mirror. Talk to yourself. Role play. Ask a friend or relative to role play with you. This is different from the actual experience, but it can help you focus your attention on proper eye contact and help you improve.

➤ 227 Posture

Poor posture while sitting in the chair during interviews is a common downfall. I have actually had feedback from a client who stated he was more preoccupied with the candidate sliding out of the chair onto the floor or falling asleep than anything else. Slouching down in the chair, supporting your head in your hand, and/or propping your elbow on a table are not acceptable. Sit up straight and be attentive in your chair at all times. You want to convey a keen interest in what the interviewer has to say throughout the interview. Don't let body language convey otherwise.

➤ 228 Voice

Speak so you can be easily understood during interviews. This is a problem for people who are naturally soft spoken. If you happen to be one of them, you will have to turn up the volume a notch or two so the interviewer can comfortably hear you. Speaking too softly can also convey a lack of confidence and timidity. Again, be aware of the impression your voice makes. People who speak clearly and at a volume a little above the average get more attention. You can achieve equal footing if you make a conscientious effort. Do not speak in a monotone voice - fluctuate the pitch, speed and volume to create interest and emphasis in your words.

➤ 229 Manners

Mind your manners at all times. This includes your table manners. Many a job prospect has died at the interview because of poor manners. If you were not trained well, you will not suddenly develop good manners. Learn, practice and exhibit good manners. Displaying good manners means you abide by rules of society which transfers into abiding by the rules of the company.

➤ 230 Enthusiasm

A lack of enthusiasm during interviews will work against you. Good positive enthusiasm will help you. That is just the way things are. You may have to psych yourself up for some tongue-in-cheek interviews. Always display interest in the person conducting the interview; show appreciation, thoughtfulness and some measure of excitement. No one really enjoys dealing with someone who just sits there like a bump on a log. Be animated, alive and lively; but don't overdo it.

➤ 231 Your Breath

Be sure to brush and floss your teeth and use a good breath freshener immediately before each interview. (Don't be obvious about the use of a breath freshener.) Bad breath and body odor can kill an interview. Both can and do happen. This is particularly true if you indulge in foods with garlic and onions. Stay away from these foods when interviewing. Don't indulge, and then make excuses.

➤ 232 Gum

Don't chew gum during an interview. People have unknowingly been eliminated from consideration because of their snap, crackle and popping. People are creatures of habit. When gum chewers get nervous, they will resort to their old habits subconsciously. Just don't chew gum!

➤ 233 Perfumes

Cologne, perfume or aftershave lotion should be very subtle while you are interviewing. Just as garlic is as a flavor enhancer to food, not an herb to overpower a meal, likewise don't over indulge in fragrances. People get so accustomed to their favorite cologne, perfume or aftershave lotion that they really don't realize their over use. The scent should not linger behind you, nor precede you. It should not fill an elevator or room with its presence. This will work against you in a business atmosphere. What you do socially after business hours is up to you. Be careful in the business arena, especially during the hiring process. You will lose points if you don't.

➤ 234 Nail Biting

If you are a nail biter, stop it. Something as little as this can be a big knockout factor. Grow out your nails so you do not appear to be a nail biter.

➤ 235 Smoking

Do not smoke during interviews or even ask if it is okay to do so. It is getting increasingly more difficult for smokers because more and more companies are banning smoking. Furthermore, a growing number of companies don't even want to talk to smokers. I know a lot of people who smoke. I used to be a smoker myself years ago, so I can relate to both sides of this issue. However, the trend on smoking is very clear. It can cost you your dream job as well as your life.

➤ 236 Alcohol

Do not drink alcoholic beverages before an interview. A faint hint of alcohol on the breath has killed interviews of a number of otherwise excellent candidates. Do not order alcoholic beverages during lunch, dinner or weekend interviews. You want to keep a clear head at all times. When asked, you can always order iced tea or orange juice.

➤ 237 Ordering At Business Meals

Do not procrastinate when ordering for a breakfast, lunch or dinner interview. Be decisive and keep it simple. The primary purpose of this meeting is not to eat but to conduct a successful interview. Do not order difficult to eat foods such as barbecued ribs or a half of a chicken. Keep it simple. Even a simple, light meal such as a salad can get you in trouble because it takes time to chew and can be messy. The easier the meal is to chew the better the meal is for an interview. You are there to talk. Eating is secondary.

I have seen people take an inordinate amount of time to order. They just can't seem to be able to make up their minds. It is as though they were making life and death decisions. What kind of impression do you think you make when you are indecisive in this area? What kind of decision maker will you be if you can't order a simple, everyday meal? I have personally been driven up the wall all too many times by people who don't know what to order. Then when they do finally order, it is something that creates a problem for them to eat. Have a simple game plan worked out in your mind beforehand, and be decisive. Don't complain about the food or service. You are the guest.

➤ 238 Profanity

Do not use profanity during interviews. Don't use it - even in a clever story with a good point to make. There are an awful lot of people who cannot utter a single sentence without using some profanity. All you have to do is watch some of the shows on TV to get this picture. It is quite normal for some young people to be fascinated, intrigued and even attracted to the use of profanity. This is probably true because they are not supposed to do it and that by itself is reason enough for them to do it. However, as one grows up, the loose use of profanity tends to fade. For others the habit lasts throughout their life time. It is as though they are proud of this "trade mark." Certainly there is profanity in the world of business; but profanity should not be used during interviews. If the interviewer uses it, don't use it as a cue for you to do the same. Just don't use it at any time during the hiring process. Don't take any exceptions to this rule.

➤ **239 Avoid Discussions On Religion Or Politics**
Do not bring up religion or politics during interviews. They are lose/lose subjects.

➤ **240 Displaying Levels Of Class**
Class shows and so does the lack of class. Different levels of positions call for different levels of class. Learn to recognize the difference, and do your best to position yourself accordingly. Everyone fits somewhere.

➤ **241 Your Car**
You are judged in many ways. Drive a clean and orderly vehicle to all interviews. If a potential employer sees you drive a dirty, grungy, cluttered vehicle inside or out, it can kill a potential opportunity.

➤ **242 Parking/Parking Meter/Parking Lot**
I have seen otherwise intelligent people put coins into parking meters to save a two dollar parking lot fee while they go on interviews. What happens during the interview when the meter runs out? The person is

nervously preoccupied wondering if the car may be towed away. I have also seen candidates ask to be excused during interviews to feed a parking meter. Some impression!!! Perhaps they didn't think this opportunity was worth a two dollar investment.

➤ 243 Family At Interviews
Do not bring your spouse, children, parents or friends with you on interviews unless you are invited to do so. Make sure that they act appropriately and do not distract, contradict or disrupt you.

➤ 244 Communication Skills
Your ability to effectively communicate, verbally and in writing, will be a definite factor in your job hunting success. You can hire someone to effectively write your resume and cover letter; however, you are on your own verbally. If this is a problem area for you, then learn to make up for it with other strengths you have.

➤ 245 Knowing When To Shut Up
Next to knowing what to say is knowing when to SHUT UP!

➤ 246 Talking Too Much
Guard yourself against talking too much if you are the gabby type. Don't be a motor mouth. Some people simply can't shut up. They talk non-stop and won't let anyone get a word in edge-wise. Some of this behavior can be out of nervousness by new job seekers. With others it is simply their nature. To be effective conversations and interviews must consist of a volley back and forth between both parties. With practice and awareness on your part you can definitely improve in this area and help your job search proportionally.

➤ 247 Interrupting
Do not interrupt while the interviewer is talking. Many

people have a bad habit of constantly interrupting others. These are people who simply insist in monopolizing a conversation. They want to be in control, the center of attention. They are convinced that what they have to say is more important than anything that anyone else can say. This is a very bad social habit that will definitely spill over into your interviews. Nervousness will augment this problem. If this sounds like you, then you have to guard yourself against habitually interrupting the other person. Otherwise this habit will work heavily against you during interviews and can cost you the job of your dreams. Be careful and considerate of the other person.

➤ 248 Interview Interruptions

In the course of being interviewed there may be times the interviewer gets interrupted by phone calls or people barging in and out of the office. To get interrupted once or twice is one thing, but when the interruptions continue they can kill your interview chances. There is no way you can maintain any reasonable flow of conversation. Should you find this happening, be very diplomatic but offer the following suggestion. "It's rather apparent that we picked a difficult time to interview with your busy schedule today. Why don't we set another appointment when we can talk without interruption? This meeting is extremely important to both of us. I'm afraid something may fall between the cracks if we continue." Or use any words to that effect. One of two things will happen. The interviewer will apologize and ask all calls to be held; or another meeting will be rescheduled. In either case, your suggestion will be taken with respect.

➤ 249 Talking Too Fast

Don't talk too fast. Slow down. Some of you are natural born fast talkers, and you will have a tough time slowing down. Things will get even tougher if you don't. You can slow down if you practice, be deliberate, use a mirror and a tape recorder to watch and listen to yourself. Turn on the tape recorder when the phone rings and record your end of the conversation. When you hang up, re-play the tape. Use a stop watch to time the pauses. How much did you let the other person say? Now, re-record some of the same things you said; say your words slower; play back the tape. Keep your enthusiasm, your pitch and your emphasis but slow down so the other person can grasp what you are saying. Often fast talkers use many fill in sounds such as well, ah, and da. They also repeat words, use run-on sentences, and add much content that is not necessary. Check yourself. Beyond being difficult to understand, there are too many negatives associated with fast talkers. Down-shift to a slower gear. It will do wonders for you. I used to talk too fast. I had to break myself of the habit. I still have to guard myself against shifting my rate of speed into overdrive to this very day. You too can slow your speaking rate with practice.

➤ **250 Effective SILENCE**

There will be times when silence; absolute silence, can speak louder than the loudest words spoken. Silence at the right time can actually be so loud it is deafening, for silence communicates in and of itself. It usually speaks assurance. Do not attempt to fill with words all voids in a conversation. Pauses are extremely effective to good communication. Absolute silence at the right time is compellingly effective! Learn to use it; for it will improve your negotiating abilities immensely. Silence works when you are pleased, as well as disappointed. A person very new to sales was asked, "How much is this item?" The salesperson did not know the exact amount; so she said nothing. The customer then made an offer to buy it for a specific amount. It was within the price range, but the salesperson was slow to respond; she still said nothing. The buyer then doubled and then tripled the offer. By the fourth offer the salesperson knew the offer was a great one, and she accepted. Her pauses earned a bonus of over $100 in that sale. Silence (even out of ignorance) paid off. The salesperson learned a big lesson in the effectiveness of silence that day. Does this story have application in all aspects of life?

LISTENING

Everyone loves a good listener. Being a good listener means more than simply being silent while the other person speaks. That is only part of being a good listener. The next part is being attentive, responsive and acknowledging what one hears without interrupting. Next comes hearing and understanding what the other person is saying, rather than concentrating on what you want to say as soon as the other person stops talking.

Another part of listening is staying with the subject being discussed, and not changing topics, shifting gears from one topic to the other. Learn to stay with the other person's lead.

Listening also means looking into the other person's eyes in a deeply attentive and interested manner throughout the conversation. Express an interest in what the other person is saying. This allows the conversation to volley back and forth between the other person and you. Never monopolize the conversation with the belief that if you keep talking you will gain an advantage. Actually, the opposite is true.

If you let people talk and encourage them to continue, they will tell you everything about themselves that you would like to know. Unfortunately, most people do not listen enough.

The human species is actually put together wrong. We have one mouth and two ears. When in reality we should have two mouths and one ear. Learn to use your two ears twice as much as your one mouth.

➤ 251   Asking And Answering Your Own Questions

Any time you ask a question, BE SILENT! Give the other person an opportunity to respond. Some people ask questions, then continue talking non-stop. They often attempt to answer their own questions. They guess what they think the answer may be and never allow the interviewer to say a word. A few examples would be as follows:

- What are your working hours, are they 8 to 5?
- When can I expect to hear from you, will it be early next week or later?
- What is your vacation policy, is it two weeks after the first year?

Get out of this habit if you have it. Most people who do this don't realize they are doing it at the time. They just can't help themselves, or so they think. A logical answer pops into the head and out the mouth. If you recognize yourself, STOP IT! Stop it right now and make a concentrated effort each time you ask a question to close your mouth and wait for the person to answer it. Answering your own questions does not set very well with people who hire (or anyone else for that matter).

➤ 252   Finishing Another's Statements

Some people have a bad habit of finishing other people's sentences whenever that other person hesitates or pauses in the slightest way while talking. They are very impatient, and this is their way to speed the conversation along. This is a bad social habit and a killer during interviews. This is different from interrupting, but it is equally bad. If this sounds like you, bite your tongue when the urge hits you.

➤ 253   Overselling On Interviews

Do not oversell on interviews. There is a fine line that you have to straddle between doing a good job of selling yourself and overselling. Be careful in this area. Too much sell and you will hurt yourself.

➤ 254 Do People Say What They Mean?

People don't always say what they mean, nor mean what they say. You have to somehow learn to read between the lines. Otherwise, you may misinterpret their intentions. Take a cold shower as you ponder what may have been said to you. It is very sobering and will help you keep wishful thinking down to a minimum. People often hear what they want to hear, rather than listen for the truth. A person could say, "You have a face that makes time stand still." You could take that as a compliment. If the person said, "You have a face that could stop a clock." You would know the meaning. Don't let subtleties pass by you.

➤ 255 Attitude Of Helping The Company

Ask not what the company can do for you, but what you can do for the company.

This should surface early in your initial interview when you ask what kind of person the company is looking for, what the individual is expected to achieve and what strengths are sought. If, indeed, they are in line with you, your needs, and your capabilities, then weave in these facts throughout your interviews. This can only be achieved when you are prepared properly before the interview.

➤ 256 Bring Life To The Company

When you are interviewing, keep in mind that companies are looking for "spark plugs" and not "dead batteries."

➤ 257 Listlessness

Lack of enthusiasm will cost you the loss of more job

opportunities than anything else. If you don't show some enthusiasm, you won't get the job despite the excellence of your educational background or work history. Make sure you get a good night's sleep and do whatever necessary to get your batteries charged up before you interview. If you are living an uninspired life and project a ho hum attitude, change your ways, overhaul yourself, do something to put spark and life into your interviews. Otherwise, do yourself and the interviewer a favor; stay home and spare yourself from another rejection.

258 Pessimism And Concerns
Don't make the mistake of conveying pessimism and concerns versus presenting a healthy optimistic outlook and expectations. Your pessimism surfaces when every question you ask is followed with a statement to the effect that... You just want to be sure you are making the right move, or... You want to be sure you don't make a mistake... After all, there's a big risk in making a job change. (Many candidates, otherwise qualified, eliminate themselves from contention because of the negative seeds of uncertainty they plant during interviews.)

259 Stating Negatives About Employers
Stating something that is negative about a present or past employer is unjustified even though the comments may be true. I have seen some people who simply beat it to death and go into a rock throwing contest that won't stop. Unfortunately, many people may feel justified in their conduct; however, no matter how justified one may be or feel, it will still go against you. You will be remembered as a person with a negative attitude. Keep your comments and thrust positive. You can learn to do this with practice. Rehearse what you want to say about the situation. Don't let anger or hurt show. Doing so can cost you the job of your dreams.

➤ 260 The Prima Dona Complex

Don't be a Prima Dona. Those bygone days of demand exceeding supply are long gone for the vast majority of job seekers. People in the job search professions refer to job seekers with a you-please-me-or-else demeanor as suffering from a Prima Dona complex. Humility and sincerity are the theme of the day. They will win the attention and respect of companies.

➤ 261 Rudeness

Don't be rude or impolite regardless of the circumstances. There is no excuse for it. This conduct can come back to take you out of competition when you least expect it. We live in a small world. You never know how your actions will follow you from person to person or place to place.

THE RELUCTANT JOB SHOPPER

Some people approach the first interview with tongue-in-cheek apprehensions. They talk themselves into proceeding with this fact finding mission on the premise that they have nothing to lose. They have an "I don't care mental attitude."

During the interview they sit back and quietly listen. They ask an occasional question in an interrogating, impersonal manner. Their attitude reflects their doubts. They are passed over from further consideration despite their qualifications for the job.

The reaction to candidates hearing this feedback ranges from disappointment to being devastated. Being rejected hurts psychologically. It leaves its mark. It ranges from a slight bruise to a major blow to one's ego. This is true particularly after job seekers find that they had underestimated the quality of the job, the people, the company, the philosophy and the potential. It is too late to change the initial impression.

To job shop properly, you must prepare yourself before you interview. In addition to researching the company, you have to psych yourself up and be mentally prepared with an enthusiastic, positive attitude. Your expectations must be positive. You should be prepared to do whatever is necessary to be victorious before you step into the competitive arena. You better accept the fact that competition is extremely keen for any worthwhile career position. And the more attractive the job and company are, the greater the competition is.

> ## 262 Interviewing Expenses

If you have the opportunity to interview with an out of town firm, do not hesitate to ask how the travel, food and lodging expenses are to be handled. This will vary from company to company. Don't assume. You should know up-front so that you are prepared.

> ## 263 Company Paid Interviewing Expenses

Use good judgement in regards to interviewing expense accounts extended to you. Do not fly first class, charge gourmet meals with imported wines at expensive restaurants, rent top of the line cars and stay at the most expensive hotels. Be moderate, fair and reasonable, even though you may normally live otherwise. You don't want to convey that you are extravagant.

A Word Of Advice On Procrastination

By the street of 'By and By' one arrives at the house of 'Never.'
Cervantes

Don't put off eliminating the <u>don'ts of good interviewing</u> one moment. Listen to yourself during ordinary conversations. How well do you really try to listen, to communicate, to be courteous, to be attentive and to enjoy the other person? Look in the mirror as you express yourself or have some one video tape you during conversations. This is difficult, but it will help correct some of your obvious and hidden bad conversational habits. Once you are aware of your specific problems, then it is easy to correct them with some concentration. Practice will help improve your interviewing and that will help you land the job you want.

20

INTERVIEW QUESTIONS THAT

CAN WORK FOR YOU

Ask not, and you may never know
what the answer might have been.

There is an art and science to just about everything. The art
of asking questions is the way you ask them and the
timeliness of your asking. The science is asking the right
questions. This chapter deals with a selection of questions
that need to be addressed if you are going to work for a
company. You will have to feel your way along as to when
and how you should ask them. A conversation is like a
tennis match. Remember, no tennis match is a match
without the other party. Be alert to the interviewer and lead
into these questions when the time seems most right.

> **264 Asking Questions**
Ask sufficient in-depth, meaningful questions during
interviews. Failure to ask questions during the
interview is normally the result of a lack of prior
research about the company. It can be a one way
monologue by the interviewer or, worse still, an
interrogation with short answers from you. Don't make
interviewers talk to themselves. Pursue the who, what,
when, where, why and how thought provoking line of
questions. Otherwise, you will contribute to killing an
interview. Be sure to read at least one book on

interviewing. It will do wonders for you if you put into practice the good interviewing techniques that you have read. If you could only see yourself during the interviewing process, you would learn much about your interviewing. A next best thing is to watch a good video on effective interviewing. It, too, can teach you much by example.

➤ 265 Ask Questions - Find Answers

Many people applying for jobs are afraid to ask questions for fear they might look stupid. Consider the alternative. If you don't ask the questions to get the information you need, then you will remain stupid.

➤ 266 Ask About Hiring Procedure

Ask the company early in the interview about the company's specific hiring procedures and normal time frames. How many interviews (with what people and in what locations) are involved. Hiring practices vary from company to company. Knowing what is expected will help reduce your anxiety level and allow you to prepare yourself properly. All you have to do is ask.

➤ 267 Ask Who The Employer Wants

Early in your first interview with a company ask about the background and type of person that is being sought to fill the specific job opening. Also ask about the strengths and skills that the person should bring to the company. Continue to find out what the company expects this person to achieve to be successful. If you persist and obtain good specific answers, not just the usual vague generalities, then you will get a solid understanding of what is expected of you if you should be offered and accept the position. You can use this knowledge effectively to tailor your presentation and answers according to the company's needs. This is possible providing the position meets your criteria, your capabilities and your interests.

➤ 268 Ask About The Position

You need to learn about the position to find out if you want it and to let the company know how qualified you are for it. The more specific information that you acquire about the position, the better off you will be. Ignorance might be bliss, but it can lead to unhappiness and dissatisfaction if it concerns your job.

➤ 269 Ask About Advancement Opportunities

Be sure to ask if opportunities for advancement are open or limited to this division or other divisions, locations, subsidiaries or other. This conveys to the company that you are interested in a long-term career commitment. It also gives you a much better picture of where you might be able to grow within the company.

➤ 270 Ask About Growth Potential

Most job hunters tend to interview only for the immediate job opening. They fail to pursue the potential for growth and the career path with ballpark time frames. At best, the average job seeker will touch upon this all important subject by asking a simple question such as, "What is the growth potential?" or "What are the opportunities for advancement within the company?"

Never settle for general answers such as "You can go as far as you like," or "There are plenty of opportunities for advancement." Don't buy this. Dig for specifics as though you planned to spend the rest of your working career with that one company. This communicates a long term commitment on your part. You will not appear to be another job hopper just passing through. Companies, today, have had more than their fill of hiring "wandering" career nomads. Show you have a specific career path in mind and are looking for the company that can offer you an opportunity to pursue it. This shows vision and planning: two characteristics that companies admire in employees.

➤ 271 Your Answers - Informative But Short

Do not ramble, give too many details or over answer questions during interviews. If you are asked the time of day, don't tell how to build a watch. A number of people feel that the more they get to talk, the better the chances are of talking the company into hiring them. This just isn't so. Keep your answers short and on target. Answer with substance and precision. If the company wants more information, the interviewer will ask for it. The sooner, the quicker, the faster that you understand and practice this, the more success you will experience in your job hunting.

➤ 272 Reasons For Change Of Employment

During the course of the interview you will be asked why you are looking to make a change of employment and/or why you have left your past employers. Always keep your answers brief and positive in nature. Long and drawn out explanations are not necessary or good. The interviewer will ask for added details if they are necessary. Avoid negative comments. Don't be maneuvered into saying anything bad about your employer or former employer.

➤ 273 Questions And Answers

Getting the right answers is a matter of asking the right questions.

PRELIMINARY INTERVIEW QUESTIONS TO ASK

Always ask the approximate length of the interview at the time you confirm your appointment. The purpose for this is twofold.

First, you should know the length of the interview so you can comfortably fit this into your time schedule. You do not want to go on an interview and be a clock watcher so that you will be able to get to your next appointment on time. Give yourself enough time to find the place, interview, and make your next appointment without being in a time crunch. Count on the unexpected to happen. Employers can often run late for interviews. A margin of safety will allow for this.

Second, you have to know how much time is allotted to you so you can plan and prepare for the interview. Is there a difference between a forty-five minute interview and a two, four or eight hour interview? You bet there is and you have to plan accordingly. A forty-five minute interview doesn't give you a whole lot of time to plead your case. As part of the pre-screening fact-finding process, most companies tend to ask most of their questions during the first interview. This leaves a limited amount of time for you to ask your questions and dove tail your background and abilities into their needs. With this thought in mind you must plan effectively.

INTERVIEW QUESTIONS TO ASK

Following is a list of some very good questions to ask. Answers to these questions will help you determine if the position is the right opportunity for you. All of these questions cannot be handled during the first meeting; so, good judgment must be exercised along the way. At least, this will prepare you to ask a number of fact-finding questions.

Question number one, "Why is the position open?" is one of the more critical questions you should ask.

1. **Why is the position open?**

    • **Expansion?** How many people do they have now? How many people are being added? What has brought this about?

- **Promotion?** How long had that person been in the position? How long has the person been with the company? To what position was the person promoted? Is this the normal career path? If it is, then you will definitely want to dig deeper into it should this lead to a hiring interview.

- **Person quit?** Why? How long had the person been in the position? How long had the person been with the company? Was it a loss?

- **Person fired?** Why? How long had the person been in the position? How long had the person been with the company? What was the problem?

- **Health reasons?** What has been the problem?

- **Retirement?** After how many years of service with the company? Is this a normal retirement or an early retirement? If an early retirement, is it a voluntary or forced early retirement? If it is a voluntary retirement, what did the company like about the individual? What are the person's strengths and where, if at all, was the person weak? Is the company looking for a "copy" of the former employee or what strengths are desired for the new person to bring into the job? When will the employee retire? (It may be some time in the future.)

- **Replacing an incumbent on a confidential basis?** Why? How long has the employee been with the company? Don't buy general answers to these questions such as, "The person just doesn't keep up with the job," or "The job has out grown the individual," or any words to that effect. Dig as deeply and as specifically as you can into this very crucial area. A common catch-all reason is "We disagree philosophically," or "There is a personality conflict."

You should ask, "Could you be more specific so that I can get a better understanding of what you mean?" Dig, dig, dig, as deeply as you can. Conduct yourself as though you were planning to spend the rest of your career in that position. You should know what pleases your potential new boss and what is expected. You should also learn what displeases the employer. Learn specifics.

2. **Just what is it that you are looking for?**
    Don't accept vague generalities. Always seek specific answers. Often times this question will be answered by telling you what the company doesn't want such as, "One thing we don't want is a clock watcher." Don't pass over this general answer. You better ask, "Can you be more specific; what do you mean by that?" Otherwise, be prepared to work long hours six or seven days a week should you go to work for the firm. Find out what the company does want in regards to the following areas:

    - **Duties**
    - **Responsibilities**
    - **Skills/abilities**
    - **Strengths**
    - **Characteristics**, special traits, qualities or attributes they feel it would take to excel in this position.
    - **All else**

3. **What is it that you wish to accomplish?**
    - What, if anything, has prevented or impeded you from achieving it?
    - Do you have a time frame objective?

4. **What is the size of your company?**
    - Total sales volume
    - Number of locations - where?
    - Number of employees

5.   **How long have you been in business?**

6.   **What has been your growth rate?**

7.   **What are your growth rate projections, if any?** Do you operate locally, regionally or nationally? (Unless it is self-evident.)

8.   **What is your standing in your industry?**
     - Locally
     - Nationally

9.   **How large is your industry?**
     - Industry projections
     - How do you stack up?

10. **Who are your competitors and how do you measure up to them?** (Ask only when applicable.)

11. **How would your competition describe your firm, as well as your products or services?**

12. **What is the career path of this position?** Where can a person go from here? Again, don't buy generalities. Get specifics in this all-important area unless you would be happy to spend the rest of your days in this position. Obviously, this question would not be pertinent for a chairman of the board or president.

There may be more than one career avenue open. Get a clear picture of these avenues along with some reasonable time frames whenever possible. However, specifics to these questions will not be possible or attempted in a one hour first interview. Save your additional questions for a later more penetrating interview that typically covers the specifics. Entirely too many people lose points in this area. It is almost as though they avoid asking these in-depth questions for fear they won't like the answers. As a result, they potentially kill what would otherwise be a promising opportunity.

13. **Is this a publicly held company or privately owned?** (Ask only when applicable.)

14. **Where is the home office located?** (Use only when it is applicable.) If the home office or divisional headquarters is in a location that is undesirable, be aware of this up front and go in with your eyes wide open. If you should decide to move ahead, get an offer, join this firm, the right promotion will lead you to a move to an undesirable location, then what?

15. **What is the turnover in the company?** Try to get a percentage or number. Then ask the reasons for this.

16. **How many (title of position) are there in the (department, branch, division, company)?**

17. **Is there any overnight travel?** If so, how much? And unless self evident, for what reason?

18. **Is the company international?** If so, would you be required to travel there? How often? Length of trips?

19. **Does the company have any operations overseas?** If so, what countries? Also, if so, would you be required to travel there or relocate there?

20. **Is a company car (or truck) furnished?** (Ask only if it is applicable.) What kind of vehicle? Strictly business, or personal use as well?

21. **Does the company provide tuition aide?** If so, get a brief explanation. (Ask only when applicable.)

22. **Does the company have a stock purchase plan?** If yes, how does it work?

23. Does the company have a profit sharing plan? If yes, how does it work? Yearly average?

24. Does the company have an organizational chart? Where would the position fit into its structure?

25. Who will be your immediate boss? (Unless this is self evident.) An initial interview may be with a vice president of industrial relations, a vice president of human relations, a personnel director, a manager or another officer of the company other than the immediate superior of the prospective employee. Do not jump to hasty conclusions when dealing with pre-screeners. A pre-screener's function is just that - to help screen out the unqualified from the qualified. How you get along with this person is very important. It can and does have an effect on how the interviewer looks upon you in this screening process. The point I am making here is that you may not like the interviewer and if you are not careful your feelings might surface. This will hurt your chances of moving to the next step. You should build rapport with the interviewer so you can get an interview with your potential boss. The important thing is how well you get along with your potential new boss. You won't meet key people unless you get past the pre-screener.

26. Is there any company literature available? Is there literature about the products or services? What about an annual report for publicly held firms?

27. Is the company centralized or decentralized? (Unless it is self evident.)
- Does the firm promote from within each division or operating company, or is it possible to move from one to the other?
- If interviewing with a division or a wholly owned subsidiary, how does this division or wholly owned subsidiary rank in growth and profits compared to the parent company?

28. **Are there any stock options?** This would be asked for appropriate level positions. If yes, get the details.

29. **Does the company have a formal salary review program?** If so, how does it work? Get specifics at the hiring stage.

30. **Does the company have a bonus plan?** If so, how does it work? Get the specifics at the hiring stage.

31. **What is the company's philosophy?**

32. **How large is the company?** How many people are there in the department, division or company reporting to (title of position for which you are interviewing)? What kinds of people? Get a breakdown.
    • Is the department, division or company on target with its quotas or budget? Be sure to dig into specifics in this vitally important area.

33. **What type of reports are required?** (Ask only when applicable.) What are their degree of frequency?

34. **How soon do you want to fill this position?**

35. **How long has the position been vacant?** (Ask only when applicable.) Why?

36. **Last, but highly important, at the offer stage, ask about the company's fringe benefit program.**

37. **Where do we go from here?** Ask this unless you have already been told what to expect next.

This should arm you with a good list of questions to ask throughout the hiring process. Asking these questions and getting the answers to them will help you make an intelligent decision concerning the job offer if it is extended to you. You will also set yourself apart from the majority of job seekers who do not ask astute questions and, therefore, seem less than interested.

➤ 274 Vacations

Do not discuss vacations too early in the interviewing process. It is a turn off for the employer. The earliest time to broach this subject would be in the middle of the hiring process; even then don't dwell on it. You can get specific details at the offer stage. The higher up the ladder you are, the more latitude you have on this subject. Smaller companies are much more flexible about vacations than are the larger ones. Most long term executives and middle managers with major corporations who have become victims of downsizing and restructuring are going to have to go back to square one in a new company and industry. They will have to accept less vacation time. It is a bummer when this happens, but it sure beats being on a full time vacation - otherwise known as being permanently unemployed.

➤ 275 Questions About Pensions/Benefits

Do not ask probing questions about the company's benefit and pension plans too early in the interviewing process. This is a turn off to the company. You are displaying too much of an attitude of "What's in it for me?" You should be concentrating on subjects that show you are interested in benefitting the company. For some strange reason, people new to the job market are guilty of this. It may be that their parents have provoked them to do this by emphasizing the importance of a good benefit and pension plan. However, there is a right time and place for this, and it is not until final negotiations are underway. This should be one of the very last areas discussed. It typically gets covered during the hiring phase. Believe me, I am fully aware of the importance of a good benefit program. I am not playing this down. It is just that if you mishandle this too early, it conveys that you are more interested in retiring than working.

➤ **276 Asking For The Job**

Ask for the job once you decide you want it. This is not being bold or presumptuous; it is being honest. There are many hiring managers who will not extend an offer to someone unless it is made known that the individual seeking the job really wants it. Some managers just cannot stand the thought of rejection. In pre-screening and sorting out the job applicants points are often added to people who say they want the job. The issue is very simple. If you want the job, ask for it. This will separate you from the curiosity seekers and game players who play their cards so close to their vests that potential employers can't read their levels of interest or lack of it. Another way of saying the same thing is by expressing your interest in proceeding to the next step.

➤ **277 Continued Interest - Continued Action**

Always ask, "Where do we go from here?" at the conclusion of interviews. Express your continued interest if you are interested. Asking this question will let you know where you stand, what is expected of you and what you can expect from the company.

Now you are armed with the questions that can carry you through one or several successful interviews to get you the job you need and want. Read this chapter several times so the questions will become automatic. You may want to write down some key questions to take with you during your interview. Refer to them at a point when the interviewer asks if there are any more questions. This will show that you are prepared and are really considering the job.

INTERVIEW QUESTIONS TO ANSWER

Take a very simple approach. If you have interviewed before, you can make a list of questions that were asked of you. Write them down with your answers. The bulk of these questions are going to come up in your future interviews. Were you satisfied with the way you handled these questions the last time around? If given a second chance, would you change some of your answers? Often people have been caught off guard due to lack of preparation. This is no different than studying and preparing to take a test. The more you study and prepare, the better the outcome will be. You have the same opportunity to study and prepare for your interviews.

If you have never interviewed before, go to your high school or college counselor or placement director, your parents, their friends or your friends. Ask them to ask you questions that an interviewer might ask. Role play. This will give you good practice. Write the questions down and then record your answers. Don't just give quick answers off the top of your head. Give this serious thought. Have someone or several people critique them. This will not only help you say the right thing during an interview, it will build your confidence.

The following general areas are suggested as a starting point for questions that might be asked of you. Use this as a guide. Use more paper to make your answers as complete as possible. Then pick out the best parts to actually say while being interviewed. You always want say just enough to interest the employer, but don't over do it or you might put your foot in your mouth. Know when you have said enough. Answer the questions below as if they were asked of you.

TELL ME ABOUT YOURSELF?

This is one of the most frequently asked questions. It is probably the most difficult to answer because it is so general and you know you cannot take an hour to expound on the subject. Be prepared to answer this question in a few short sentences. Make them summarize the most important points concerning your work experiences, education, strengths, skills, goals and what you can offer the company.

You need to really think about this question. Devote some time to it, so you can structure your answer to be brief, but still make a great impression.

_____
_____
_____
_____
_____
_____
_____
_____
_____

Prepare to answer job related questions.

Most of the questions asked will be centered on the specific job and your ability to handle it. However, many interviewers go about gathering that information in non-direct ways. Some companies are more interested in your work habits than they are your direct skills.

Your Interest In The Company

- Why are you looking for a job?

_____
_____
_____

- Why are you leaving your present position?

_____
_____
_____

- Why do you want to work for this company?

_____
_____
_____

- What do you know about this company?

_____

_____

_____

Your Experience

- How does your experience relate to this position?

_____

_____

_____

- What skills do you have? Would you mind taking a test to demonstrate your effectiveness as a _____?

_____

_____

_____

- What have you enjoyed most about your work?

_____

_____

_____

- What have you enjoyed least about your work?

_____

_____

_____

What You Offer The Company

- What do you have to offer?

_____

_____

_____

- What is your most outstanding accomplishment?

_____

_____

_____

- What accomplishments do you wish to make here?

_____
_____
_____

- What are your greatest strengths?

_____
_____
_____

- What are your greatest weaknesses?

_____
_____
_____

- If you were me, why should I hire you?

_____
_____
_____

Your Work Ethic, Dedication, And Loyalties

- What motivates you most (money, accomplishments, ego)?

_____
_____
_____

Your Goals

- What are your short term goals?

_____
_____
_____

- What are your long term goals?

_____
_____
_____

- To what degree have you been successful in achieving your goals?

_____

_____

_____

- Do you set New Year's resolutions and keep them?

_____

_____

Your Education

- Where did you go to school/college?

_____

_____

_____

- Why did you choose it?

_____

_____

_____

- Why did you choose to major in_____?

_____

_____

_____

- What was the most exciting thing you learned in _____?

_____

_____

_____

Money Questions

- What kind of money are you looking for?

_____

_____

_____

- What are your long range financial expectations?

_____

_____

_____

Your Interaction With People

- How well do you get along with people, your associates, your superiors and those you might oversee?

_____

_____

_____

- What are your civic interests?

_____

_____

_____

- Why did you choose them?

_____

_____

_____

Your Special Interests

- What are your hobbies, sports, leisure-time activities and special interests?

_____

_____

_____

Time And Place Questions

- Would you have any difficulty with relocation, travel, extended hours, working on the weekends or at night?

_____

_____

_____

- When can you begin work?

_____

_____

_____

Remember these questions are just a few general ones. There will be many more.

Prepare to deal with unethical and illegal questions.

- Do you plan on having a family right away? How will this impact your work at our company?

_____

_____

_____

Be prepared for the future projection type questions.

- When you retire, what do you want this company to remember most about you?

_____

_____

_____

Be prepared for "What If" or political questions.

- What if you were the president of this company, what would you do to ease social tensions in the world?

_____

_____

_____

Role Playing

Also be prepared to role play. You may feel shy and self-conscious at first, but practice will help you overcome this. When the interviewer places you in a hypothetical situation, really let your mind absorb the situation. Take this seriously.   Forget about yourself.   Play the roll the interviewer has placed you in. Answer honestly. Think before you speak, but do not hesitate too long before you give your appraisal of the situation.

Methods and styles of interviewing are as varied as companies, employers and employees.

Interviews literally run the gamut from one extreme to the next, from rigidly patterned interviews, to totally informal and off-the-wall casual, friendly conversations. You should be prepared to deal effectively with all of them. This section is intended to provide a good broad overview only.

Much success in your interviewing. You know what to do. Practice to become the best you can be and get the job you want.

21

ARTFUL NEGOTIATING, ACCEPTING

OR REJECTING THE OFFER

*Successful negotiating consists of
achieving balance that is fair to both parties.
If the deal favors one side more than the other,
you will never come to terms.*

NEGOTIATING

Negotiating is like a poker game, you don't know what cards the other person has until they are placed on the table face up. Draw out of the interviewer all the information you need to determine what the company thinks you are worth. Then you have to present your merits so the company thinks you are worth what you think you are worth. A compromise is usually the result. Don't look at only one aspect of the negotiations: the immediate salary. There are many areas to consider, discuss and come to an agreement upon. Negotiate from a position of strength. This chapter will help you do exactly that.

➤ 278 Logic Versus Emotions

A major difference exists between logical decisions from the head and emotional decisions from the heart. People tend to believe what they want to believe. Many people will literally con themselves into thinking that if they want something badly enough they can influence the outcome simply by wishing it. Emotions complicate the decision making process.

➤ 279 Salary

Salary desired. Inevitably during the course of the interviewing and/or hiring process you will be asked about your salary needs. It is a mistake to give your desired salary expectation. First, if the salary figure you give is too high, you may eliminate yourself from consideration. If this should occur during the first interview before you have been adequately assessed, then you could be passed by. Later on after your capabilities are known, you may be a bargain. Secondly, if you give a figure that is too low, you could be selling yourself short. The third possibility, of course, is to coincide with the salary range the company is willing to pay. However, the odds of you hitting the right figure at best are one chance out of three, which is not very good.

Whenever a company asks you about salary, it is far better to put the question back in the lap of the company. If employed, you can state what your current earnings are. Then you can say something like the following:

Certainly we're all interested in making more money. The position we are discussing carries with it a level of responsibilities that commands a certain salary level. Your company has a reputation for being more than fair; so I'm confident if we get together and an offer is extended it will be a fair one.

The salary question can be handled on job applications by writing the word "open" in the "salary desired" space. Then you can discuss it when the company addresses it during the interview.

➤ 280 Salaries And Realities

Make realistic salary assumptions. Research the industry and appraise your worth in today's market of supply and demand. Unrealistic salary demands will work against you, no matter who you are. The laws of supply and demand will dictate your worth in the marketplace. Your demands will not. Too many people are victims of their imaginations working overtime. Some fellow workers find new jobs and make parting statements to the effect that they have received job offers they simply could not refuse. This implies that they have received a "substantial" increase in pay.

At breakfast in a restaurant the other morning, I overheard a group of friends and family celebrating the fact that one of them had received and accepted a new job offer. One thing led to the other in their conversation until the person who had received the new job stated that her job offer was more than double her previous earnings. Anyone would call that "substantial."

As it turned out this woman had been the supervisor over a crew of eight cleaning ladies for the past four years. She was joining another company doing the same thing. We live in a highly competitive world. No matter what industry one might consider, there is not that much difference in pay scales from company to company for the same job in a given industry. There is no such thing as any company being able to afford to pay a fifty percent or more pay increase, let alone double for the same job. This episode is an excellent example of gross exaggeration on the woman's part. No one in the party questioned her because of friendship or gullibility. So, what are people to believe?

You must truly be unique to command a "substantial" increase. In actuality there are not that many unique people in today's job market. If you want to get in step with the rest of the world, all you have to do is a little research at your local library. It is absolutely amazing how much you can learn if you seek and ask.

Don't Let A Nickel Get So Big
That It Hides The Dime

> ### 281 Salary Differences
>   Don't allow a nickel to get so big that it hides a dime.
>   Don't allow a five percent or less difference in a salary
>   offer alter your career path and your life. Many people
>   make this mistake in spite of the fact that all of the
>   other career needs in a job offer would have been met.

I have seen some otherwise intelligent people make serious
career blunders by allowing offers that were a few dollars
less than they anticipated dictate their career destiny. I am
not talking about making a lateral move or taking a cut in
pay. I am talking about receiving a fair and reasonable
increase in pay, but one that falls short of some pre-
conceived dollar offer that they set for themselves, their self
appraised worth. Where did this dollar assessment come
from? God only knows because the typical person can't
answer the question.

To go one step further I have seen people who have been
faced with more than one offer automatically accept the
highest salary offer on the premise that "all things being
equal" one should accept the highest offer. Really! All
things being equal??? Is there really such a thing? All you
can do is get yourself into more trouble believing that hog
wash. This is one of the reasons this book was written: to
help those of you who set dollars above everything else to
come out of that black and white world and step into the 888
shades of gray of the real world. To allow a few dollars a
week to dictate where your career destiny lies will come back
and bite you where it hurts. In selecting your career
position learn to look beyond the money as the prime
determining factor.

Money is important to everyone; no one will argue the point.
This is true particularly if you are out of work and need to
support yourself, your family and pay the mortgage on your

house. If this is true, temporarily take what you can get while you keep looking for your desired career position.

It is in this latter context that I say that money should not be the only factor in the decision making process, nor should it be the cornerstone of your job hunting foundation. First and uppermost in your mind should be whether or not your career needs will be met and whether you will be happy in your work. If not, you will live to regret your choice. "Money can't buy happiness." This is not just some cute cliche. It is a fact of life. There are rewards that go well beyond money. *Man does not live by bread alone.* All of one's basic career needs must be met including job satisfaction. Everyone also has an ego to feed. Just remember this, the best dollar offer and the best job are not synonymous.

➤ 282 Salary Offer - Silence
After receiving a dollar offer from a company always silently count to ten S---L---O---W---L---Y before giving a response. Companies have been known to kick up their offers during these moments of golden silence.

➤ 283 Salary Review
Make sure to ask when the first salary review will take place after an offer has been extended. Depending upon whether you are dealing from a position of strength or weakness, initial salary reviews can be negotiated at the ninety day or six month mark based upon performance, then on a yearly basis thereafter. There are a number of factors that come into play. However, mentioning the subject during negotiations will definitely improve the likelihood of receiving this added consideration.

➤ 284 Seniority And Advancement
Find out how much seniority plays in advancement opportunities within the company. The line to the top may be considerably longer than at your present firm.

What then? Maybe you really don't want to know. If you don't ask, you won't know; what you don't know can't hurt you. People who follow this line of logic get into trouble all the time as a result.

ACCEPTING/REJECTING THE OFFER

Desire

Over the years I have observed companies compromise their hiring standards out of sheer frustration because they absolutely needed someone but could not find the exact person they needed. The single biggest hiring factor (beyond credentials, chemistry/personality) is the individual's strong interest and desire in joining the company. It does not matter if the prospect earns above the top of the salary range, has less experience than required, lacks the right kind of degree, has no degree at all, has not worked in the preferred industry previously or any variety of criteria expected, both the company and the candidates can compromise themselves in the end. They may settle for less than what they had determined they would; and that is a fact. Each start out from a position of "absolutes" and end in the real world of compromise. Desire breaks the tie in the competition. Sheer desire (the company wanting the candidate badly enough to win the person over or the candidate wanting the job badly enough to fight for it) can be the deciding factor.

The person who wants the job the most and is able to communicate that desire to the company most effectively usually gets the job.

➤ **285 First Job Offer**
Don't accept the first job offer that comes along unless it meets your career needs. Many inexperienced job seekers are inclined to accept the first offer (for better or for worse, whether it really meets their career needs

or not) just because it was offered. Don't make this mistake. Unemployed people who may be getting desperate will more than likely accept the first offer. That is understandable. People who are about to lose their jobs also fall prey to a tempting but not fully satisfying job offer. People who are unhappy and miserable in their present employment are subject to this, too. Any new job looks considerably better than their present position even though their career needs will not be met in the new position. The last group may accept the first job offer simply to avoid further rejection in the marketplace.

If you are unemployed, go ahead and accept your first job offer which can serve as an interim job while you continue to search for the job that really meets your career needs. This makes good sense. The rest of you should keep your present job until you find the right job. If you accept a job that does not meet your needs, you will be back in the job market repeating your same mistakes and presenting a less stable work history.

➤ **286 Timing Concerning Acceptance Of Job Offer**
Taking too long with your decision after you have been extended an offer can cost you a job. Most people will not give an immediate decision to a job offer. They usually want to sleep on it or talk with their family and friends. They may ask for time to make a decision until the next day, the end of the week or in some instances for a full week. Any additional time delays on your part will head you towards potential trouble. After all, you have gone through an entire hiring process by this time. All questions or concerns, if any, should have already been addressed by this point in time. Any additional delays on your part will convey that you still have some doubts and uncertainties about the company or that you are interviewing with other companies.

I have seen many offers rescinded because of delays.

Entirely too many companies associate heel dragging with game playing candidates who try to play one company against another. Some of these people ask for one extension of time after the other and never accept. However, you are at risk if you delay your acceptance.

When the job meets the career needs, a decisive candidate will accept the offer when it is made. After all, when you find that which you are pursuing, take it. There are times when the company might give several days or a week for you to respond. That doesn't mean you have to take the entire response time. If your needs are being met and the offer is a fair one, then by all means accept. This conveys a positive message of confidence and commitment to your new employer.

➤ 287 Counter Offers

Some of you may be given a counter offer by your present employer after you have accepted a new job and proceed to turn in your resignation. Often companies are surprised and caught off guard. Depending upon the person and the circumstances the present employer may "promise" you the moon, the stars and the sky above to stay with the company. There are many different reasons that people will leave for a new job. However most leave for one of two major reasons. First, the company did not live up to their promises. Second, their expectations were not met. As a result they are no longer happy.

All I can say at a time like this is that what you can expect from any company can best be measured by their past. Both of you started with the best of intentions and for whatever reason, things did not work out. It is very much like marriages and divorces. You both start out with an oath that, "For better or for worse or until death do us part," and something changes, then one mate gives notice to the other that he or she wants a divorce. A percentage of the persons receiving notices may fight to prevent this from occurring by "promising" to change whatever they may have done to contribute to their problem. As much as everyone would like to see a magic button to punch so all-will-be-well-forever-more, the truth of the matter is life doesn't quite work that way. When you reach the point where you are no longer happy, then move on with your life. I have seen numerous people hope against hope that things just might work out and fall prey to a counter offer. I have yet to see the first person who did not live to regret it. Don't conduct your lives as though you have a thousand years to live. The meter is ticking off for all of us. Move on with your life.

> **288 The Total Offer**

After receiving a job offer, review the <u>total offer</u>, not just the money. Take every detail under advisement, or you might regret it. Consider the following factors.

- Company - size, growth, reputation, industry standing. Local/regional/national. Public/private.
- Position
- People
- Potential
- Philosophy
- Dollar offer
- Location
- Benefits - perks
- Lifestyle

Routinely each of these factors are covered with all final candidates for corporate clients as part of standard procedure in our executive search business. While it is true that executive search firms are always retained by corporate clients, and never by individuals seeking employment, there is a dual moral obligation to insure that the needs of the candidates, their spouses and families are met, as well as the company client's needs. It does little good to fill a need for the company, only to find out later that the candidate or family is not happy. It is not good for the company, the candidate or the search firm when the person hired has to be replaced.

➤ **289 Right Reason For Accepting A Job**
There are right reasons for accepting or rejecting a job and wrong reasons. Learn to recognize the difference.

➤ **290 Personality Persuasion**
Don't decide to accept a job based on the personality of the person who interviews you or even your new boss. Some interviewers and/or potential bosses are very glib and out-going and fun to talk to. They can overshadow all other important areas that you need to consider to make a job into a career. Put things into proper perspective, or you will accept the wrong job.

➤ **291 Too Good To Be True**
Try to sort out the salesmanship from the legitimate opportunities that exist at a company. Be alert. If you feel like you are being sold a bill of goods too good to be true, you probably are. Beware.

➤ **292 Look Before You Leap!**
Be careful, the best job for you may be the one you already have.

Sometimes you will wonder if you are making the wrong or right decision. You have to see the pluses and minuses on a ledger sheet logically and see that the company is meeting most of your career needs. You have to feel that you can offer the company the caliber of work that it wants, needs and expects. Most important is you have to feel like you want the job. There should be an excitement, not just that an offer is made and that you negotiated favorable terms, but that you want to work for that company. You should feel an eagerness to get started. If this is so, then you know you are accepting a job that is right for you.

FOLLOW UP AND

ACHIEVING DESIRED SUCCESS

Somebody said that it couldn't be done,
  But he with a chuckle replied
That "maybe it couldn't," but he would be one
  Who wouldn't say so till he'd tried.

So he buckled right in with the trace of a grin
  On his face. If he worried he hid it.
He started to sing as he tackled the thing
  That couldn't be done, and he did it.

It Couldn't Be Done - Edgar A Guest

Almost everything you do in your job search will call for follow up action by you. The more thorough you are in follow up the more successful you will be in achieving your goal. Yet, if you have done everything right, you have followed up on every detail and a job still hasn't come through for you, don't despair; it will.

This chapter will help you with a few pointers on re-adjusting your marketing plan to get a job despite all odds. The main factor is to expect success no matter how hard it may seem. Use those inspirational books, quotes and ideas around you and talk to people who believe in you. They will help you see the true value in you, and this will transfer to others. Never say "Never." Go for it as if it were the first

day of your job search. Weariness causes the race to slow
down and perhaps end half finished. Heads up! Keep on
going, and you will finish the race with a job if you know you
can and work at it until you do.

➤ 293 A Job After All

Remember, it is not over until it is over, when it comes
to being in competition for a job. I can state many
success stories about candidates who had been informed
that the position had been filled. They were very
gracious about it and were called back later with a job
offer. The reasons this happens are too numerous to
mention. One thing is for certain. These candidates
made strong, positive, lasting impressions and stayed
positive and in touch with the company with follow up
letters expressing their continued interest. I doubt
seriously if one person in a thousand does this. Perhaps
that is why it works as well as it does.

➤ 294 Stupidity

A good definition of stupidity is doing the same things
the same way over and over again and expecting
different results. This applies to your job search, your
job, your life and everything else. Look for things that
re-occur in your life. Ask yourself, "Why do they?" Be
alert, so you will be able to identify the problem and
correct it.

➤ 295 Change Job Hunting Techniques

If you have made the job hunting rounds for some time
without securing interviews in spite of a good level of
activity, it is time to change your resume, cover letters
and/or career options. Your sense of urgency will
dictate the proper timing. Do whatever is necessary to
take a new approach, do something different to
potentially change the results rather than doing more of
the same. You may need to read a selection of different
books on resumes and cover letters to help present

yourself with a different slant. During difficult recessionary times in some parts of the country, you may need to repeat this process again. Being a fisherman has taught me a thing or two that makes this type of readjustment easier to understand. Sometimes the fish have lock-jaw; therefore, you have to keep changing your lures or bait and your presentations or other variables in order to catch fish. The same applies to job hunting. There are so many variables that can make all of the difference in the world. These techniques are scattered throughout this book. Try as many different approaches as it takes until you get the job you are looking for. As the expression goes, "You can take it to the bank," your competition for these jobs will be doing everything within their power to gain an upper hand on the available positions.

➤ **296 Problem Solving - 101**
If you have a problem which you are working to resolve, but it persists, could it be that the reason the problem remains a problem is because you attack the problem in the same ineffective manner all the time?

➤ **297 Problem Solving - 102**
I used to think that the first step to problem solving was to identify the problem. This served me well for the better part of my life when I made a quantum leap forward and changed my ways. The first step in problem solving is to admit you have a problem. It is much like the approach AA, Alcoholics Anonymous, uses in helping its members. All new members must first openly admit that they have a drinking problem. The great success of their program is based upon this same principle.

➤ **298 Problem Solving - 103**
Every problem has its own solution built within itself. Start digging deep enough, and you will uncover it. A

favorite quote of mine is from the late Charles Kettering, the famous inventor who made so many contributions to the automobile industry including high compression engines and the electric starter:

"Solutions to the most difficult problems, once found, are always simple."

Insurmountable Problem Solving

I am reminded of a basic philosophy that has served me well and that I taught my three children. My son, Mitch, came to me with a problem back when he was a junior in high school. He was faced with what he felt was an unsolvable problem. I asked him if he had ever experienced any similar problems where it appeared there were no solutions, or was this his very first insurmountable problem.

He said, "Dad, you have got to be kidding. No way is this my first real problem. I have had a number of them along the way."

I asked him "What happened to those other insurmountable problems of the past?" He opened up and said that somehow, some way, the problems diminished. Time had a way of helping him find solutions and make it through the obstacles. He simply moved on with his life as the problems faded away. I pointed out that just as this was not his first real problem, it would surely not be his last and that the problem solving lessons he had learned in the past would help him with future problems. Life goes on. It always has and always will. Just keep the faith, and you will do just fine.

➤ 299 Study

The more you get to know about what you are doing the easier things will go for you in your job search. The same applies after you get the job or in anything you do.

WHEN LIFE GETS YOU DOWN

God provides feed for the birds,
but he does not throw it into the nest.

The Birds, The Bees,
The Fishes In The Seas,
And All Of God's Creatures
Have To Work At It To Survive.

Whenever I get to thinking about how tough and difficult things can get in the world of business or life, I fall back on a very uplifting experience I have had with a sparrow hawk.

A sparrow hawk flies from the woods across the street to my side of the street in search of food on a routine basis. He perches on the power line strung between the utility line poles that run beside my building. He starts at one end of the building property line. Perched on the power line he scans the sloping bank and searches for food. He does this despite the weather: rain, shine, sleet or snow. However, it is during the stark cold winter months that he stands out most vividly. At times this small bird will shiver and shake to keep the rain drops or snow from accumulating on him.

He will sit there perched for a minute or two. When he sees some sign of food, he darts to the ground. He then flies back to the power line and lands about fifteen feet further down the line. He repeats this process each time and continually darts to a new location to the sloping bank in search of food. At times he will find some food, but most of the time he misses out. Sometimes the pickings are good. Other times they are not, particularly in the winter. Times can get tough. After the sparrow hawk gets his bill filled, he heads back to his nest in the woods across the street to feed the rest of the family.

God provides feed for the birds, but he does not throw it into the nest. All the birds, the bees, the fishes of the seas and all of God's creatures must get out of the nest and get on the hunt for their daily food in order to survive. They have to do this in spite of shrinking forests and woodlands; they do this despite the fact that their hunting grounds are vanishing due to civilization. They do this in spite of the fact that streams, lakes and oceans are getting more polluted on a daily basis. And yet species like the little sparrow hawk adapt and survive. They have no refrigerators, freezers, canned goods, smoke houses, banks, savings accounts or assets of any kind upon which to rely except the good earth. They all have to somehow make it one day at a time as they have been doing since the beginning of time.

Why should it be any different for the human species? It isn't. We all have to get out of bed and get on the hunt for our daily bread, each in our own way. Somehow, someway, the human species will prevail, and somehow make it through yet another day.

So, when things get a little rough and you are feeling a little sorry for yourself, look around and just think of this sparrow hawk, the birds, the bees, the fishes in the seas and all of God's creatures. They will serve as a friendly reminder to you. We are all in this world together. Count your blessings each day as you get out of bed and get on with your hunt.

Persist until you find the job that's right for you.

➤ 300 Doing
You gotta do what you gotta do. The sooner, the quicker, the faster you come to grips with this reality, the better your job search will go.

➤ 301 Learning/Earning Curves
First comes the learning curve,
then comes the earning curve.

FORMULA FOR SUCCESSFUL JOB HUNTING

First is knowing or learning what has to be done.
Second comes knowing or learning how to do it.
Third is doing what has to be done in a timely manner.
And last is following through to a successful completion until you find the job you want.

We have covered a whole lot of ground in this book and all of it is important. Each specific secret by itself can make or break your search efforts. So don't let a single one-liner slip by you without paying attention to it. These job search lessons came at great expense. You are not going to be able to make a single sweep through this book and capitalize on all the points in it. Some sections of this book will come easier for you than others. Other sections will call for a lot of review and practice over and over again until you become comfortable doing the uncomfortable. This is a key to your becoming successful in your job search. Keep this book at your side every step of the way to insure you are on track and doing the necessary things that have to be done along the way. Again, all these methods are tried and proven over the years. They work.

Use a highlighter to mark special points that you need to work on. Paper clip the pages so you can return to them easily. Fill out the lists that are suggested in the book. Get started on the "Things To Do Today". Set up your base of operations. Buy the necessary items to get your job search organized. These are crucial. Don't put it off. As you begin to accomplish each specific item, you will enjoy a sense of accomplishment as you complete each task and check it off your list.

Mustering up the necessary self discipline will be a major factor in your degree of success. The sooner, the quicker, the faster you come to grips with what has to be done and do it, the better off you will be. Keep the faith and apply everything you have learned until you find the job of your choice. The best of success to you.

WORDS TO WORK BY

I will try to live through this day and this day only one day at a time, because that's all each of us are given at best. I will conduct this day as if it were the most important and only day of my life. I will not conduct myself as though I have a thousand years to live.

I will not live or think in the past because I cannot change it. My present actions are the only thing that I can change. Beyond that whatever I do today will dictate my future and the future is where I'm going to spend the rest of my life. I may have to do something today that would appall me if I felt I had to keep it up for a lifetime. But, for today only, I will do it.

I will maintain a positive mental attitude and keep the faith in spite of any obstacles or negatives I may encounter. The obstacles or negatives I overcome today will strengthen me for tomorrow. I will not allow negatives to enter my life as I have no room for them.

I will plan my work and work my plan to the best of my ability. I may not achieve it 100 %, but I will make progress over yesterday.

I will muster up a new-found discipline to do the things that have to be done, whether I enjoy them or not. I may never develop the discipline to love everything that has to be done, but I can surely develop the necessary discipline to at least do those things. I will save myself from two bad habits: procrastination and excuses.

I will work to control my circumstances rather than allow circumstances to control me.

I will be happy. As Abraham Lincoln once said, "Most folks are as happy as they make up their minds to be."

I will work at self-improvement daily. I will study; I will learn something useful. I will read something that requires effort, thought and concentration. I will not be a mental loafer. I will exercise my mind and continue to grow or I will surely vegetate.

I will make a total commitment as I have never made in the past. I will achieve whatever I set my mind to. I will not allow rationalizations to deter me from achieving my goals. I will fight to win and will not settle for anything else.

I will crystalize my goals to a sharp focus. Whatever I do today will move me one step closer to the realization of my dreams; nothing will deter me.

I will not complain, find fault or criticize no matter how justified I may feel in doing so, because experience has taught me it does not pay. Whatever I say will be positive or complimentary or not at all.

I will take special pride in my work; knowing my fingerprints are my signature on work I have done for others. I will not worry. Worrying does not solve problems; taking corrective action does.

I will count my blessings for being alive and well, and living in this land of opportunity that rewards and recognizes each person according to individual contributions.

I will keep a smile on my face, a twinkle in my eye, a spring in my walk and enthusiasm in my voice, even though I may be bleeding on the inside because of wounds inflicted upon me. No one enjoys dealing with the walking-wounded moving with a slow shuffle and a gaunt look or speaking in somber, lifeless tones. I won't conduct myself as such no matter how great the pain may be at times.

I will concentrate my efforts and enjoy my job while at work and concentrate on enjoying my family, friends and social life while at home without allowing each to take away from the other. I will work to achieve that balance.

I will have a quiet half-hour each day all to myself and relax. During this half-hour, I will try to get a better perspective of my life; I will then adjust my ways accordingly.

I will conduct myself with the knowledge that from the time I was born and for a good part of my life I was 100% on the receiving-end enjoying all the fruits of labor by my family and society; food, shelter, clothing, education, religion, medical and recreation were all provided for me. Equally if not more important was the love, support, guidance, motivation, values and understanding given to me. I owe something back and will work to even things up to help make this world a better place to live. I will give of myself, knowing full well that as I give to the world, the world will give back to me.

Michael Latas

INDEX

TOP 40 JOB HUNTING FACTORS
FOR RECENT COLLEGE GRADS

On Learning

Perhaps the most valuable result of all education is the ability to make yourself do the thing you have to do when it ought to be done, whether you like it or not; it is the first lesson that ought to be learned; and however early a man's training begins, it is probably the last lesson that he learns thoroughly.

Thomas Huxley

Short of the luck factor, such as knowing the right people with the right connections, you as a recent college graduate need to acknowledge the fact that a variety of factors will determine the success of your job search.

First things first. Knowing what these diverse factors are will at least let you begin your job search on a level playing field. Some of these factors are within your control; others are not, nor can they be controlled, altered or eliminated at this point in time. Armed with this information you can compensate for the ones you cannot control and effectively control those that are within your power to master.

The following list of the Top 40 Job Hunting Factors will provide you with valuable knowledge about your job search. Read them, analyze yourself honestly in regards to how each applies to you and then use this knowledge to move your job search ahead to achieve success - getting the job you want and in which you will prosper.

FACTORS TO SUCCESS

1. **Your College:** The quality, standing, and overall reputation of the college or university that you attended will be a factor. The better the school, the better your opportunities are.

2. **Your Grades:** Your class standing, grade point average and honors, if any, are important determining factors. The higher your rank in each of these the better off you will be in your job search. Unfortunately, it is too late to change these at graduation.

3. **Degree And Major:** How much of a demand is there at this point in time for your specific degree, area of specialization and major? Certain fields are hot with excellent demands, such as environmental engineering and health care. On the other hand banking and aerospace are tight. Again, this is unchangeable at graduation time. Surely, you must know by now that demands will change over the years for various fields. Defense industries are downsizing. Every indication points to the fact that they will continue to do so. Students graduating in defense related fields will probably need to pursue alternatives.

4. **Advanced Degrees:** MBA's, PhD's or other advanced degrees can be a plus or a minus in your job search. Much depends upon your field. If you are continuing your education to avoid looking for work, the advanced degree might not be as beneficial as you hoped it would be.

5. **Extracurricular Activities:** This area was definitely within your control while you were in school. An active list of accomplishments is a very good plus to show to an employer. Most levels of participation and leadership can help you. This voluntary activity shows an ability

and interest in getting along with people which is important in any business.

6. **Networking:** Your friends and friends of their friends are most important. This area is in your control and one in which you can still make improvements. If you do not have a large network of friends and family willing to help you, then you should start immediately to develop a network of people that are able and willing to help you. I cannot begin to write enough about the importance of networking. The deeper you probe for names the better your results will be. This is the oldest tried and proven method for successful job hunting. It is not enough to list whom you know. You also should ask all the people you know to supply you with contacts that could help you. This list of connections can become quite impressive and can place you in touch with prospective employers.

    Everybody knows somebody that can be of help to you; no matter who they are. Be sure to include your alumni in your networking. Your college alumni who went out into the world and made a name for themselves can help you. Ask your college for a list of alumni who are successful in your field or related fields; then start contacting them. They will be happy to help you. Be sure to include your select college professors in your networking. Set up orderly files and develop a functional follow-up system. Make it a point to add new names to your networking list on a daily basis.

7. **Your Work Experience:** Employers like to see students who have interned or have had part-time and summer jobs. Many students have pursued careers upon graduation with the firms for which they had worked on an intern, part-time or summer jobs basis. This activity gives you an added advantage. It moves you ahead of other students who have yet to work in this work-a-day world particularly in your field. If you

have worked prior to graduation, you have a much better grasp of the working world, and employers will respect that. You also will have recommendations from your employers which can state your skills and your desirability as an employee.

8.   **Your Charisma:** This is your chemistry/personality (charm) that attracts people to you. It is unbelievable how important this area is in job search. It is such an important factor in hiring that a separate chapter or even a book can be written on this subject. Setting the "all things being equal" myth aside, nothing, besides base credentials, will carry more weight. Employers will hire candidates they like and get along with over ones with stronger credentials whom they don't like. How can you be more personable? How can you make people like you more? There are good books on improving your personality; read, learn and apply what they say.

9.   **The Economy:** Is the state of the economy expanding or contracting? It is always much easier to pursue your job hunting campaign when the economy is expanding, not contracting. When I graduated from the University of Dayton in Dayton, Ohio, in 1960, the country was in a prolonged period of expansion. Demand for college graduates was very high. There simply were not enough college graduates to meet the needs. The supply and demand ratio was way out of whack.

I had a friend of mine who had interviews with 50 different companies, including 35 who recruited on campus during his last 18 months before graduation. He was an electrical engineer and received 27 job offers. Some of your parents may have related similar stories to you. I am sad to say that as of this writing the supply/demand factor has gone the other direction. Consequently, you will have to work hard to get good interviews. This can be done; it just takes more networking, more research, more flexibility and more ingenuity than it did in the past. Plan on conducting a thorough job search campaign, and work at it.

10. **Your Naivete:**
> *To be conscience that you are ignorant of the facts is a great step to knowledge.*
>
> Benjamin Disraeli

Naivete and ignorance on how to find a job by recent college graduates are two of the biggest factors in their success or lack of it. This affects the success rate much more so than the lack of sufficient job opportunities. This holds true in all types of market conditions. The times have changed in the job market; unfortunately, the job seekers have not. Tight job markets call for even more know-how and "know-who" coupled with a lot more activity required than in the past. As you learn, so shall ye reap.

The untrained person follows entirely too many pre-doomed paths.

11. **Your Athletic Ability/Fame:** Your sports or other outstanding public centered achievement will carry with you into the world of work. Some college athletes have become so famous that they are eagerly sought, not only in their chosen field of athletics, but also in other areas. Your past will create your future or at least open doors for you. You may be one of the fortunate ones.

12. **Your Location:** Different parts of the country offer differing degrees of job opportunities in selective fields. Geographic location is an important factor. Are you limiting your search to your own local area, regionally, or nationally? Or are you attempting to get a job in another specific city. The broader and more flexible you are concerning location the better your job prospects are. Consider the position of the area in which you desire to work. What percentage of the total population is that city? That is your job market percentage if you

limit it to that city.

13. **Your Job Campaign:** A well planned job hunting campaign can make a difference. It is in your control. Rate your campaign at this moment, and state what you can do to move your campaign up the scale to reach your highest possible level of success.

High - A Top Rated Plan _____
An Above Average Plan _____
An Average Plan _____
A Below Average Plan _____
No Plan At All _____

Grade yourself. This area here is totally within your control. You can excel in this area to compensate for areas you can not control.

14. **Your Placement Office:** Both the size and the quality of the job placement office at your college are factors. The degree of activity generated by you and the placement office will definitely affect the results of your job search. How much and how well you put it to work for you is up to you. Make your placement office really want to help you. Keep on the good side of the placement director and associates.

15. **Your Job Hunting Activity:** The degree of your total job hunting activity will determine the outcome. The more you do, the more involved you become, the more in depth your search is, the more successful it can become. Think about this: how far in advance of graduation did you begin your job search? If you started your job search after graduation; don't regret; proceed with it, now!

16. **You:** Your physical and personal characteristics can also make a difference. This statement might raise an eyebrow or two. What in the world do these have to do

with a person's ability to do a given job? Not a darned thing! However, they can and do play a big part in getting a job. For better or for worse people are victims of the impressions they make on others. Plus points in some areas and minus points in other areas are given nearly automatically to every person one meets.

Some of you will be more fortunate than others because of your natural good looks and presence. You can do what you can to improve your looks and professional appearance. Some of you have a special gift of gab, outgoing friendly personalities, and some of you don't. People come in all sizes and shapes. Some are better looking than others. It is just not fair, but it is the way things are. You better get used to it if you are not already conditioned by now. Everyone has one's own personal viewpoint.

Learn to capitalize on whatever strengths you have to compensate for your weaknesses. Exceptional grooming, dress, manners, along with a firm handshake and a friendly cheerful smile are all within your control. Don't compromise in this all important area. I can't begin to emphasize strongly enough the importance of you looking your best during interviews and throughout your career. Often students interviewing with companies on and off campus tend to dress and conduct themselves as students; they, thereby, convey the wrong first impression. Most people proceed along the lines of what you see is what you get. If you look like a student, act like a student and talk like a student; then, what are you?

Companies are only interested in hiring students for part-time jobs and summer employment. If you expect to be hired as a full time salaried professional by any company, you are going to have to conduct yourself as such or lose out to others who do.

Suppose you were selected to participate in a national television program dealing with college graduates on the job market. During it you were to be interviewed. What would you wear? What would you do? What would you say? And how would you conduct yourself? Surely, you would do your best to be prepared and look your best. Put your best foot forward and keep it there, now, and throughout your career. Two good looking professional business outfits will get you started in the right direction. There are those who will do all of the right things to project a strong successful professional image and gain an unfair advantage over others who do not.

Grade yourself in each of these areas before and after you have read this section. Then, do whatever is necessary to bolster your strengths to compensate for your weaknesses.

Personal Factors

	Advantage	Neutral	Negative
Height/weight/stature			
Personality/charisma/charm			
Voice			
Outgoing/introverted			
Sparkle/twinkle			
Smile			
Laugh			
Energy			
Confidence			
Professional Attire			
Grooming: Hair/nails			
Demeanor/presence			
Social Graces/manners			
Other			

Ask others to assess you, too. These should not necessarily be your contemporaries. People who are the same age and hold parallel type jobs to your prospective employers would give you a fair evaluation.

Two young college students were applying for summer jobs. One was dressed in a business type dress, hose, heels, make up, and her hair was tastefully groomed. The other had on a blue jean mini skirt, sport top, flats, no hose, big loop earrings, no make up, and her hair was loose, long and flowing. She looked cute, but not like an adult ready for work. Both had equal work experience, recommendations and grades. Which one got the office job and which one got the popcorn server job at the local theater?

17. **Your Resume:** A good clean, crisp, well thought out and critiqued resume is an important factor. Be sure to read at least one good book on the subject. Your active work experience might be limited but your skills from activities in high school and college are transferable to work. List them and your accomplishments.

18. **Your Cover Letters:** Make your cover letters stand out from the rest. Customize each to fit the specific job. One general cover letter just will not do. You will need different types for different occasions. Each must be attention getting. Get help from your placement counselor. Have other business friends read and critique your letters.

19. **Your Attitude:** This is a catch all. Is your attitude upbeat and positive, neutral, or down and negative? Do you suppose it makes a difference? Do you suppose you have control over it?

20. **Your Ambition:** Your degree of ambition will dictate how much effort you are willing to expend to get the right job and advance in your career path once you get the job. How hard do you want to work?

21. **Military:** ROTC, ex-military personnel, military reserves and other experience you might have that is related to the military can be a plus in your job search. This is particularly true when in contention for federal jobs.

22. **Employment Agencies:** Find out which employment agencies in your area handle the type of work you are interested in pursuing. Get registered with one or more of these agencies. It might take a couple of dry runs before you make the connection with the right firm. Just be patient, persistent and do it. The right ones can help you.

   Please understand, your degree of marketability can differ from one agency to the next. Some of you may have a problem because the type of degree you have is not common or in demand. The right attitude on your part in this area will make the employment agency really want to help you. Interviewing with the agency will give you experience at interviewing. Your interviewer can help you in the art of interviewing and assist you with your cover letters and resumes.

23. **Interim Employment:** Depending upon your circumstances you may have to accept interim employment while you continue your career search.

24. **Your Independence And Desire:** If you worked your way through college and paid for part or all of your college expenses, these are indications of a strong sense of self reliance which employers respect and admire. Everyone realizes the strength it takes to work and go to college at the same time.

25. **Your Income Expectations:** Are your income expectations realistic or unrealistic? How can you know what to expect? You need to ask friends and relatives and explore all they know about salaries. Ask your

placement counselor what other recent graduates have been paid. Read and investigate salary trends. Rank yourself objectively.

26. **Interviewing Skills:** Be sure to read at least one book on this subject before your first interview. Make a list of do's and don'ts about your speech habits and mannerisms. Study this area until you have control over it. Then rate yourself.

Rating Your Interviewing Skills

Excellent _____
Above average _____
Average _____
Below average _____

How can you improve?

27. **Confidence Level:** Your level of confidence will be a major factor. The more you get to know about how to conduct your job search effectively, the more your confidence will improve.

28. **"Know Thy Prospective Employer":** Thoroughly research the companies to secure interviews and before you interview. Don't be caught by surprises. The more you know about a company the better you will be able to place yourself in it. You would not think of marrying a stranger. Don't accept a job interview like it is a blind date. Careful research about the company will pay dividends.

29. **Getting In Touch With You:** Having a backup phone number and an answer machine or phone mail service are very important. Make sure your phone message is businesslike. Coach your friends and family to answer the phone in a businesslike manner, take accurate messages and give them to you.

30. **Following Up:** Making follow-up phone calls and writing thank you notes are critically important in securing a job. You cannot keep a friend if you don't return calls and express thanks. How can you expect to get a job if you don't follow up, return phone calls and express thanks?

31. **Reality:** Facing reality earlier versus later will move you forward in your job search. How hard is it going to be to get a job, and how should you prepare yourself for your job search? The answers to these questions will be the reality in your job search.

32. **The One Hundred Percent Rule:** Remember, nothing is one hundred percent... no rules... no requirements... no logic...

33. **Smoking:** Look at today's society. Even if the interviewer smokes, don't.

34. **You Are Special - Show It:** Special attributes, characteristics or qualities that help set you apart from the crowd will work for you in getting a job. Make a list of yours. Ask your friends, parents and professors to help you list characteristics that will show how you would make a good employee. Keep them in mind and insert them into your presentations.

> *There is a kind of greatness which does not depend upon fortune: it is a certain manner that distinguishes us, and which seems to destine us for great things; it is the value we insensibly set upon ourselves; it is by this quality that we gain the deference of other men, and it is this which commonly raises us more above them than birth, rank, or even merit itself.*
>
> Francois de La Rochefoucauld

35. **Looking Within Your Field:** The availability of jobs in your given field will determine if you can selectively pursue a career within your degree field or if you need

to look outside it. This factor will be of great importance to you. Keep your options open.

36. **Persistence:** You need to persist until you acquire the job that is right for you. This will help overcome your weaknesses and factors that are not in your control.

37. **Rejection Tolerance Level:** How high or how low is yours? Say, "I need some help. Can you, please, help me?" Don't be afraid to ask for help routinely. Don't let rejection be a personal matter.

38. **Number Of Interviews:** Avail yourself of all reasonable opportunities to interview with companies recruiting on and off campus. The number of interviews you have is a primary factor in your job search success. The more interviews you have the greater your success.

39. **Degree Of Motivation:** There are those who will give it the old college try, and there are those who will do or die. Which are you? How badly do you want a job? Face facts, appraise yourself and determine what you want and how you can get it.

40. **All Other Factors:** Other factors will be instrumental in your job search success. I won't argue that point. However, the above factors will hold true for the vast majority of you. Last but not least, luck needs to be understood: the importance of being in the right place at the right time is not just luck. You personally play a bigger part in this area than most people realize. You improve your odds of being in the right place at the right time to the degree that you generate opportunities by talking to people about your need for a job.

Network. Network. Network.

As you can see, there are many different factors that can affect your success rate in job hunting. Not everyone

316 Job Search Secrets

graduating side by side from the same school with th\
degree and grade point average from the same side of t\
will have the same degree of success in job search. Each o.\
you should evaluate yourself on the above top forty job
hunting factors and use your strengths to the fullest. This
will compensate for your weaknesses. No one is perfect.
One or two of the right strengths will make a difference.

Don't be mislead by the experiences of others. Complaints
are common about the jerk that beat the good guy out on a
job opportunity. It is not fair. I won't argue the point.
These things happen, and indeed life is not always fair. But
you better get used to it because this will not be your first
nor last brush with fairness. The sooner, the quicker, the
faster that you recognize this reality, the better.

Oh yes, there is one more point to remember regarding the
Top 40 Job Hunting Factors and that is that many of these
factors will apply to future job hunting throughout your life.

DOOMED FROM THE START!

Entirely too many entry level people seeking employment
simply don't have any idea of what they want to do with
their lives. You may be one of them. If so, read on. If your
answer to the question, "What kind of job are you looking
for?" or "What is it that you would really like to do?" or any
words to that effect at the beginning of an interview is "I
really don't know," you are doomed from the start.
Employers will look upon you with puzzled looks while
asking themselves why you are wasting their time. If you
don't know what you want to do what are you doing there?

The proper way to handle this question in an interview is to
tell the interviewer that you are not familiar with all the
possible job opportunities that may be available within the
company and job titles vary from one company to the next.
You could add that there could be a number of opportunities

within the company that would be of mutual benefit to both of you.   Proceed to briefly state your strong points (strengths) along with a highlight of what you enjoy doing most.   Saying that you enjoy working with people is not enough of an answer by itself because virtually all people have to work with other people.   I am reminded of the mortician who was asked why he chose that profession, to which he responded, "Because I like to work with people."

All people need to take an inventory of their "wares" before they go out into the streets to sell them.   These "wares" would consist of an inventory of your skills, strengths and accomplishments along with a list of duties in which you excel or enjoy.   This could also include the type of degree you have if it is pertinent; otherwise, don't bring it up.   You should be ready with a summary of your capabilities that you could bring to the company to contribute to its continued growth and profitability.   A word of caution is in order.   DON'T DWELL ON THIS QUESTION, KEEP IT SHORT AND BRIEF.   Then proceed with your interview.

You will be surprised how well you will be received when you plan your job hunting approach properly.   You will be facing stiff competition from others who have planned properly and have crystallized their objectives.   Do the same and you will be playing on the same level playing field.   There is considerably less risk in hiring people who know what they want to do versus those that don't.   This latter group tends to hop, skip and jump from one job to the next hoping to get lucky somewhere along the way and find a job that will last. Others simply never find themselves and end up as career nomads.

Take the necessary time NOW, before it is too late and take inventory of yourself, then go out and sell yourself in the marketplace.   There are needs for every conceivable types of "wares" imaginable, and then some.   Getting yourself organized first is the key.   This will help you crystallize your approach in a good businesslike manner.

OVERCOMING A LACK OF EXPERIENCE

This special section would not be complete without discussing the lack of experience issue. Fresh college graduates (high school grads, too) become nearly paranoid when they hear, "You just don't have any experience." How is anyone without experience supposed to get it unless someone is willing to hire them without it.? People in this situation fail to realize that no one is going to be qualified or in demand for all job openings. Those without experience will only acquire jobs that do not require experience.

Let's look at all job openings across the land at any given time. They will cover the gamut from jobs requiring no experience or education at one extreme to college degrees and top level positions at the other end. So, each job seeker, regardless of how impeccable each person's credentials are, will only be qualified for a small percentage of all existing job openings. *The U.S. Dictionary of Occupational Titles* lists over 22,000 different job descriptions. They call for different education and background.

Most job seekers will not be qualified for most jobs. The majority of their inquiries will result in rejection. The only difference will be the reason for the rejection. The reverse is also true. Most job seekers are NOT interested in most jobs. They, too, are highly selective in their fields of interest. They just won't take any old job opening that comes along; both companies and job seekers are entitled to their preferences. On a brighter note, recent college grads will find more and be qualified for a greater number and variety of job openings than any other group of job seekers. That is a fact; therefore, count your blessings.

Now that you have read this special section for recent college grads, you should go back over the book and read and re-read selected chapters of interest and application to you. Work at your job search daily as if it were a job, and this will give you an advantage over others less informed.

NOTES:

NOTES: